PRODUCTIVE PROLOG PROGRAMMING

Limits of Liability and Disclaimer of Warranty

PRODUCTIVE PROLOG PROGRAMMING

Peter Schnupp

Lawrence W. Bernhard

HANSER

Library of Congress Cataloging-in-Publication Data

Schnupp, Peter.
  Productive Prolog programming.

  (Prentice Hall International Series in Computer
  Science)
  Translation of: Prolog, Einfuhrung in die
  Programmierpraxis.
  Includes index.
  1. Prolog (Computer program language)
I. Bernhard, Lawrence.   II. Title.   III. Series.
QA76.73.P76S3613   1987   005.13'3   86-30437
ISBN 0-13-725110-6 (pbk).

British Library Cataloguing in Publication Data

Schnupp, Peter.
  Productive Prolog programming – (Prentice
  Hall International Series in Computer
  Science)
  1. Prolog (Computer program language)
  I. Title   II. Bernhard, Lawrence
  005.13'3   QA76.73.P7

  ISBN 0-13-725110-6

This book was originally published in German under the title *PROLOG: Einführung in die Programmierpraxis* by Dr Peter Schnupp.
Copyright © 1986 Carl Hanser Verlag, Munich and Vienna.

This translated edition is co-published by Prentice Hall International (UK) Ltd, London and Carl Hanser Verlag, Munich and Vienna.
Copyright © 1987 Carl Hanser Verlag and Prentice Hall International (UK) Ltd.

Printed and bound in Great Britain for
Prentice Hall International (UK) Ltd,
66 Wood Lane End, Hemel Hempstead,
Hertfordshire, HP2 4RG
by A. Wheaton & Co. Ltd., Exeter

1 2 3 4 5   91 90 89 88 87

0-13-725110-6

CONTENTS

PREFACE

Prolog is probably the most interesting new programming language to have emerged from the field of 'artificial intelligence' with great practical import for software engineering.

Not only does Prolog, compared with its competitors, promise an increase in productivity in the programming of expert systems and knowledge-based applications; in its more recent implementations, properly adapted to the underlying operating systems and armed with interactive debugging tools, as well as simple means of extending the language via procedures written in other programming languages, Prolog reveals itself as a general-purpose language, suitable for almost any application and for all phases of software development, from specification up through prototyping to the final implementation.

Consequently, we have sought, in this book, to introduce you to Prolog via practical examples from as many different application areas as possible. Furthermore, our emphasis is not merely on the syntax and semantics of the language, but more on the practical aspects of programming in Prolog: how to modularize and debug your programs, how to access utilities of the underlying operating system from within Prolog programs, or how to extend the language by facilities typically not found in standard implementations, e.g. connection to a database.

The reader for whom this book is primarily intended is the experienced programmer or software engineer, who is familiar with a modern, higher-level programming language and one of the more common operating systems. Should these happen to be C and Unix, then you will find the book particularly rewarding.

But even the reader *without* practical programming experience should find the book quite useful, since Prolog is itself so different from conventional programming languages that experience with them does not necessarily provide any serious advantage in learning the language — indeed, many claim that it is something of a disadvantage. In your first reading, you should merely skip over those sections which seem to assume such experience. In the bibliography you will find some books which can help you bridge the gaps at your leisure. In the meantime, just use Prolog 'normally', i.e. without any concern for how it might compare to a traditional solution to the same problem. At some later date, you can then pull out this book once again and tackle those parts that require the skill gained by experience.

A third group of readers addressed by this book encompasses students of computer science, participants in workshops, seminars, etc., be they about Prolog *per se* or, more generally, artificial intelligence, expert systems and knowledge-based software or related fields of software engineering, such as formal specification, system modelling and (rapid) prototyping.

We hope that Prolog will help the reader to both a qualitative and a quantitative improvement in software-development productivity — measured, of course, in running programs per unit time rather than lines of code, since Prolog programs are an order of magnitude more compact than most other programming languages.

We would like to take this opportunity to thank the many people involved directly and indirectly in the birth of this book. Although we cannot mention all by name, we wish to give particular recognition to the publishers, Messrs. Spencker and Niclas, who encouraged us to write this book and gave us much invaluable support in its production. Likewise, many thanks to our colleagues here in Munich at InterFace GmbH and InterFace Computer GmbH for the many suggestions, fine examples, illustrations and criticisms, as well as production support: Ute Leibrandt, Claus Mueller, Cosima Schmauch, Josef Schreiner.

Perhaps the greatest indebtedness, however, is to the developer of our excellent Prolog system, Preben Folkjaer. Thanks to his fine implementation, what started out as a special tool for experimentation and specification has turned into an indispensable programming language for daily use.

The examples in this book were, for the most part, developed and tested on an *HP Integral*. We wish to express our thanks to the Hewlett-Packard company for use of the computer. This portable system was instrumental in turning much otherwise wasted travel time into productive work and made it possible to keep to schedule for this book.

Last but not least, a very personal thanks to the friends and family members who raised our spirits when they were flagging, and without whose support this book might never have gone to press.

P.S.
L.B.

INTRODUCTION

During the first decade of its existence, Prolog was considered to be a purely academic language. It was used in the education of computer scientists to illustrate how a model for a programming language could be derived from formal logic. Beyond that, it was used for such esoteric applications as *artificial intelligence* or for *proving the correctness* of programs.

Around 1980 these areas of application suddenly became of great practical interest – in the development of expert systems and in the field of software engineering. It was in this context that the applications-oriented members of the computing community discovered Prolog. It proved to be a particularly powerful production language for the more complex 'knowledge-based' applications, especially for those programmers with access to an implementation of Prolog tailored for practical use. Such systems were just beginning to appear on the market for the first time.

Prolog as a production language, a software tool for software engineers: this is the perspective from which we present Prolog to you in this book!

Prolog is, like LISP, Forth, and APL, an unusual programming language. This has one disadvantage as well as numerous advantages.

The disadvantage is that Prolog requires learning programming anew, even for persons with a command of many of the more traditional languages. Whereas an experienced Pascal programmer can grasp a language such as C in a matter of hours, producing useful programs within days thereafter, such experience is (generally) of very little use in learning Prolog. Indeed, many claim that the *algorithmic approach* acquired through programming in the "classical" languages more often than not proves to be a handicap when trying to learn Prolog. In fact, it is the programming novice who often has an easier time learning Prolog, because he does not have to 'unlearn' the algorithmic bias! Kowalski, one of the fathers of the *programming-in-logic* paradigm, reinforces this view on the basis of his experience with elementary school children constructing a knowledge base (in Prolog) about repairing bicycles.

Before those of you who are experienced programmers begin to despair, let us consider the advantages of Prolog!

To begin with, Prolog is probably the 'highest'-level programming language to date. Prolog comes closer than any existing language to achieving the ideal wherein a program developer only has to specify *what* task is to be done and not *how* it is to be realized computationally. As a result, Prolog programs are typically much shorter than programs performing the same task implemented in other languages.

Moreover, the Prolog versions serve, at the same time, as *formal specifications*. Whereas modern software engineering discourages the program developer from writing his implementation "directly into the computer" until he has carefully prepared a detailed specification thereof, using Prolog one can hardly avoid such procedure. The implementation is the specification! The fact that his specification is immediately executable and testable certainly cannot be held against him!

Another advantage of Prolog is its minimal syntax, by far the smallest of any of the well-known languages. There are but a handful of language constructs which one must learn. Prolog's expressive power derives from the large collection of *predicates*, similar to the built-in *functions* of traditional programming languages, which a good implementation provides. Furthermore, the fact that the user can extend his pool of predicates at leisure brings Prolog close to the ideal of a language which can be extended at will.

In order to take full advantage of this feature, be sure that the Prolog system which you select allows you unrestricted access to the interface for defining new, built-in predicates in the implementation language of the system itself, e.g. C in a Unix environment. You will find that most of your own predicates can be easily defined using the standard built-in predicates, while some require access to the underlying system, e.g. querying a database system whose interface must then be accessible to Prolog.

A third advantage lies in the multi-faceted and consequently *multi-purpose* nature of Prolog. Colmerauer designed and implemented the original language around 1970 in order to do *prog*ramming in *log*ic (hence the name). If you have a strong theoretical inclination, you can consider Prolog a special style of expressing *first-order predicate logic*. But if you have a different focus, you are more likely to see Prolog in another light.

A view popular among many users is that of Prolog as a very intelligent *relational database*. The notion of intelligence derives from the nature of the database: It contains not only the hard *facts*, which are analogous to *relations*, but also includes *rules*. With these rules, you can 'program' the database, turning it into a *knowledge base*. If you intend to use Prolog to implement an *expert system*, this is presumably the most useful view for your purpose. This will be the first view of the language presented in this book.

Another view of Prolog, essentially the one taken by the Prolog interpreter itself, focuses on the *procedural interpretation* of the rules. In this case, a rule is treated as a series of procedure calls to be made in a particular order. The order is a fixed part of the interpreter and, as such, represents an element of the semantics of Prolog.

For many typical programming problems, such a procedural interpretation (usually referred to as *dynamic semantics*) is often the easiest for the software engineer who already has a great deal of programming experience with conventional languages. For this reason we shall subsequently examine Prolog from this second perspective as well.

A final, crucial aspect of Prolog is the principle of *unification*. Unification embodies *pattern matching* applied to data structures of, essentially, arbitrary complexity. This view is useful if you must solve complicated search problems. Also, if you want to trace the path of computation in the procedural interpretation, you must understand the nature of this process. This will be the third view of Prolog presented.

Having laid the above foundation, we shall then take a look at what programming in logic really entails. This is necessary in order to truly understand Prolog and its underlying theory. The concept of programming in logic should prove relatively easy to grasp once the aforementioned views of the Prolog language have been understood.

We are obliged, at this point, to draw your attention to one small problem: there exist a number of different implementations of Prolog. Consequently, we would like to briefly specify the one upon which the discussion here is based.

To begin with, one distinguishes between two major dialects. On the micros, one will occasionally encounter *Micro-Prolog*. It may be characterized as being a subset of full-blown Prolog. Moreover, it may not conform exactly to the standard syntax at the interactive level. From those running on workstations under MS/DOS to those on mainframes, virtually all implementations conform essentially to the quasi-standard, a standard which, as has often been the case for many of the more recent programming languages, was established by the first good textbook describing it. In the case of Prolog, it was the book by Clocksin and Mellish.

Almost everything described in this book can be expected to apply to any of the newer Prolog systems which you encounter on larger machines. There are, however, a number of features of the language which either had not yet been conceived or were only superficially described in the aforementioned textbook. These were subsequently implemented differently in the various Prolog systems. Nonetheless, we shall deal with the following topics, as they are vital to a discussion of the language in the context of professional, commercial applications:

- testing aids

- Prolog and the host operating system (embedding).

With respect to the latter topics, we base our description on the IF/Prolog implementation under UNIX. We have been careful to indicate, wherever appropriate, that particular features may be implemented differently, or perhaps not at all, in other systems. In these rare cases, you should consult the manual and documentation for your specific system.

With no further ado, let us turn our attention to the first of the above-mentioned views: that of Prolog as a *relational knowledge base*.

1 PROLOG AS A DATABASE

In this chapter you will learn how to start your Prolog system and how to conduct a dialog, i.e. a session, with it. Typically, you begin a session by consulting one or more Prolog (program) texts with which you intend to work. You can practice this procedure using a very simple Prolog database. This will familiarize you with Prolog as an interactive database query language.

1.1 The User Dialog

Prolog is conceived as an interactive programming language. If you have had any contact with Basic or APL or Lisp, you should find this interpretive approach less foreign than a reader who has had experience only with the 'classical', more batch-oriented language.

You start the Prolog system from your terminal. The precise starting command will depend on your host operating system and the Prolog implementation which you are using. Check your manual for the exact information. Under Unix or MS/DOS it should suffice to simply enter a command like

prolog

to activate a standard version. You can later refer to your manual to see if there are any optional parameters, such as desired workspace size or the name(s) of Prolog text file(s) which should be loaded into the internal database at initialization. For the time being, however, you need not concern yourself with such 'extras'.

Since Prolog is not exactly small (a professional system typically requires a minimum of 100 kilobytes) loading and initialization takes a little time. This pause is usually used to greet you with a number of lines indicating the producer, copyrights, version number and other notable facts; no doubt to distract your attention from the load time delay!

Things get interesting once the system writes a prompt on the left-hand

1

edge of the screen and the cursor comes to rest just behind it, indicating that
Prolog is awaiting your first command. Most systems use the string

     ?–

as the prompt. Prolog now expects to read one *clause* from your terminal,
which it will then immediately execute.

We have just used a very common term, specific to Prolog. To avoid
your having to later readjust your terminology, we shall be continually introducing the necessary language concepts as they have practical bearing on the
discussion. Prolog draws on a language model based on formal logic.
Consequently much of the nomenclature derives from concepts native to
that field rather than from the field of data processing, with which you are
doubtless more familiar. Our reason for 'talking Prolog' from the start,
rather than conducting the discussion in terms to which you are likely more
accustomed, is that most Prolog terminology cannot be simply translated,
one-to-one, into data processing terms. If we were looking for an analogous
concept, in traditional programming terms, e.g. for *clause*, we would find
that, depending on the context, it could be interpreted as either a 'command', a 'procedure' or a 'logical record'.

As we mentioned in the introduction, Prolog is an unusual language.
And here we have a prime example: Prolog makes no formal distinction
between commands, procedures and logical records. Once you have
accustomed yourself to this fact, you will be delighted how much this
simplifies the syntax. What you once had to learn, in other programming
languages, as rote formalism, can be replaced, in Prolog, by a little common
sense.

The seemingly diverse meaning(s) of *clause* is best grasped, if you
conceive of a clause as a *logical statement* defining a circumstance, i.e. a state
of affairs. Such a statement acquires a meaning when it is interpreted. Thus,
a given Prolog clause acquires its functional meaning through its interpretation as either a command, a procedure or a record.

So if you enter a legal clause after the prompt, then Prolog interprets
it as a command, and therefore it is an command. In a quality implementation of Prolog, there is no difference between the command language for
system control and the programming language Prolog itself. Every Prolog
clause can be used as either a system command *or* a program statement *or*
even as a record in the database.

Naturally, you must first learn what constitutes a 'legal' clause. But
before we get involved with a detailed description of the syntax, we should
first look at some simple examples. And before we do that, we should note
how you inform the interpreter that you have finished your input, i.e. *ended
your clause*, so that it resumes its job: executing your commands! If

your clause is not syntactically correct, not to worry, Prolog will let you know!

A clause in Prolog always ends with a *period* ('.'). Whatever you might enter in response to the Prolog system prompt '?–', you must terminate it with a *period*. If Prolog responds to your input with silence, then chances are you forgot the closing period, so just enter one to see if that is the problem. The system should respond, at the very least with a message regarding some syntax error. In any case, you will then be able to continue your dialog.

Before we make any suggestions as to *which* clauses you could experiment with as commands, we had better let you know how to end a session with Prolog and get back to your operating system. This is the most trivial of actions, and probably for that very reason one for which no standard clause as yet exists. Consequently, you will have to check your manual on this one. If you do not happen to have it at hand, you might just try some popular ones, like **halt.**, **bye.**, **end.** or, if you are running under Unix, even an *end-of-file*, i.e. *<control>D* or *<control>Z*.

1.2 Prolog Texts and their Consultation

Just as you do not, as a habit, re-enter your program and data for each run in an interactive language like Basic or Lisp, neither do you ordinarily do so in Prolog. Instead, it is common practice to enter those clauses which you regularly use into a file, using your favorite editor. To make these clauses available to the interpreter, you issue a command, typically at the beginning of the session, instructing it to load the contents of such files into the system's active, internal database.

Now, since Prolog, as already mentioned, makes no distinction between procedures (or 'code') and data, we should avoid trying to artificially classify Prolog files into different types. We prefer a more general term, referring to all files in the context of this language as *Prolog texts*. They are, in fact, ordinary text, i.e. character files, their contents, however, restricted to clauses and comments. The comments are, as you might expect, purely for documentation purposes and are therefore ignored by the interpreter.

Most Prolog systems permit two kinds of comments:

- Comments *parenthesized* by the symbols /* and */, a convention familiar to those who know PL/I and C. Such comments may extend over several lines and appear anywhere in the file, even in the midst of a clause.

- *End-of-line* comments, beginning at an arbitrary point in a physical line, indicated by a percent character and extending to the end of that respective line. Such comments may also appear in the middle of a clause, in which case the clause 'definition' resumes quite normally on the following line.

Having mentioned the in-line comment facility this once, we shall hereafter ignore it, just as the interpreter does, and assume that, basically, our Prolog texts consist of an arbitrarily long sequence of clauses. The use to which you put your clauses, the order in which you write them into your text and whether or not you distribute your clauses over numerous texts is left to your discretion. In all fairness, however, you should be aware that the arrangement of clauses within a text and the sequence of text input is not entirely without significance.

For one thing, as in the case of any programming language, it is in the interest of clarity of objective and ease of maintenance, particularly in larger program packages, that one attempts to arrange the information into logical units. Even more important, the order in which the texts are read in determines where they are stored in the active workspace. The later they are encountered in the reading-in process, the further back they appear in the internal database. This, in turn, determines the search sequence followed by the interpreter. As we shall shortly see, this physical order affects not only the efficiency of your program, i.e. how fast it performs, but also its semantics, i.e. what it performs.[1]

To avoid this inherent pitfall, we recommend that you observe the following rules, whenever you create a Prolog text:

● Treat individual Prolog texts, i.e. *files*, as the equivalent of a *module* in a traditional programming language. It should be a homogenous unit, with a single well-defined task or function in the total application. Naturally, it is best to keep such modules as small as possible. This is best achieved by carefully considering, in advance, what the actual task is and then including only those clauses into the text which play a role in that functional frame. Writing a brief description of the task dispatched by the module into a *standard heading* in the file is a good way to reinforce this process.

---

[1] Theoretically , the semantics of a program should be independent of the order in which the clauses occur in the database. Logic tells us that the meaning of a set of logical expressions (which are represented by clauses in Prolog's language model) is independent of their arrangement, with respect to one another in a file or workspace (logic does not assume a 'workspace'!). In order to avoid this discrepancy, one often distinguishes between the so-called *static semantics* of a Prolog text, which is a *purely logical perspective,* and the *dynamic semantics* of the text, which views the text in its *procedural interpretation.*

• Always write clauses which are related, e.g. clauses describing a particular data relationship or a given procedure, together in one place in one file. If you must depart from this convention, be sure you have a good reason for doing so and document it with comments in the text. Gathering the clauses in a given text into clusters is more than just a convenience for the potential reader of the text. In the testing phase one often instructs the system to read the contents of a given Prolog file into the workspace again (*reconsult* built-in) after some bug therein has been modified. This action results in the deletion of any clauses in the workspace which match any clause names that occur in the workspace which match any clause names that occur in the Prolog text being read in again. The idea is to allow modification of errors detected in modules during the interactive test session, without having to abort the session entirely. This, however, works as expected *only if* all clauses with the same name come from the same file. If not, you often end up inadvertently eliminating clauses from other sources (modules) as well, which usually leads to inconsistent program behavior and general confusion.

A Prolog text can be loaded at any time by issuing the command

   ?– **consult***(filename).*

or

   ?– **consult***([filename_1,filename_2,...]).*

in the event that more than one text file is to be consulted at once. Remember that the order of consultation may be significant! If the filename contains special characters other than the underline symbol ('_') or if the name starts with an upper-case letter or the underline symbol, then you must enclose that filename in *single quotes* ('), so that Prolog recognizes it as an *atom*, i.e. an identifier. This is especially true of Unix *pathnames*. They should be written as follows:

   ?– **consult(['prologfiles/xyz', abc, 'MyProgram']).**

Since consulting is a relatively common event in an interactive session, most systems permit an abbreviated form of the *consult* command, i.e. simply a list of filenames as input. Thus

   ?– **['prologfiles/xyz', abc, 'MyProgram'].**

does the same as the previous, more complete form.

   In order to experiment with *consult*, you must first have a Prolog text to read in. We shall therefore begin with a concrete application implementing a *relational database* in Prolog.

1.3   Facts and Functors

The entries, i.e. 'records' in our Prolog database are referred to as facts. A *fact* is the most primitive form of a clause. The very name 'fact' characterizes its function: a *fact* is used in Prolog to define a circumstance which is always considered to be *true*. This is in sharp contrast to *rules*, which are (typically compound) clauses which are *true only when defined conditions* prevail. We shall discuss rules in detail in the next chapter.

Facts take the following general form:

    functor(Argument_1, ..., Argument_N).

Once again, we encounter the formal logic-oriented terminology of Prolog:

- a *functor* might be seen by a database specialist as the name of a record type or the identifier of a particular relation, and
- the *arguments* as fields or attributes.

Ignoring the unusual terminology, we could say that a fact in Prolog is simply a (relational) record. This equivalence is quite plausible from the perspective of 'programming in logic', as well. After all, what is a record, e.g. in a master file for personnel, but a documentation of the *logical statement*, i.e. the *fact* that a person of the description contained in that record is an employee of the respective enterprise?

The number of arguments in a fact is referred to as the *arity* of the functor. The *arity* of a functor can, theoretically speaking, be arbitrarily large. In fact, however, every implementation sets some limit on the maximum number of arguments which can be dealt with. This is generally large enough, in our experience, to present no real problems. And if only for the sake of readability, one usually tries to keep the number of arguments to a maximum of about ten; most systems permit many more.

Arity is a significant attribute of a functor. For example, if two facts have the same functor name, but a different number of arguments, i.e. arity, then the system treats them as distinct, despite the apparent similarity. Thus, given

    film(Title, Producer, Director, Actor)

and

    film(Manufacturer, Format, Sensitivity)

Prolog 'sees' these two functors *film* as being completely distinct.

This is actually quite reasonable from a functional point of view, as they actually refer to two very different record types or relations in our database. Nonetheless, it is a common source of errors, as you easily leave out an argument or accidentally include one too many when programming.

Keep this in mind when, in testing your programs, Prolog cannot seem to find some clause that you are absolutely positive is there.

Relations, i.e. functors, of arity *null* (zero) are also possible and often quite useful. You could, for instance, include the fact

prologcourse.

in your database, to provide a reminder to yourself of something having to do with a Prolog course; somewhat like tying a string around your finger!

As long as you use Prolog exclusively as a database system, you will actually find little use for such reminders. You are more likely instead to associate additional information with a given fact, e.g. the date on which the Prolog course is taking place.

On the other hand, once you begin programming in Prolog, you will find yourself using null arity facts more regularly. They are actually a very practical way of setting *flags* as state indicators. For example, you wish to make the execution of a procedure, a trace for instance, contingent upon whether you are currently testing a program. You would then enter the fact *test* into your database, and write the trace procedure such that it executes only when such a fact is present. How one writes such a program will itself be discussed in a later chapter.

1.4 Atoms, Variables and Constants

You may have noticed in the above description of the basic syntax of *facts*, that we always wrote the *functor* name all in lower-case letters and all the *argument names* starting with an upper-case letter. This is a convention observed by most Prolog implementations. It serves to quickly and easily distinguish between *variables* and *constants*. Those are two *lexical units*, or *atoms*, in Prolog terminology, which are recognized by the interpreter.[2]

Variables are identified by names consisting of alphanumeric characters (A–Z, a–z, 0–9), as well as the underline character. The names may be arbitrarily long, but must always begin with an *upper-case* letter or an underline. Some permissible variable names are:

X
Lastname
_address
_

The latter, the *atom* consisting of the underline symbol all by itself, is

---

[2] *Strings* are not a lexical unit recognized by the interpreter. Prolog represents strings as a list of individual characters, which are written and manipulated as such.

referred to as an *anonymous variable*. An anonymous variable is a sort of placeholder. It appears in positions where an argument is expected, but where the actual value of the argument is not of particular interest, serving, as it were, as a kind of wild card or joker. It saves the user the bother of having to invent named, dummy variables and, even more important, makes the irrelevance of the variable's value for the given task immediately evident to the reader.

Constants fall into four categories:

names:
> written like variables, except that they are not allowed to start with upper-case letters or the underline symbol. Nor may they consist purely of digits. They may be arbitrarily long.

integers
> integers are distinct from *names* in that they consist exclusively of digits and that they can participate as operands in mathematical computations.

operators
> operators are lexical tokens (atoms), which have a special meaning for Prolog, e.g. '+' or '−', used in arithmetic expressions, or such symbols as '=...' or '\='. These, like integers, will be discussed in greater detail in a more suitable context.

quoted names
> as the category name indicates, these are character strings of arbitrary length enclosed in *single quotes*, e.g. *'Smith'* or *'error message'*. They generally serve one of two purposes: either to mark as constants strings which would otherwise be interpreted as variables or to delineate text which is intended to be stored as one unit, despite intervening blanks, e.g. strings used to write messages to the user (errors, prompts, etc.).

Returning to the original topic, the general format of *facts:* the *functor* name is written entirely in lower-case letters to indicate that it, in essence, must always be a constant. Each *formal argument*, on the other hand, is written with an initial upper-case letter, because arguments may be *variables*, as well as any constant value which a variable may assume.

An actual argument is an arbitrarily complex expression or, drawing on Prolog's logical roots, an arbitrary *term*. The term can be a

- constant,

- variable,

- nested *structure* or *logical function* (synonymous here) of arbitrary depth, i.e. a term with the same syntactic structure as a fact,[3] or

- *list*, of the form [*Entry_1,..., Entry_N*], whereby each entry may itself be another term (recursion or nesting). A list may also be empty, which is written as '[]'.[4]

If you are familiar with the terminology of the relational database model, you might say that a fact in Prolog need not be of any normal form whatsoever. As in the case of a function, a fact may exhibit an arbitrarily complex, hierarchical (tree) structure.

1.5   A Personal Databank

The database we would like to construct is a kind of appointment calendar, in which we can record data regarding people, places and events. Typically the entries concern future events, but they can also refer to past ones, giving the database the character of a diary.

The entries themselves are actually facts. They may be broken down into three relations, yielding as many functors:

person*(Keyword,Name,Town,Telephone),*
place*(Keyword,Locale,Town,Telephone)*

and

event*(Keyword,Date,Time,Locale,Name).*

As we have already seen, any one of the individual arguments, such as *Keyword* or *Name*, could just as easily be a complex structure, as long as it is a syntactically correct *term* in Prolog. The problem with such complex terms arises when you wish to query the database: namely, that you must formulate your request observing exactly the same structure. This is due to the nature of the fundamental *pattern-matching* process, called *unification*, which is used to extract the information in the respective database entries. We shall explore this in greater detail later.

Suffice it to say here that given this search mechanism, one cannot find an entry such as

---

[3] Semantically speaking, a function differs from a fact in that whereas the latter is always two-valued, i.e. either *true* or *false*, a function, can be multi-valued, i.e. represent, at least in principle, any number of values. Thus, a function *wife(Name)* stands for a distinct value from the set of all married women.

[4] A list is interpreted semantically as a term represented by the functor '.', i.e. a period, which has an arity of 2. Thus [*Element_1,Element_2,Element_3*] could be written as ".(*Element_1,.(Element_2,.(Element_3,*[]))). This notation is rarely used, however, as it is difficult to read and write, particularly when lists get very long.

person(customer,[fred,smith],[chicago,'Main St.'],5679810).

with the following query:

?–**person(_,smith,chicago,Phonenum).**

You will recall that '_' and 'Phonenum' serve as variables. The *anonymous variable* '_' was used because we were not interested in the value associated with *Keyword*. It is Mr Smith's *Phonenum*ber in Chicago whose value was to be extracted.

To find the entry, however, you would have to formulate the query mirroring the entry in every structural detail:

?–**person(_,[_,smith],[chicago,_],Phonenum).**

This is because we are using Prolog here like a conventional 'dumb' databank. In the next chapter we shall see how we can make it more intelligent, removing the limitation described above.

For the time being, we might establish the convention that only simple constants or variables will be used as arguments of the clause. The one exception to this rule to be the *Date*, which we shall always enter as a list:

Date = [Month,Day,Year].

Since the telephone number is a constant, we can only give the local telephone number without the area code, as the two taken together would require a list or some other (complex) structure.

We resolve this issue in a way which actually leads to a better problem definition altogether. We introduce a fourth relation in the form of the functor *areacode*, with an arity of 2, e.g.:

areacode(Town,Code)

This effectively creates an area code index in the database, containing such entries as:

areacode('new york','212').
areacode(london,'0044/1').
areacode(munich,'089').
. . .

Note that we placed not only the area code for London in quotes, due to the special character '/', but that of Munich as well. We did this because, as mentioned earlier, an atom consisting strictly of numerals is normally, automatically interpreted as an integer. Under most circumstances this would not matter, except that Prolog always suppresses leading zeroes in numeric output. This would cause the Munich's area code to be printed as 89. By placing the numerals in apostrophes, we make a *quoted name* out of the value, causing the interpreter to accept the string as is, i.e. without doing any of the conversions which would otherwise occur to transform the expressed value into a computationally manipulable representation of the corresponding integer.

Figure 1.1 shows an excerpt from the personal database created.

```
person(customer,schulz,'new york',7963470).
person(customer,smith,boston,4236796).
person(customer,miller,boston,4241796).
person(customer,williams,berkeley,8371623).
person(supplier,andrews,'new york',7815944).

event(invitation,[5,2,1985],20,fridays,schulz).
event(invitation,[6,6,1985],19,pier46,smith).
event(invitation,[6,7,1985],12,bigboy,williams).
event(overnight,[6,6,1985],evening,hilton,myself).
event(birthday,[12,7,1934],'?','san francisco',smith).
event(birthday,[6,8,'?'],'?','?',williams).

place(restaurant,fridays,'new york',7625899).
place(restaurant,pier64,boston,4556766).
place(restaurant,bigboy,berkeley,8417234).
place(hotel,hilton,boston,4738000).

areacode('new york','212').
areacode(berkeley,'415').
areacode(boston,'508').
areacode(munich,'089').
areacode(london,'0044/1').
```

Fig. 1.1   Some sample entries in the personal databank

Arguments whose actual values are unknown are indicated by a question mark. Being a special character, it too is always enclosed in apostrophes, as explained above. This use of the question mark in the database is arbitrary and is *not* part of the definition of Prolog. You could choose some other constant to serve as such a placeholder for the 'unknown' value associated with a particular record, i.e. fact in the databank. You might think that the standard *anonymous variable* ('_') would be more appropriate. Actually, though, using it for placeholding in these *facts* would have the undesirable effect of matching any value the user entered in the query in the respective position. This would cause the thus formulated fact to be returned *regardless* of the search value the user might enter for that field — hardly the behavior of a good database system.

As you may recall, the original reason for creating this small database was to make a Prolog text which we could then consult as part of our interaction with the Prolog system. If you enter the sample text from Fig. 1.1 into a file named *database*, then you can always respond to the Prolog system prompt with

?–consult(database).

or

   ?–[database].

and have Prolog load the contents of that file into its workspace for
immediate use. If you should happen to make a syntax error, your system
should, it is hoped, return a relatively unambiguous error message as to
where in your input the error occurred.

   A good Prolog system should resume its interpretative activity at the
place (state) where it had been prior to the entry of the invalid clause. This
prevents erroneous clauses from appearing in the database. We shall see
shortly how you can interactively add clauses to the workspace as the need
arises. Many people, however, prefer to abandon the current session when
it is evident that there is an error in the text loaded and immediately correct
the original source file.

1.6   Prolog as a Database Query Language

Once you have successfully loaded, i.e. consulted your database, and Prolog
has written a prompt to the screen, you can begin to experiment with some
simple queries. Figure 1.2 shows you a few examples.

   ?–person(_,smith,Town,Tel).

   Town = boston
   Tel = 4236796

   yes
   ?–person(Key,smith,london,Tel).

   no
   ?–place(hotel,Hotel,Town,Tel), areacode(Town,AC).

   Hotel = hilton
   Town = boston
   Tel = 4738000
   AC = '508'

   yes
   ?–

Fig. 1.2   Queries on the personal databank in Fig. 1.1

   The first query causes Prolog to search for a particular *person*. As you
can see, a query is also formulated as a clause. Because the clause is entered
in response to the system prompt, it is interpreted by Prolog as a *goal*, i.e.
the object of its search.

The only constant argument in the clause is (the name) *smith*. Prolog proceeds to search in the workspace (database) for a *fact* with the functor *person* and an atom *smith* in the same position as in the query and then *unifies* the variable arguments in the goal with the corresponding arguments (values) of the *fact* found. The result shows the value assigned each variable by the unification. Note that the first query argument, an *anonymous variable*, is not mentioned in the result.

If you try this out at your terminal, you will see that, after printing the values for *Town* and *Tel*, the cursor is positioned at the end of the second line of output. In order to have Prolog continue, you must hit the carriage return key. The system should reply with *yes*, indicating that its search was successful, or in Prolog terminology, that the *resolution* of the last goal was successful. The concept of *resolution* is derived from formal logic. In this context it means that the *truth* of a particular goal, with the given values for logical variables, could be established by the resolution algorithm based on the facts in the active database.

Treating a search in the database as a 'proof of a logical statement' may seem peculiar to you. The following discussion will, it is hoped, make the method appear plausible. The advantage of the 'proof' approach lies in the fact that it allows you to integrate logical *rules*, as well as *facts*, into the database. Just how you do this is explained in the next chapter.

Returning to our example, we see that, after returning a *yes*, the interpreter continues the dialog by issuing another prompt. The second goal which we entered *cannot* be resolved according to the facts in the current database, or, to use conventional data-processing terms, no record could be found satisfying the request, and Prolog indicates this by responding with *no*. From a database point of view, this answer is most reasonable. From a logical perspective, however, this response raises a problem: we typically interpret it as meaning the statement is (logically) *false*. Clearly, the fact that our database contains no entries for a 'smith' in 'boston' cannot be construed to mean that there is no one named Smith in Boston, but rather that Prolog is not aware of such a person's existence. Thus, the *falseness* of a given statement in Prolog must be interpreted as meaning that the statement is *not demonstrably true* rather than *provably false*. The implication is one of logical *undecidability*. This idea is of crucial significance when dealing with programming in Prolog, where the absence of needed information (facts) causes a statement, speaking now in conventional programming terms, to be interpreted as being *false*.

Looking at the third query in the examples in Fig. 1.2, we see the first use of a *built-in* Prolog *operator*, the comma (','). The comma represents *logical and*. As used in this goal clause, it indicates that a place *and* its area code is to be searched for. The connection between the two sub-goals, *place* and *areacode*, is established via the common variable *Town*. During *unification*, the first sub-goal is associated with a particular value, e.g. *boston*, and this value is then used as a constant in the second sub-goal to *limit the search*.

In terms of logic, the resolution of the entire goal becomes a matter of satisfying a *conjunction*. Given the constant *hotel* as the *Keyword*, one must find a *place* clause whose value for the variable *Town* is the same as the variable *Town* in an *areacode* clause, i.e. the town in the first *and* the second are identical, making the goal *true*.

The use of the comma as the logical *and* connector of terms enables you to formulate queries of arbitrary complexity. As we shall see later, it is one of the most important components for the definition of procedures in Prolog programs. Figure 1.3 shows another example of a query using the *and* operator. In this case, two of the arguments in the *person* goal are *anonymous variables*, i.e. they match any value, indicating that they are not of particular interest.

?–event(What,Date,Time,Where,Who),person(_,Who,berkeley,_).

```
What = invitation
Date = [6,7,1985]
Time = 12
Where = bigboy
Who = williams ;

What = birthday
Date = [6,8,?]
Time = ?
Where = ?
Who = williams ;

no
?–
```

Fig. 1.3 *A query with alternative responses*

If you examine the database in Fig. 1.1 you will see that there are two possible responses to the query. In the dialog shown in Fig. 1.3 we see both answers. How was this achieved?

The second result was obtained by entering a *semicolon* (';') and then hitting the <*return*> key. The semicolon is also a built-in Prolog operator. It stands for the logical connector *inclusive or*. When used interactively, it causes the interpreter to search for another, *alternative* solution to the current goal. This may be repeated as often as you like, i.e. until the set of possible answers in the database has been exhausted. If no further solutions can be found the system responds, as you might expect, with the reply *no*. In other words, based on the information in the workspace, i.e. database, there are no further combinations of variable values which correctly satisfy the request.

2 FROM A DATABASE TO A KNOWLEDGE BASE

The Prolog database in the last chapter contained only *facts*. By adding *rules* we shall now convert it to a knowledge base capable of *producing* new facts from the existing ones. Rules correspond to the procedures of conventional languages. They will enable you to really program in Prolog and not merely access data.

2.1 Production Systems

In the previous chapter we said that facts, seen as records of a relational database, need not be stored in any particular normal form. And yet we built our personal database using only relations of the third normal form. We omitted the telephone area code from the person and place facts, because it is always a function of place and would therefore be redundant. Similarly, we did not permit the use of lists as argument values, except for the date, although they would seem most appropriate for such entries as the name of a person or persons involved in a specific event. For example, if the event is a conference, then we invariably associate several participants with the fact, i.e. the occurrence.

We left the area code out to save space and reduce the time and effort needed to enter and/or change the information. Had we included it in each fact, then if the phone company were to change the area code for a particular city, we would have to modify it in every entry for a person living there.

We prohibited the use of lists as arguments because of the problems it causes in querying the database. If we were to allow for a list of participants at a conference in the fact

    event(conference,[5,3,1985],15,ibm, [williams,miller,schulz]).

then the user would not only have to know that three people took part in the event, but even worse, s/he would have to know that *miller* was the second one named! Otherwise, how would s/he be able to formulate the goal

?–event(What,When,_,Where,[_,miller,_]).

which s/he would need to extract the above fact?

In the last chapter we promised you that in Prolog we could furnish the database with sufficient intelligence to solve this problem itself. To this end, the database must contain enough 'knowledge' to *produce* new information, which is not directly accessible and yet necessary to process a specific goal. Systems which have this ability are called *production systems*.

Your Prolog interpreter is such a production system.

2.2   Rules and Predicates

A production system generates new knowledge using *production rules* or, simply, *rules*. A database which contains rules, as well as facts, is called, in contrast to conventional databases, a *knowledge base*. Programs which use such a knowledge base and a production system are called *knowledge based software*. Having digested this dose of terminology, let us take a look at how you formulate a rule in Prolog.

As you may have suspected, rules are *clauses* too. A rule consists of a *head* and a *body*:

rule_head: − *rule_body*.

The head is orthographically, i.e. formally, identical with a fact: it is a functor with (optional) arguments. As such, the rule's functor has an *arity*. Rules may have the same functor name but different arity. Such rules are distinct in the eyes of the Prolog interpreter!

The rule body consists of one or more terms. In the latter case, the terms must be connected by the previously discussed logical operators ',' (*and*,) or ';' (*or*).

It is important to note that the comma, i.e. *and*, has a higher precedence than the semicolon, i.e. *or*. Keep this in mind, as it is a common source of error for novice Prolog programmers. You can override this built-in precedence, just as you do in many other languages, by using *parentheses* '(...)'.

```
telephone(Name,Role,Town,AreaCode,Number) :-
        (          person(Role,Name,Town,Number)
        ;          place(Role,Name,Town,Number)
        ),
        areacode(Town,AreaCode).
```

Fig. 2.1   A sample rule

Let's look at the sample rule in Fig. 2.1. You can see the meaning of this rule most easily if you add it at the end of your database from the previous chapter and then consult the modified database. Figure 2.2 shows two *telephone* queries using the new rule.

?–telephone(Who,_,_,AreaCode,Tel).

Who = schulz
AreaCode = '212'
Tel = 7963470

yes
**?–telephone(Restaurant,restaurant,Place,ACode,Tel),
  person(_,williams,Place,_).**

Restaurant = bigboy
Place = berkeley
ACode = '415'
Tel = 8417234

yes
?–

Fig. 2.2   Some queries for the telephone rule of Fig. 2.1

As you can see, this rule 'produces' a new *telephone* relation

> from a *person* fact
> *or* a *place* fact
> *and* an *area code* fact..

You can use this rule in a query just as you would use a fact.

As you see, facts and rules are indistinguishable from without. They may both be used in queries and in the formulation of other rules in a like fashion. Recognizing this functional equivalence, we refer to both by a common name: *predicate*. The concept of a *predicate* is, like many others, drawn from formal logic. We shall use the term *predicate* whenever we wish to specifically avoid stating whether the information in the knowledge base is represented by a fact or a rule or some combination of both. As in the case of facts and rules, we shall also speak of *arity*, i.e. the number of arguments, of a predicate. The arity corresponds to that of the predicate's functor.

In a formal sense, a predicate is a logical function which can have only one of two values:

● *true* or

● *fail*.

The values *true* and *fail* may themselves be used in the body of a rule. Indeed *fail* is an important and commonly used value in practical programming applications! We shall show you some examples later.

2.3 Alternative Notations for Rules

Let us, however, return to the telephone rule. You may have noticed that in our explanation of the rule's meaning, we strictly observed the formal structure of the rule body in Fig. 2.1, but disregarded the precedence of the operators *and* and *or*. In writing the rule, however, we accounted for this by using parentheses. We had to do so, otherwise the rule would not always produce the correct results. You might want to see what does in fact happen if you naively translate the verbal description into a rule without any parentheses.

Speaking of parentheses, perhaps our ordering of them, as well as of the semicolon in Fig. 2.1, struck you as being somewhat unusual. You could, if you prefer, write the rule in a different format, e.g. as in Fig. 2.3. From our experience, however, we recommend the original format, as it accents the use of the *or* and the scope of its effect.

```
telephone(Name,Role,Town,AreaCode,Number) :-
    ( person(Role,Name,Town,Number);
      place(Role,Name,Town,Number) ),
    areacode(Town,AreaCode).
```

Fig. 2.3   The conventional style of writing rule 2.1

The advantage of this style will become clearer as you go on to write more complex rules and must debug or maintain them. Tracing the interpretation of rules containing the *or* operator, particularly in nested predicates, seems to be inherently difficult.

Many purists, in fact, recommend that one avoid semicolons in rules altogether! It is indeed possible to express the logical *or* connection merely by writing a series of clauses one after the other. This sometimes requires a certain amount of redundancy or even the inclusion of an additional, intermediate predicate. This is best illustrated by example. Figures 2.4 and 2.5 show two such *or*-free alternatives to our original telephone example.

In Fig. 2.5 we introduced an auxiliary predicate which has the same name as the original predicate, i.e. *telephone*, but of *arity* 4, as compared with *arity* 5 for the original. For the interpreter, it is as if the predicates had two completely different names, because the functors differ in arity.

```
telephone(Name,Role,Town,AreaCode,Number) :-
    person(Role,Name,Town,Number),
    areacode(Town,AreaCode).
telephone(Name,Role,Town,AreaCode,Number) :-
    place(Role,Name,Town,Number),
    areacode(Town,AreaCode).
```

Fig. 2.4   An or-free formulation of rule 2.1

```
telephone(Name,Role,Town,AreaCode,Number) :-
        areacode(Town,AreaCode),
        telephone(Role,Name,Town,Number).

telephone(Role,Name,Town,Number) :-
        place(Role,Name,Town,Number).
telephone(Role,Name,Town,Number) :-
        person(Role,Name,Town,Number).
```

Fig. 2.5   An or-free formulation of rule 2.1 using an intermediate, auxiliary predicate of arity 4

It is certainly of questionable style to have functors and predicates which can be visually distinguished only by the number of arguments which they take. One easily makes such mistakes as including one argument too many or too few when referencing one or the other predicate. And in Prolog this does not necessarily mean you will get an error message, but often merely that the wrong predicate will be applied! This could mean hours of debugging, if you should notice the problem at all![1]

The use of auxiliary predicates has other advantages: the individual rules are generally shorter and thus more readily comprehended. This is particularly true if you are able to find names for the predicates which reveal the contextual function of the rule to the human reader.

Briefly stated rules are of advantage should your interpreter offer a full-screen, interactive debugger. Such tools display the rule associated with each state as the interpreter moves from state to state, processing successive, subordinate rules. The shorter a rule, the more likely it is that it will fit in its entirety in the debugger window!

2.4   'Intelligent' Search Rules

Having discussed the formal aspects of rule writing, let us proceed with the development of rules which will bestow our database with enough intelligence to render it a knowledge base. It should be capable of processing lists as attributes of a relation, i.e. as arguments of a query predicate, to use Prolog terminology. A list might be the names of the participants of an event, or perhaps all the parts, including titles of a person's name.

In Figs. 2.6(a) and (b) we see a new knowledge base. We have intentionally reduced and simplified the contents. Once again, it represents a sort of diary or log, but the entries are merely persons and events. We dispense with the places and area codes, that we might better illustrate the essential aspect.

---

[1] The situation is worsened by the fact that some Prolog interpreters do not even inform you that a predicate which you have referenced has not been defined. Such interpreters consider such a reference to have the value *fail*. Should your interpreter be so generous, then not even the best programming style will help you!

```
%    Rules for handling lists entered for names in queries.
%    When more than one name is included in a query, it is
%    interpreted as a logical AND:

person(Role,Name,Town,Telephone) :-
        var(Name),
        p(Role,Name,Town,Telephone).
person(Role,Name,Town,Telephone) :-
        nonvar(Name), atom(Name),
        (        p(Role,Name,Town,Telephone)
        ;        p(Role,[Head|Rest],Town,Telephone),
                 member(Name,[Head|Rest])
        ).
person(Role,[Name],Town,Telephone) :-
        nonvar(Name),
        person(Role,Name,Town,Telephone).
person(Role,[Name,Name2|Additional],Town, Telephone) :-
        nonvar(Name),
        person(Role,Name,Town,Telephone),
        person(Role,[Name2|Additional],Town,Telephone).

%    Facts about People

p(customer,[carl,schulz],'new york',7963470).
p(customer,[frank,schulz],berkeley,8235921).
p(customer,smith,boston,4236796).
p(customer,miller,boston,4241796).
p(customer,[miller,frank,dr],'new york',7759657).
p(customer,williams,berkeley,8371623).
p(supplier,[dr,andrews,inc],'new york',7852011).
p(supplier,[frank,andrews],berkeley,8240456).
```

(a)

```
%    Rules dealing with the participation of more
%    than one person at an event.
%    When more than one person is included in a
%    query the interpretation is as logical OR

event(What,Date,Time,Place,Who) :-
        var(Who),
        e(What,Date,Time,Place,Who).
event(What,Date,Time,Place,Who) :-
        nonvar(Who),atom(Who),
        (        e(What,Date,Time,Place,Who)
        ;        e(What,Date,Time,Place,[Head|Rest]),
                 member(Who,[Head|Rest])
        ).
```

```
event(What,Date,Time,Place,[Who|_]) :-
        nonvar(Who),                    %    Recursion for var !
        event(What,Date,Time,Place,Who).
event(What,Date,Time,Place,[Who,WhoElse|Additional]) :-
        nonvar(Who),
        event(What,Date,Time,Place,[WhoElse|Additional]).
```

```
%       Event Facts
```

```
e(conference,[7,2,1985],10,boston,
        [smith,williams,andrews]).
e(conference,[7,5,1985],14,'new york',
        [schulz,miller]).
e(invitation,[6,7,1985],12,bigboy,williams).
e(overnight,[6,6,1985],evening,hilton,myself).
e(birthday,[12,7,1934],'?','san francisco',smith).
```
(b)

Fig. 2.6   A knowledge base about people and events: (a) Part 1 – people;
(b) Part 2 – events

The essential aspect is that the predicates *person* and *event* are expressed as rules and no longer as simple facts. These rules must implement the 'intelligent' search mechanism.

Naturally we still need a database of actual facts in addition to the search rules. The database of facts now contains entries of the following form:

   p*(SearchKey,Names,Place,Telephone).*

and

   e*(SearchKey,Date,Time,Place,People).*

In contrast to the corresponding facts in the database of the previous chapter, the values of the arguments *Names* and *People* in the new database may also be lists of values, as you can see in the example in Fig. 2.6a.[2]

Queries should naturally be possible using either atoms or lists. For instance, if we suspect that there are but a very few persons with a particular last (or first) name in our database, then we should like to be able to give the one name as an atom and not be forced to enter a list. On the other hand, if we think there may be many entries with the single name, we should like to be able to add qualifiers, such as

---

[2] For the remaining arguments (excepting date), we continue to restrict the allowed values to atoms, in order to keep the rules simple. We suggest, as an exercise, that you attempt to similarly extend the allowed value set for these arguments!

[miller,frank]

or

[dr,miller]

given as a list. And the user should, of course, be allowed to enter the
qualifying data in any arbitrary order!

2.5 List Processing

In order to understand the rules in Fig. 2.6(a) we must briefly discuss the
Prolog syntax, i.e. notation for lists.

As we have already mentioned, a list in Prolog is written as an enumer-
ation of its elements, each separated from the next by a comma, and the
whole thing enclosed in square brackets:

[*Element1, Element2,..., Elementn*].

The *empty list* is represented by brackets enclosing nothing at all: '[ ]'.

The three periods used in the original example are not part of the Prolog syntax, but rather our informal way of indicating that an arbitrary
number of some object, i.e. elements in this case, may be substituted in the
corresponding position.

You can imagine, however, that one often needs a rule which is general
enough to process each element of a list of arbitrary length in a particular
fashion. Prolog provides us with the notation for just such situations by
conceptually treating a list as consisting of *Head* and *Tail*:

[*Head*|*Tail*].

Head stands for the first *element* of the list and *Tail* stands for a list (!)
consisting of all the remaining elements. For example, given the following
list *L*:

L = [frank,miller,dr],

then the expressions on the left result in the unifications shown to the right,
respectively:

L = [frank|R]	R = [miller,dr],
L = [frank,miller|R]	R = [dr],
L = [X|R]	X = frank, R = [miller,dr],
L = [frank,X,dr|R]	X = miller, R = [],
L = [frank|[N,T]]	N = miller, T = dr,
L = [frank|[N|T]]	N = miller, T = [dr].

Before you attempt to analyze the rules in our sample knowledge base, be sure you really understand why the above examples yield the results they do. Without a firm footing in the list notation you will have endless difficulty with list manipulation!

2.6 Classifying Predicates

To follow the rules in Fig. 2.6(a), you must, for one thing, know the function of those predicates which are used in it and yet are not explicitly defined. Indeed, the only things defined there are the facts *p* and *e*.

As you may already have suspected, the aforementioned predicates are of the so-called *built-in* sort, i.e. predicates which are predefined in a standard Prolog system. A comprehensive Prolog system provides more than one hundred such standard, built-in predicates. In the appendix you will find a list of all the built-in predicates used in this book, as well as some additional, very common ones. We shall actually discuss only those built-ins which are absolutely necessary to understand the examples presented or which exhibit some characteristic particularly worthy of scrutiny.

Let us then begin by examining the built-in predicates used in Fig. 2.6(a). For example, *member*(X, L) checks if the element X occurs anywhere in the list L. We will treat this predicate in greater detail in the next chapter. Instead, let us turn our attention to the other built-in predicates used in the example, like *var, nonvar* or *atom*, as they belong to a group of predicates whose arity is 1 and whose function is to check the 'type' of their respective argument. We do not mean type, however, in the sense in which it is used in conventional languages, such as Pascal, where a variable is associated with a particular data object, i.e. internal representation such as integer, real, character, etc. Prolog, like Lisp, is a *typeless language*. A variable can represent, i.e. may be unified with, an arbitrarily complex Prolog term.

We use the term type in the sense of an *abstract data type:* a classification of data objects according to what can reasonably be done with them, how they can be logically manipulated. And this is precisely what typifies the use of these, what we like to call selector or classificatory predicates, as our example illustrates.

Often one of the first and most important functions of a predicate is to determine its applicability based on the results of the unification of one or more variables in the rule head with the corresponding arguments of the current goal. If we look at the *person* predicate, for example, we see that it must 'do something different', depending on whether the argument *Name* is unified with a variable, an atom, a list or a logical function.

The typical structure of a predicate whose definition must deal with several slightly different versions of a common problem is illustrated in our example: the rules are written in immediate succession and consist respectively of essentially two parts.

It is the second part that defines the actual purpose of the rule, i.e. the determination of values via unification, or side effects, which we shall discuss later in more detail, such as input and output or the storage of results in the database.

In contrast, the first part fully specifies the particular case dealt with by the second part. This is typically accomplished via classificatory predicates, which identify some unique characteristic of the respective case, although it is sometimes possible to express the selector in some other way. Many times, particularly in the case of structures such as lists or logical functions, the classification can be made via the formulation of the argument in the rule head. The third and fourth rules of the *person* predicate are excellent examples. The notation

[*Name*] and [*Name2*|*AdditionalNames*]

limit the respective rules to those cases (goals) where the second argument is a list of one or more elements.

Should such clear-cut structural type characteristics be lacking, you will find the built-in predicates mentioned above quite useful for classifying the respective cases to be dealt with:

var(X)
> is *true* if the argument X is a variable, i.e. can still be unified with an arbitrary data structure.

nonvar(X)
> is *true* if the argument X is *not* associated with a variable. Nonetheless X could still be associated with a complex data structure which is itself not a variable and yet contains variables! Thus, if X is unified with [*Y*|*Z*], then *nonvar(X)* is in fact true! And yet X will unify with no problem whatsoever with [*miller,frank,dr*] (Why?)

atom(X)
> is *true* if the argument X is a genuine Prolog atom, and not numeric or a variable.

integer(X)
> is *true* if the argument X is *numeric*, i.e. is an integer. You can perform calculations with a numeric argument, as we shall see later.

atomic(X)
> is *true* if the argument X is any arbitrary atom, including numeric ones. It *fails* if X is unified with a variable. Arguments for which it yields true may, among other things, be used as a functor.

struct(*X*)

    is *true* if the argument *X* is a structure, i.e. is *not* an atom.

All these predicates can be inverted, i.e. transformed to mean the complement of their original test. This is accomplished by applying the built-in unary operator *not* to them.[3] Thus,

    not integer(*X*)

tests if *X* is something other than an integer.

    Please note that it is extremely important that you *completely* delimit the specific case for which a given rule applies, using the classificatory predicates and structural pattern matching discussed above, *in each and every rule!*

    You will often encounter a certain degree of carelessness in this regard: since Prolog works through the rules in top-down fashion, programmers mistakenly leave out the selector predicates in rules further down, under the assumption that the respective alternative cases were already 'checked' by the previous rules. Thus, if the first rule already screened out the case where the characteristic argument is a variable, using the predicate *var*, in the subsequent rules they neglect to exclude that possibility by checking their characteristic argument with the predicate *nonvar*.

    This is always, under all circumstances, bad Prolog programming style. The reason for this is really quite simple, although perhaps not immediately evident: should the earlier (higher up) rule *fail*, then the *backtracking* mechanism in Prolog causes the subsequent rules also to be (inappropriately) applied.[4] The variable will then be unified with the strangest things, as the subsequent rules expect some nonvariable argument. The consequences will at best (?) be incorrect results and at worst (?) an endless recursion, which will abort when some memory allotment has been exhausted.

    We recommend that you introduce such errors into the example in Fig. 2.6 (a) and (b) by, for instance, deleting a *nonvar* predicate. You can then test the sloppy version with some complicated queries (goals), to see what happens — particularly when you respond to a given result with a semicolon, causing the interpreter to backtrack for an alternative answer. This exercise will give you a chance to familiarize yourself with the typical (mis-)behavior of Prolog in reaction to such programming errors.

    At least when you make the mistake yourself, and even the best of us do, after a few times you will almost instinctively recognize the problem as being a missing selector predicate and will not have to search very long for the deficient rule(s).

---

[3] The *not* operator has some subtle pitfalls! We will deal with them later. You can use it with the above classificatory predicates, however, without any hesitation.

[4] We shall later introduce the language component known as *cut*, which can be used to avoid this problem. This increases the temptation to be somewhat sloppy in this regard. *But don't give in! You will certainly regret it.*

2.7 The Unification and Instantiation of a Variable

Let us examine the predicate *person* with arity 4 (four) in order to see how the rules in Fig. 2.6(a) function. Having done so, you should be able to dissect the *event* predicate with arity 5 by yourself. In other words, we shall attempt to develop a general scheme or model for rules, which you can apply to all Prolog programs.

As we have already seen, a rule consists of a *rule head* and a *rule body*. The rule head has the same notational form as a fact, except that it is terminated with the ':-' operator.

> person(Role,Name,Town,Telephone) :-

postulates, in our example, the existence of a specific person, characterized by the attributes *Role, Name, Town* and *Telephone* formulated as variable arguments, *if* the conditions presented in the rule body as *goals* can be satisfied: i.e.

> var(Name),
> p(Role,Name,Town,Telephone).

The operator ':-' stands precisely for the *if*; you should get used to reading it that way as soon as possible. The goals in the rule body are evaluated in just the same way as those which we used interactively at the terminal. The operators ',' for logical *and* and ';' for logical *or* also have the same meaning and function as their interactive counterparts.

What happens with the variable arguments in the rule head and the respective goals, when the rule is tentatively applied? By entering the goal (query)

> **person(_,[dr,miller],'new york',Telephone)**

at the terminal we activate the first rule.

As was the case with facts, Prolog *unifies* the variable arguments of the goal (query) with those of the rule head, inasmuch as this is possible: i.e.

Role	with the *anonymous variable*,
Name	with the list [*dr,miller*],
Town	with *new york* and
Telephone	with *Telephone*.

Please note, however, that in the last unification the variables *Telephone* in the rule head and *Telephone* in the goal are actually two *separate* ones, despite their common name. This is because Prolog, upon reading the goals and rules in, immediately replaces all the variables with unique internal names. Later you will see that a good Prolog implementation, for example during interactive, symbolic testing or debugging, will only show you the unique, internal name and not the original, symbolic name, to avoid confusion arising from the identical names.

The 'inasmuch as this is possible' limitation mentioned above refers to the fact that Prolog only carries out a *unification* if the structures 'match'. If you look at the rule head of the third *person* rule, you will notice that the second argument is defined as

[Name]

specifying explicitly that it only deals with lists consisting of *exactly one* element. Clearly this will not unify with the second argument of our stated goal (query),

[dr,miller] .

Consequently Prolog will immediately skip the third rule in its unification attempt and ignore it in its search for possible solutions. In contrast, the second argument of the fourth rule

[Name2|AdditionalNames]

permits a unification, the result of which is

dr	for *Name* and
[*miller*]	as a list (!) for [*Name2*|*AdditionalNames*]

The variables in the rule body are subject to the same unifications as their counterparts in the rule head. Moreover, unification also works *in the opposite direction*: if some as yet non-unified variable should become associated with some value during evaluation of some goal at a deeper level in the rule body, this unification 'floats up' to the higher level. Thus, in our example, the sub-goal

p(_,[dr,miller],'new york',Telephone),

from the evaluation of the first *person* rule, acquires, via the lower level unification with the fact

p(customer,[miller,frank,dr],'new york',7759657),

the value

Telephone = 7759657

which gets associated with the corresponding variable in the rule head and our goal (query) subsequently returns the result shown in Fig. 2.7. Try it out!

?-**person(_,[dr,miller],'new york',Telephone).**

Telephone = 7759657 ;

no
?-

Fig. 2.7   Querying the knowledge base of Fig. 2.6(a) and (b)

The process by which a variable acquires a value via unification is referred to as *instantiation*.

Thereafter one speaks of an *instantiated* variable, whereas prior to the unification one calls it *uninstantiated*. Only uninstantiated variables can acquire a value via unification! The modification of the value of an *instantiated* variable, such as one routinely does in most conventional programming languages with an *assignment operator* like '=' or ':=', is not possible in Prolog. This means that you must write many procedures in Prolog quite differently than you are accustomed to. This 'feature' is not necessarily a disadvantage — indeed many software engineers consider the undisciplined reassignment of variable values to be almost as problematic as the undisciplined use of *goto*s.

2.8   Resolution, Backtracking and Choice Points

At this point we suggest that you take the time and effort to 'walk through' the process involved in responding to the query shown in Fig. 2.7 (and perhaps some others of your own making). The general principle is quite simple: Prolog works through the goals of the rule body, one at a time and in the order in which they were written. The evaluation of a goal implies the attempt to unify a goal's uninstantiated variables with facts and heads of rules, etc. in the manner discussed above. This continues until one of two situations arises:

- either no further unifications are possible and uninstantiated variables still exist — a result called *fail*, or

- all applicable rules (possibly implying several levels of *recursion*) have been successfully processed and the uninstantiated variables of the original goal unified with some value so that a result has been reached. The working up of the individual rules and subgoals is referred to as the process of *resolving* their implicit propositions. As such, one calls the underlying algorithm of the Prolog interpreter *resolution*. We shall deal later with the logical underpinnings of the resolution principle.

Right now, we should consider what the *resolution algorithm* does when it, at some arbitrary level, encounters a predicate for which a unification is impossible? It applies the following two strategies in precisely the order given:

1.   It attempts a unification with the next rule or fact which has the same

functor, i.e. the same name and arity (number of arguments). This means that, in our example, it is the four distinct rules for *person*, taken *together*, which actually constitute the predicate defining a person. Furthermore it implies that writing several rules of the same name and arity, one after the other, is equivalent to formulating a single rule with the same rule bodies connected by ';', i.e. the *or* operator, and parenthesized to form a disjoint selection. That the former is preferable for reasons of clarity has already been mentioned. At the risk of being pedantic, we repeat ourselves, however, since writing rules which are too long and therefore too complex to comprehend and test is one of the prevalent errors among novice Prolog programmers!

2. If there is no alternative, satisfactory clause for the currently active (sub-)goal, then the Prolog interpreter switches to another strategy known as *backtracking*. Assuming the active goal is not the first clause in the rule body, the interpreter goes back to the goal immediately preceding the unsatisfiable current one, i.e. to the last successfully evaluated goal, and attempts to re-satisfy it, in the hopes that it will deliver alternative values and thus allow the aforementioned, 'problematic' goal to be satisfied and ultimately allow the entire chain of goals, in the case of rules, to unify to a final result. Naturally, if the previous goal is not resatisfiable, backtracking recursively attempts to resatisfy its predecessor, and so on, always seeking to find a set of values which ultimately allow it to fully satisfy all the (sub-)goals of a rule and thus reach a viable conclusion. Thus, in the case of the fourth *person* rule, backtracking would cause the attempt to resatisfy the sub-goal

    person(Role,Name,Town,Telephone)

    if its successor

    person(Role,AdditionalNames,Town,Telephone)

    had proven unsatisfiable (non-unifiable), i.e. had *fail*ed using the values generated up to that point.

The goal to which the Prolog interpreter moves back to in its attempt to come up with a viable alternative (set of) value(s), i.e. the last successfully satisfied goal, is referred to as the *choice point*.

An important feature of backtracking is that whenever it occurs, all the variables which had become instantiated *after the choice point* get *uninstantiated* again, so that they may be unified with new values, should the attempted resatisfaction allow the interpreter to proceed. In a sense, backtracking is the only means Prolog has to reassign or modify values of a variable.

If you really tried to apply these strategies of *unification* and *resolution* to walk through our example, you surely noticed that even in this relatively simple case things get quite confusing. That is why a good, interactive testing tool (debugger), which allows you to follow the actions of the interpreter step-for-step, is indispensable! In Chapter 5 we shall discuss such tools in greater detail. If your system has such an aid, you may want to jump ahead briefly to try it out, especially if you found the above little exercise too frustrating!

3 A PROCEDURAL INTERPRETATION

In this chapter we illustrate the close relationship between a Prolog *predicate* and a *procedure*, or routine, as you know them from other programming languages. This alternative interpretation is the reason that you can use Prolog as a query language for a database, or as a language for formal specifications, or simply as an everyday programming language, all depending on your intended application.

3.1 Predicates as Procedures

Not all the predicates which we treated as *built-in* in the example in the previous chapter perform a classifying function. At least one of them, the predicate

member(Element,List)

is much more like your customary procedure. Indeed, depending on how the arguments are unified at the time the predicate is called, it may be considered a

test procedure:
   testing if *Element* appears in the given *List,*

query or access procedure:
   fetching the respective *Elements* in the given *List*, or

generating procedure:
   producing a *List* containing the given *Element*.

In view of the diverse interpretations, you might well object, now, to our referring to this predicate as comparable to the 'usual procedure'. It is certainly unusual that a programming language does not clearly distinguish between these very different tasks executed by a single procedure. This merely demonstrates the fact that the *algorithms*, i.e. the computational instructions, designed to fulfill these three goals are themselves very different, and that therefore the bodies of procedures carrying out the three actions are each distinctively different.

Since Prolog describes *what* a 'procedure' is to do, rather than *how* it is to achieve its end, i.e. *what* the characteristics of the arguments must be, in order that the predicate make a *true* statement, the determination of the correct algorithm to determine the appropriate or legitimate values of the argument(s) is entirely the task of the Prolog interpreter. Consequently, the distinction between the three procedure types is (almost) irrelevant to the Prolog programmer.[1] Thus, Prolog is considered a *non-algorithmic language*. For many computer scientists this is identical with *non-procedural*, a term frequently associated with Prolog. This, however, causes a justifiable confusion, since the concept of *procedure* is frequently used as a synonym for *predicate* in most Prolog-related literature.

In this book we intentionally use the term 'procedure', but emphasize that procedures in Prolog distinguish themselves from their conventional counterparts, in that, due to the fact that the programmer in Prolog does not write algorithms, they typically serve a number of different purposes. Therefore, perhaps in contrast to other languages, in the context of Prolog we cannot consider the concepts of *procedure* and *algorithm* to be synonymous.

Let us now examine the procedure *member* more closely in view of the above. It is an appropriate example also, because it is *not* included as a *built-in* predicate in all Prolog interpreters, and therefore you might well have to write one in Prolog yourself, so that you can run the examples of the previous chapter.

How does one *program* a procedure such as *member* in Prolog?

3.2   The Procedure *member*

Figure 3.1 shows the predicate *member*, as it is defined as a built-in in your system, or as you yourself would include it in a private collection of standard procedures which you can then routinely consult, should your interpreter not provide them automatically.

```
member(Element,[Element|_]).
member(Element,[_|RestOfList]) :-
          member(Element,RestOfList).
```

Fig. 3.1   The procedure member

---

[1] 'Almost', because of the *cut* mechanism, which we have as yet mentioned only in passing. The *cut* mechanism makes Prolog more procedural than necessary, and we therefore prefer to put off talking about it until much later.

These clauses are best understood, if you read them, i.e. interpret them, 'procedurally'. This is true for each of the three cases previously mentioned: as test, query, and generating procedure, separately. The procedural interpretation depends entirely on which arguments are *variables* and which are *constants* at the time of the procedure call.

Most programming languages require a strict distinction between the input and output parameters of a procedure: the input parameters are those arguments which must have a value at calling time, while the output parameters, by contrast, are assigned values during the procedure's computational activity.[2] Although the terms are used analogously in Prolog, it is important to realize that the attribute input or output is not a fixed characteristic of the procedure. In other words, an argument in Prolog is an

- *output parameter*, if it is an *un*instantiated variable, at the time when the predicate is applied, and it is unified with a term as a value when the predicate is evaluated.

Otherwise the argument is treated as an

- *input parameter*, which passes the term with which it is instantiated as a value into the 'procedure body'.

The distinction is not ideal, however, since procedure arguments are often structures, e.g. lists, which themselves contain *un*instantiated, variable elements. Such arguments serve as input as well as output parameters. Consider the queries which you formulated for our simple knowledge base.

Thus we cannot unconditionally apply this distinction within the Prolog model, primarily because Prolog appeals to a more natural, contextual value-passing mechanism, which most other programming languages cannot deal with. Nonetheless, we would like to have you practice using the concept as it is frequently used. Indeed, some Prolog systems even provide syntactic constructs with which you can declare arguments to be of the input or output type.

Let us see exactly how the *member* predicate in Fig. 3.1 works in the three different applications.

Test procedure

member exercises a test function, if both arguments are instantiated, i.e. *input parameters*, from the start.[3] The first clause

---

[2] Some languages, e.g. the Unix-Shell or C, do not even have output parameters. They require other mechanisms to acquire return values from within procedures.

[3] We assume here that the second argument itself contains no internal, uninstantiated variables, e.g.

```
member(want,[we,X,steak]).
```

Already the distinction we have made no longer functions properly! Do you see why? If not, simply try calling *member* as above.

```
member(Element,[Element|_]).
```

is clearly true, when the second argument is a list whose first *element* is a term identical to the first argument to the procedure. In this case, the test is successful, i.e. the goal is reached. If the two terms are not identical, then the procedure continues on to the second clause:

```
member(Element,[_|RestOfList]) :-
        member(Element,RestOfList).
```

Again, the second argument must also be a list. Its first element, however, is of *no* interest. This is indicated by the *anonymous variable* in that position. Instead, it is the remainder of the list which is subject to further scrutiny. The processing continues here via a *recursive* application of the *same* procedure *member*! This *recursion*, i.e. the calling of a procedure from within itself, is the most important mechanism for controlling the flow of control in Prolog procedures. If the notion of recursion is not familiar to you from your experience with other languages, you should take the time to walk through the above example to learn the principle. Only after this repetition mechanism has become as much second-nature to you as, let us say, a *while* loop, will you be able to program effortlessly in Prolog.

Query procedure
member behaves like a query procedure, if, at call time, the first argument is an *un*instantiated variable, i.e. an *output parameter*, and the second argument an instantiated list, i.e. an *input parameter*. The first clause of the predicate

```
member(Element,[Element|_]).
```

then unifies the first argument with the head, i.e. first *Element* of the list. If the procedure is re-activated via backtracking, then the recursion mechanism causes, as in the test procedure, a sequential access to each (head, or first) element in the respective remainder of the list. This continues until the *RestOfList* is itself the empty list, i.e. '[ ]', at which point the procedure *member* returns the truth value *fail* — indicating that it has accessed each list element exactly once.

Generating Procedure
Finally, *member* is a procedure which generates a list, if the *second* argument, *List*, is an uninstantiated variable, i.e. an *output parameter*. In this case, the call and *each instance of backtracking*, using the recursion mechanism, produces a new list which contains the first argument (an instantiated variable, or constant, i.e. input parameter), each time one position further to the 'right'. You should experiment with this procedure, which is invaluable for your understanding of the way in which the Prolog interpreter and the unification process works. For one thing, such generating proce-

dures are excellent for producing data structures of a given type, but with varying contents, e.g. for use in test generation for software verification. Furthermore, it is instructive to see that the recursion goes on here (theoretically) indefinitely, since there is no break condition as in the case above with the empty list. Instead, the second argument returns a list which becomes, with each recursion, one element longer.

Such an *endless recursion*, due to a programming error, is almost always the reason that Prolog, after much churning away, reports that some resource, e.g. memory, has been exhausted.

If you have a good Prolog interpreter, then this message may never appear! In this case, your system has been implemented with the so-called *end-recursion* resolution. This mechanism converts a recursion at the end of a clause into an internal iteration, i.e. a jump to the beginning of the affected clause, and thus can loop endlessly, without exhausting any physical resources. This is useful, if you want to program a *recursive loop*, e.g. as a run-time frame for an interpreter or, in process-control situations, where a measuring instrument is to be repeatedly and continuously polled.

In any case, it is valuable to have experienced such an infinite recursion once; it will certainly help you detect, if not avoid, such errors in your programs.

3.3 Arithmetic

In our discussion above of the different types of Prolog procedures, you probably miss one of the most common programming tasks: the calculation of values. Naturally such operators or primitives exist in Prolog as well, but in view of the typical application areas for the language, these are less frequently used here than in other languages.

Every Prolog interpreter provides arithmetic operators. Many implementations, particularly for smaller machines, however, allow only for integers as numerical values. Depending on the machine, these are typically 16- or 32-bit/word values. This is, as a rule, sufficient for most Prolog applications, since they are usually of a non-numeric nature and arithmetic is needed only for running counters or for similar purposes.

In the scientific–technical fields, where large machines with floating-point hardware are common, the users are increasingly interested in extensive numeric applications. The *floating-point arithmetic* in Prolog is always *typeless* and generally transparent to the user. This means that numeric values, be they variables or the results of a computation, are converted internally into float representation automatically whenever integers are not adequate. The same holds true for output.

In this book we restrict our discussion to *integer arithmetic* only.

Indeed, we will present you with only a small but very typical *computational procedure*. You will encounter instances of arithmetic operations in later examples, but, as already mentioned, more for flow of control and similar purposes than as the main task of a procedure.

In the next example, however, the computation is the heart of the procedure. Fig. 3.2 illustrates a Prolog program called *euclid*, which calculates the *greatest common denominator* of two integers passed in as the first and second arguments, returning the result via the third one. The algorithm is due to Euclid.

```
euclid(X,X,X).
euclid(X,Y,GCD) :-
        X < Y,
        euclid(Y,X,GCD).
euclid(X,Y,GCD) :-
        X > Y,
        X1 is X − Y,
        euclid(X1,Y,GCD).
```

Fig. 3.2   Procedure euclid(Num_1,Num_2,GCD) for computing the greatest common denominator GCD of two integer values

Notice that the three arguments can be clearly classified into two input and one output parameter. This is atypical for Prolog but typical for computational procedures: an indication that arithmetic represents a (to be sure indispensable) 'foreign body' in the overall language structure.

Because of the asymmetric nature of the arithmetic assignment operator *is* it is necessary to clearly define the arguments in the procedure as being either input or output parameters.[4] Thus we *cannot* generate all possible number combinations for a given GCD!

The three clauses in *euclid* distinguish between three possible relationships between the first two numeric arguments:

1.   the values are equal, or

2.   the first argument is smaller, or

3.   the first argument is larger.

In the first case, the clause is a trivial fact. If both values are equal, obviously *X* is also the GCD.

---

[4] One could, however, employ the classificatory predicates *var* and *nonvar*, in order to formulate appropriate clauses respectively for the various combinations of input and output parameters. Perhaps you could try to write *euclid* such that, given the *GCD* and either the first or second argument, it would recursively generate all the numbers which share the GCD with the given argument.

The second case is derived from the third, in that we simply call the procedure again after reversing the first and second arguments. Here we use our first numeric operator: the comparator < for the 'less than'. Corresponding operators exist for the other common comparisons: > for 'greater than', =< for 'equal to or less than', and >= for 'greater than or equal to'.

In addition, there is an *equivalence* operator =. This operator differs somewhat from the others in that its operands may be non-numeric terms or even variables. In the latter case, the result is a unification of the two operands with one another, regardless of whether they are numeric or non-numeric. If, however, both operands are numbers, then the operator functions as a test for equality between them!

Finally, there is the operator \=, which tests for *non-equality*. This operator may also be applied to non-numeric terms. Take note that the slash involved is a backslash and *not* the usual slash used to indicate division.

Goals containing these operators are successful, or true, if the intended relationship between the operands holds (or in the case of the *equivalence* operator, if the unification can be made). Otherwise the goal *fails* and backtracking ensues, just as in the case of other 'normal' goals.

In the third clause of the procedure you find a corresponding comparison operation as the first goal:

```
euclid(X,Y,GCD) :-
      X > Y,
      X1 is X − Y,
      euclid(X1,Y,GCD).
```

If the first goal succeeds, then according to the Euclidian algorithm, the smaller of the two numbers must be subtracted from the larger; the GCD of the smaller number and the result of the above subtraction will be the same as that of the original two values. This is expressed in the last two goals of the clause, whereby the last goal employs the techniques of recursion, as described earlier.

The second goal serves as a typical example of the notation used in Prolog for numerical computation. The operator *is* is the arithmetic assignment operator. It is characterized by the following strict syntax:

Result is NumericStructure

where *NumericStructure* implies an expression containing only arithmetic operators, i.e. '+', '−', '*', '/' or *mod*. These operators have their usual meaning and precedence. The operation *mod* is an abbreviation for modulo, i.e. the integer remainder after integer division of the first operand by the second. The operands must themselves always be either numeric constants or variables instantiated as corresponding numeric structures.

The assignment operator *is* causes the evaluation of the *NumericStructure* according to the usual rules of arithmetic. If the leftmost operand of *is* is a variable, then it will be unified with the *Result* of the numeric calculation and the goal is by definition successful. If _Result_ itself is a constant value, or if it is a variable which already has been unified with some value, then the value of _Result_ is compared with the value generated by the computation and the goal returns _true_ or _fail_ depending on the truth of the implied equality.

Try out the algorithm, both on paper and as a Prolog procedure, using a few different values!

3.4 The Operator _univ_ and the Predicate _functor_

As a final example for the procedural interpretation of Prolog predicates, we would like to return to the personal knowledge base, which we worked with in the first two chapters of this book. We hope to illustrate how a procedural view of the processing of predicates often gives us insight into how they can be formulated in a more generally applicable fashion.

This 'advantage' is probably a consequence of the fact that the algorithmic approach ('first we do this and then we do that, repeating the latter until...') has been more strongly internalized by programmers solving complex tasks, than the 'abstract specification' method, underlying the pure, non-algorithmic approach in Prolog.

The examples of the two predicates _person_ and _event_ in the previous chapter illustrated that different predicates may be implemented in essentially the same way. These two predicates differ primarily in their functors. As we know, the arity of a predicate is a crucial attribute of a functor; when it is different, then it is sufficient to distinguish two functors which are, by name, the same. In addition, these two predicates interpret lists appearing in the query differently, i.e. in the one case as logically _and_ed conditions and in the other as logically _or_ed.

Naturally we wish to exploit every opportunity to write 'generalized' procedures. It is useful if the language provides the means to write identical clauses for different functors, and in our procedures we merely need to reference the clauses with different names and arity in order to select the appropriate behavior. The most obvious way to implement this is to allow for variables whose values represent the desired functor name. This, however, is not possible in most Prolog implementations, for the following reasons:

- the different arity of the functors would render this solution not generally applicable.

- since variables can be instantiated with arbitrarily complex structures, such as lists, the semantics of functors in the Prolog context would have to be extended to account for functors which are non-atomic.

- Finally, for the reader with a more theoretical bent, a logic containing variable functors is no longer decidable. This is an impractical basis for a problem-oriented programming language.

The desired effect can, however, be reached in Prolog, through the use of the *universalizing* operator **univ**, (=..) without sacrificing the logical consistency of the language. The operator *univ* transforms a functor of arbitrary arity into a list, a universally interpretable structure, or vice versa. Since this operation represents such a powerful and practical feature of the language, we shall devote some space to it right here.

$$Structure =.. [Functor|Arguments]$$

specifies a unification, whereby the *Functor* of the *Structure* to the left of the *univ* operator (=..) becomes associated with the first element of the list on the right. The functor arguments are associated with the remaining members of the list.[5] If the above unifications can be made, then *univ* succeeds, otherwise it *fails*. The direction of the unification is dependent only on the application, i.e. it is irrelevant whether *Structure* or the list to the right contains *un*instantiated variables, or if individual arguments, or even the first member of the list, *Functor* (or even more deeply embedded terms, in the case of more complex arguments) are themselves variables. The only thing of significance, as always in Prolog, is that they can be successfully unified with some value. This is illustrated in Fig. 3.3.

Another operator closely related to *univ* is the predicate of arity 3 called *functor*.

$$functor(Term, Functorname, Arity).$$

This operator also unifies in two directions. If applied with *Term* instantiated to some value, then the second and third arguments are unified with the name of the functor and the arity thereof, as derived from *Term*. In the opposite direction, given a *Functorname* and a numeric value for the *Arity* argument, if *Term* is uninstantiated it is unified with the given *Functorname* and this functor is provided with as many variables as requested via the *Arity* argument. This use of *functor* always succeeds! Figure 3.4 illustrates the way in which *functor* works in a short interaction. The variable arguments you see in the *Terms* generated in the first and last cases are generated automatically by the Prolog interpreter. These are the unique, internal identifiers created by the system, serving as placeholders for as yet uninstantiated values. If you experiment with this example on your own system, you will probably find different, but functionally equivalent, names in those positions.

---

[5] If the functor is of arity null, i.e. *Structure* is a constant, then the list derived by unification contains only a single member, the name of the functor, and no arguments.

```
?- F =.. [flight,510,nyc,boston].

F = flight(510,nyc,boston)

yes
?- flight(510,nyc,boston) =.. [F|Args].

F = flight
Args = [510,nyc,boston]

yes
?- flight(510,nyc,X) =.. [_,_,_,boston].

X = boston

yes
?- flight(510,nyc,X) =.. [_,_,_].

no
?-
```

Fig. 3.3   Sample dialog for unifications using univ *operator*

```
?- functor(p(customer,miller,Town,Tele),Func,Arity).

Town = _G28
Tele = _G32
Func = p
Arity = 4

yes
?- functor(3 + 4,Func,Arity).

Func = +
Arity = 2

yes
?- functor(Term,p,4).

Term = p(_G62,_G63,_G64,_G65)

yes
?-
```

Fig. 3.4   Use of the predicate functor

3.5   A Generalized Search Procedure

When we go to program a generalized search procedure for our personal appointment calendar, it should become quite clear as to how useful it is, that the interpreter, via the *univ* operator, is able to treat a predicate as either a structure consisting of a functor with arguments (for searching and activating our database), or as a list to be manipulated or processed. As in the previous chapter, we store the facts via the functors *p* for 'persons' and *e* for 'events'. Any single argument may itself consist of a list.

The knowledge base should be extended, however, to allow the following possibilities for each argument of a given *person-* or *event*-query:

- An (*un*instantiated) variable as argument, i.e. an *output parameter*, should be unified with the value of the corresponding argument in the respective fact.

- An atom or a list should be accepted as the value of an argument only if the respective argument in the fact can be unified. This implies that the atom must be identical with the one in the fact, or, in the case of a list, that the number of members is the same, and they in turn are all unifiable with those in the fact's list argument. If variables appear in the query list argument, then these should become instantiated with their associated list members in the fact. This rule insures that the three-element list [*Month, Day, Year*] is treated as a well-defined *pattern* for entering the date, and can be used as such in the context of a query.

- Beyond these rules, it should be possible to formulate a search expression for any argument, which captures alternative value combinations via the use of the functors of arity 2 *and* and *or*, e.g.

  and(or(maier,meyer),or(dr,professor))

These primitive operators have the usual connotations: *or* requires that at least one of the requested values in the 'compound' argument exists (be it an atom or a list argument), while *and* requires that both exist. It should be possible to nest such logical expressions to any arbitrary depth when formulating such search expressions.

In Fig. 3.5 we illustrate how a dialog using such complex queries could proceed, based on two sample queries. Note the response to the second query! Here the system responds with '*no*' to the request for alternative solutions, indicating that the first answer was the only one fulfilling all the given conditions. This is certainly the result of the specification of the street as well as the city, since in the first query in our example, where we only selected solutions based on the city *berkeley*, several alternatives were generated.

?– person(or(customer,supplier),Name,berkeley,Tel).

Name = [frank,shulz]
Tel = ['415',8235921] ;

Name = [dr,williams]
Tel = ['415',8371623] ;

Name = [frank,andrews]
Tel = ['415',8240456] ;

no
**?– person(or(customer,supplier),[_,Name],
       and forgot (berkeley,'telegraph ave'),Tel).**

Name = williams
Tel = ['415',8371623] ;

no
**?– event(What,Date,_,
       or(or(bigboy,hilton),'new york'),_).**

What = [invitation,conference]
Date = (7,5,1985] ;

What = invitation
Date = [6,7,1985] ;

What = overnight
Date = [6,6,1985] ;

no
?–

*Fig. 3.5   A dialog using logical search expressions (based on database
in Fig. 3.6(a) & (b))*

As we see in Fig. 3.5, it would be desirable to be able to formulate the different possible search arguments simply as arguments in the respective predicate, *person* or *event*. The next step would therefore be to implement a *search procedure* which accepts as its argument the facts which are in fact being sought, e.g.

```
        search(p(Role,Name,Town,Telephone))
```

or

```
        search(e(What,Date,Time,Place,Persons))
```

This search procedure is most easily understood in a 'procedural' sense, i.e.
a stepwise, sequential comparison of the individual arguments of the query
with the corresponding arguments of the stored facts.

```
        person(Role,Name,Town,Telephone) :-
                search(p(Role,Name,Town,Telephone)).
        event(What,Date,Time,Place,Participants) :-
                search(e(What,Date,Time,Place,Participants)).

        search(Query) :-
                Query =.. [_|Arguments],
                functor(Query,F,A),     % Query -> F, A
                functor(Fact,F,A),      % Fact <- F, A
                Fact,
                Fact =.. [_|Values],
                match_up(Arguments,Values).

        match_up([X|Arguments],[Val|Values]) :-
                comparison(X,Val),
                match_up(Arguments,Values).
        match_up([ ],[ ]).

        comparison(X,Val) :-
                var(X),X = Val.
        comparison(X,Val) :-
                nonvar(X),atomic(X),
                (       atomic(Val),
                        X = Val
                ;       Val = [_|_],    % Val is a List
                        member(X,Val)
                ).
        comparison(List,[X|Rest]) :-
                nonvar(List), List = [X|Rest].
        comparison(AND,Val) :-
                nonvar(AND), AND = and(X,Y),
                comparison(X,Val),
                comparison(Y,Val).
        comparison(OR,Val) :-
                nonvar(OR),OR = or(X,Y),
                (       comparison(X,Val), !
                ;       comparison(Y,Val)
                ).
```

(a)

%   Facts about Persons

```
p(customer,[carl,schulz],'new york',['212',7963470]).
p([customer,supplier],[frank,schulz],
        [berkeley,'prince st',11],['415',8235921]).
p(customer,smith,boston,['508',4236796]).
p([customer,supplier], miller,
        [boston,commons,25],['508',4241796]).
p(customer,[miller,frank,dr],'new york',['212',7759657]).
p(customer,[dr,williams],[berkeley,'telegraph ave',40],
        ['415',8371623]).
p(supplier,[dr,andrews,inc],'new york',['212',7852011]).
p(supplier,[frank,andrews],berkeley,['415',8240456]).
```

%   Event Facts

```
e(conference,[7,2,1985],[morning,10],
        [boston,commons,25],
        [smith,williams,andrews]).
e([invitation,conference],[7,5,1985],14,'new york',
        [schulz,miller]).
e(invitation,(6,7,1985],12,[bigboy,berkeley],williams).
e(overnight,[6,6,1985],evening,
        [hilton,boston],myself).
e(birthday,[12,7,1934],'?','san francisco',smith).
e(birthday,[5,3,1925],'?',berkeley,
        [dr,carl,williams]).
```

(b)

Fig. 3.6   The personal knowledge base with generalized search procedure (a) Part 1 — Procedures; (b) Part 2 — Facts.

Figures 3.6(a) and (b) show the modifications made to our knowledge base to equip it with the desired functionality.

In the following discussion of the mechanics of the implementation in Figs. 3.6(a) and (b) it would be instructive to consider the behavior illustrated in Fig. 3.5.

The fundamental mechanism is embedded in the single *search* procedure, of arity 1, which is called by both query predicates, *person* and *event*. The sole argument is respectively the 'function' which is being sought. Its functor is, depending on the query, either *p* or *e*, and their arguments are the same as those which were given in the original query.

search thus does essentially two things:

- it fetches a *fact* with the corresponding functor, *p* or *e*, from the data base and

- it uses the predicate *match_up*, of arity 2, to test if the *Values* in the fact fetched are compatible with given query *Arguments* (which possibly contain logical expressions formulated by use of the operators *and* and *or*).

Let us examine more closely just how *search* finds the (next) respective fact with the desired functor. The first of the four goals of the rule,

Query =.. [_|Arguments]

serves merely to generate a *List* of the query arguments, which is required by *match_up*. The remaining three goals

```
functor(Query,F,A),          % Query −> F,A
functor(Fact,F,A),           % Fact <− F,A
Fact
```

serve to locate the fact. As is indicated by the in-line comments, the first *functor* predicate is evaluated 'forwards', the second one 'backwards', corresponding to the respective variable instantiations. Thus, if the query reads

p(or(customer,supplier),Name,berkeley,Tel).

then the first *functor* predicate unifies

F = p   and   A = 4.

Using these values, the second *functor* predicate 'constructs', i.e. instantiates

Fact = p(_,_,_,_),

a predicate with the functor *p* and four (anonymous) variables. This is precisely the structure needed as a goal, in order to fetch per unification every *p*-fact of arity 4 existing in the database. And this is precisely what is done in the fourth and last goal!

This 'trick', i.e. the generation of a suitable goal, followed immediately by its application, is indispensable for *knowledge-based* applications in Prolog. Of the popular programming languages, only Lisp provides a comparable mechanism.

The remainder of the *search* predicate uses the *univ* operator again, this time in the other direction, to generate a list of argument values from the respective *Fact* fetched, since these attributes are the ones needed by the *query* predicate.

The predicate *match_up* itself uses the typical, recursive approach to process the two argument lists (from *Query* and *Fact* respectively) of equal length. The terminating conndition is reached when both lists have been emptied, i.e. reduced to the empty list.

The actual work in the predicate *match_up* is done by the predicate *comparison*. Once it *fails* to establish equality between the corresponding elements of the two lists, then *match_up* returns a *fail* as well and *search* must then generate the next potential fact.

The predicate *comparison* itself embodies essentially the same mechanism as that which was included directly in the bodies of the rules of the respective *person* and *event* predicates used in the example in the previous chapter. It determines the type of its arguments in order to apply an appropriate comparator. The extension to deal with combined and alternative argument values, i.e. with possibly nested *and* and *or* operations, is reduced to a recursive call of the *comparison* predicate for each of the two arguments involved in each instance.

Take careful note of the fact, however, that even for such cases as when the first argument of the *comparison* predicate is a structure like $and(X, Y)$, this argument is specified to be *nonvar* in the corresponding clauses. You might be tempted to formulate this more simply and elegantly, e.g.

comparison([X|Rest],[X|Rest])

but you will discover that this leads to undesirable effects when backtracking occurs. Can you figure out why? If not, try modifying the predicate accordingly and see just what happens.

3.6 Control Flow in Procedures

The language constructs used in *comparison* should all be familiar to you by now, with the exception of the *cut* operator, which is represented by the exclamation point (!) found at the end of the first *or* branch in the *or* clause of the *comparison* predicate. Although we shall deal with it in greater detail later, a brief introduction here should allow you to understand its function. The *cut* operator is used to restrict backtracking. Normally, the failure of a clause leads the interpreter to back up to previous clauses in search of alternative choices for variable instantiations in a search for another solution. The *cut* operator sets a marker, and once this marker has been passed, the backtracking mechanism may no longer return beyond it in order to generate another solution.

In this particular case this means that once a comparison with X has been successful, *no* attempt to make a comparison with Y shall be made, even if we explicitly demand an alternative solution (backtracking) by entering ';' at the terminal. This conforms with the logical definition of the *or* operator. It returns *true* if its first argument is true; the second argument need not be tested.

Perhaps the best way to see how *cut* influences the behavior of this clause is to simply remove the '!' (and the preceding comma too, of course) and then try a query containing an *or*-expression, where both arguments involved are present in a single fact in the knowledge base. Figure 3.7 illustrates the effect. Note that the solution *new york* appears twice, because the first *p*-fact in our knowledge base satisfies each of the alternative values for *name* and therefore is selected a second time during backtracking.

?– person(_,or(carl,schulz),Where,_).

Where = new york ;

Where = new york ;

Where = [berkeley,'prince st',11] ;

no
?–

Fig. 3.7   *Repeated selection of the solution* new york *as the result of leaving out the cut in the* comparison(or(X,Y),Val)

Let us close our discussion with a few remarks regarding the role of backtracking in our *search* predicate, which is initiated when the user requests an alternative solution by entering a semicolon at the terminal. Backtracking effectively causes an iteration of the sequential processing of the facts in the knowledge base. The key to understanding this process lies in recognizing where, in the body of the rule, the so-called *choice point* is located. The *choice point* is the goal to which the backtracking mechanism returns in order to find the alternative values for a different solution.[6] In the *search* predicate the choice point is the fourth clause, i.e. *Fact*. Since *Fact* is generated by *functor*, such that all its arguments are *un*instantiated variables, these variables allow the structure to unify with every fact in the knowledge base which has the same functor name and arity. Thus, every time the rule backtracks, it fetches the next respective, corresponding fact, i.e. makes a sequential access to the person or event facts according to the user's request.

The goals preceding the goal *Fact* can only be satisfied in one particular fashion (Why?). They are not choice points and consequently will be executed only once when *search* is called. In this sense, they have little bearing on the run-time performance of the search process.

This rather detailed discussion of the sample procedure should serve to prevent a common misconception with respect to the performance issue: The fundamental algorithm in Prolog is a search procedure with respect to

---

[6] Try to understand why there is *only one such choice point* in the *search* procedure. Our experience indicates that determining which goals are eligible for alternative unification is one of the few difficult things to learn in Prolog programming.

a given database. Many people confuse this orderly search with some sort of random sampling and assume (indeed, even pronounce publicly), that Prolog is therefore inefficient.

As we have seen in the above example, the flow of control is essentially that of your typical sequential access in any other programming language, and thus fundamentally no less efficient.

On the other hand, we cannot deny that formulating extremely inefficient algorithms is just as easy in Prolog as in any other programming language, particularly if one is not sufficiently familiar with the procedural perspective of the interpretation. We shall illustrate this in an example in Chapter 11.

4   INSTANTIATION AND UNIFICATION

In the previous chapter we briefly explained the notion of instantiating variables and unifying Prolog terms. It is now necessary to take a more detailed, formal look at these mechanisms, as they are the only data-processing operations directly available in this language. Even string handling is not available as primitives, but rather is realized via the instantiation of lists and their members. Once you have understood the unification operation, you will have mastered half of Prolog! The other half is related to control flow — the topic of the following chapter.

4.1   The Instantiation of Variables

Fundamentally, Prolog 'computes' values via one single mechanism — the unification of two terms. We have illustrated this informally in previous examples. Here we shall discuss unification more formally and provide more detailed examples.

Unification is not the same as the *assignment* of a value to a variable, as in conventional languages. It is the process of *instantiation*, which comes closer to fulfilling that function in Prolog. But even instantiation differs in several aspects from a conventional assignment operation:

- The operation is type free, i.e. a variable can be instantiated with a Prolog term of arbitrary complexity.

- Backtracking causes variables to become *un*instantiated again, i.e. variables which have been instantiated after passing a *choice point* are returned to their uninstantiated or unbound state when the interpreter backs up to the previous choice point.

- On the other hand, once a variable has been instantiated, no subsequent predicates can modify its value.

It is the latter characteristic of the instantiation process which programmers accustomed to traditional algorithmic languages initially consider to be a bothersome limitation. The experience of modern software engineering indicates, however, that this characteristic indeed contributes to the production of correct programs. The lessons of the past show that the indiscriminate modification of variable values can be as dangerous as the undisciplined use of *goto*s.

4.2   The Unification Algorithm

Unification employs the instantiation of variables merely as a primitive operation. The process of unification itself involves the structural comparison and matching of two terms. Typically, one of these terms is a *goal* received as a query from the terminal or taken from the body of the currently active clause, and the other is a *fact* or a *rule head* stored in the database. Unification can also be initiated explicitly by the use of operators, such as the equivalence operator '='.

Regardless of the cause, unification is a process which is completely symmetric with respect to the two terms involved. Whereas in conventional languages the 'left' term traditionally assumes the value of the 'right' term, and the 'right' term itself remains unchanged, with unification the direction of influence is dependent upon the current state of the terms involved.

There are three possible results:

1.   If both terms are identical in structure, and all constants, substructures and instantiated variables in their respective positions in both terms match as well, then the unification establishes this identity and no further processing need be conducted. The unification is successful.

Differences consisting of a value in one term and an (uninstantiated) variable in the other term in the corresponding position may be detected, in which case the attempt is made to modify the discrepancy by instantiating the variable with the other term's constant, or perhaps more complex, structure.

2.   A unification is possible when the corresponding structures in the respective terms are *compatible* and instantiations can be made; otherwise

3.   the unification fails due to the inability to find suitable instantiations for the respective variables.

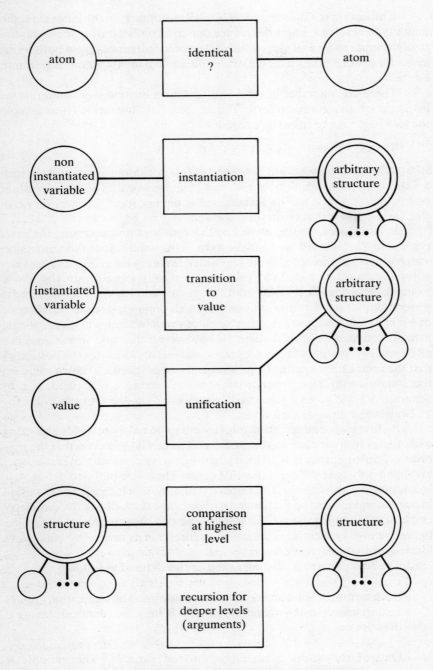

Fig. 4.1   The different possibilities for unification

Unification is a discrete event, i.e. all or nothing. In the latter case, the inability to resolve a single difference due to a conflict during the instantiation attempt renders all successfully attempted instantiations in both terms invalid, i.e. none take place, and the unification of the two terms is rejected, i.e. *fails*.

There are a number of ways to effect the adjustment of two terms via instantiation to a common form. For purposes of illustration let us assume the two following terms to be unified:

f(otto,X)   and   f(Y,Z),

where variables are involved as the respective positional arguments. In such a case, only the instantiation $Y = otto$ is unequivocal. The precise values with which X and Z will be instantiated is unimportant, i.e. arbitrary. All that can be said is that they must be identical.

In such cases, Prolog abides by the convention of choosing the *most general unifier*, should alternatives exist. This implies that the unification which finally gets accepted is the one which leaves as many variables as variables, i.e. without a defined value, as is legally possible. In the above example, this means that the unification instantiates $X = Z$. This most general unifier is, of course, not entirely well defined, since in the absence of *left* and *right* values in Prolog, we cannot yet determine whether X will be instantiated as Z or Z as X. This is, however, a question which does not affect the executability of the programs, but merely indicates the possibility that the predicate may either pass a value down *or* receive a return value via the instantiation. This depends on how the predicate is applied, e.g. to generate X via Z given a value for Y, or given Z via X establish a value for Y. Both possibilities are left open.

At first glance, unification might seem to be a very complex algorithm with many different cases to choose from. The fact is, however, that the procedure implementing it is a logically quite simple, albeit recursive one, involving only four different possible cases. These are outlined in Fig. 4.1. It is important to note that the terms *left* and *right*, which are to be unified in our example, could be exchanged without any effect, due to the symmetry emphasized in our previous discussion. The two cases in the middle of the figure are non-symmetric and each also represents its respective equivalent form, specified with the terms reversed.

The four cases to be distinguished can be defined as follows:

1.   Both terms (or sub-terms) are constant atoms. The unification implies a comparison of the values, successful if they are identical, failing if they are not.

2.   One of the terms is an *un*instantiated variable. The variable is automatically instantiated with the corresponding term, regardless of the correspondent term's structure.

3. One of the terms is an instantiated variable. In this case the value of this variable is unified with the other term. Since the value may itself be an instantiation of another variable, this could lead to a recursion.[1]

4. Both terms are structures. As a first step, the two structures are compared. If they are alike, i.e. both terms have the same functor and arity, then the next step entails an attempt to unify their respective corresponding arguments. This implies the recursive application of the four cases just described.

Again, the unification is successful (if and) only if a unification at all levels of recursion, i.e. all substructures, can be achieved.

4.3 The Unification of Complex Structures

The ability of unification to instantiate variables in both of the two terms involved is one of the keys to Prolog's elegance as both a basis for information systems and a programming language for more conventional applications.

To illustrate this more clearly, let us assume we wish to create a system for real estate agents, which matches housing for sale with a potential buyer's requirements for a particular kind of real estate, and determines under which conditions interest in a particular object might lead to a sale. In this knowledge base we could store the offers and requests respectively in the facts *supply* and *demand* using the following structures:

```
supply(meyer, single_family_house(Conditions,
                    rooms(6),
                    [baths(2), workshop])).

demand(miller, single_family_house(price(50000,
                    ModeOfPayment),
                    rooms(6),
                    Extras)).
```

Variables appearing in a structure mean the respective detail in question is open to discussion. Thus, the seller *meyer* is willing to talk about the *Conditions* of sale. On the other hand, *miller*, the potential buyer is pre-

---

[1] In the actual implementation of this algorithm instantiations are typically embodied in pointers. The efficiency of a Prolog system depends greatly upon the speed with which a chain of pointers can be de-referenced. This explains why the same Prolog system may exhibit great differences in performance when run on different computer architectures.

pared to spend $50 000 for a house with six rooms, but has no specific conditions with regard to the *ModeOfPayment*. Furthermore, she does not care about any particular *Extras* in the house, i.e. the number of baths, swimming pool, etc.

The rule for determining a potential sale *psale* might be formulated as follows:

```
psale(S,B,Object):-
        supply(S,Object), demand(B,Object).
```

With the above rule and the given facts, unification would lead to the following instantiations:

```
S = meyer
B = miller
Conditions = price(50000, ModeOfPayment)
Extras = [baths(2), workshop]
Object = single_family_house(price(50000,
                              ModeOfPayment),
                              rooms(6),
                              [baths(2), workshop])
```

To be sure, the query predicate *psale* is somewhat primitive for actual professional use. As in the case of our personal knowledge base, we should write more 'intelligent' predicates, capable of recognizing, for example, that a house for sale for $45 000 also represents a potential sale when the buyer is willing to spend $50 000.

Nonetheless, even our primitive predicate illustrates some fundamental features. The points still open to discussion, i.e. the variables on *both* the selling and buying sides, are satisfied via unification by the corresponding values stipulated by the buyer and seller. The *ModeOfPayment* remains clearly undecided as indicated by the fact that in the response it appears as a still uninstantiated variable.

Nonetheless, even our primitive predicate illustrates some fundamental features. The points still open to discussion, i.e. the variables on *both* the selling and buying sides, are satisfied via unification by the corresponding values stipulated by the buyer and seller. The *ModeOfPayment* remains clearly undecided as indicated by the fact that in the response it appears as a still uninstantiated variable.

You may have noticed in the previous section's discussion that we consider complex structures to be exclusively functors (perhaps nested) with a defined arity. There are, however, certain Prolog structures for which this description, at least with respect to their superficial syntax, does not seem to hold, and yet they are indeed treated as structures. One such structure which we have seen already on numerous occasions is that of the *list*, i.e. a syntactic structure characterized by its square brackets:

```
[a,list,may,contain,an,arbitrary,number,of,elements]
```

Another such counter-intuitive, atypical structure is an arithmetic expression:

X is Y + Z − 1.

Or even a clause or rule itself, e.g.

member(Element, [_|RestOfList]) :-
            member(Element, RestOfList).

is a term and must therefore be treated as a processable structure!

The interpretive mechanisms illustrated in Fig. 4.1 are capable of 'digesting', i.e. unifying the above, seemingly syntactically inappropriate expressions, because they are all only abbreviations which are automatically transformed internally to conform to conventional functor structures.

In the next two sections we shall discuss this in greater detail. Not that you should use the internally used form, because the abbreviations are intended to ease the writing of such expressions and to improve their legibility, but because your understanding of how these apparently diverse structures get processed is best achieved by seeing how things get stored and how those stored units are involved in the unification process.

4.4 Operators

Expressions are structures involving unary or binary *operators*. Typical examples are the arithmetic operators: **is,** +, and − as in

X is Y + Z − 1

which could be expressed more formally as

is(X, −(+(Y,Z),1))

but this is certainly not as easy to read.

Similarly, the operators like :- in

member(Element, [_|RestOfList]) :-
            member(Element, RestOfList).

or other built-ins like **not** or \== or even your own operators may be defined such that they may be written as more conventional infix expressions. Ultimately, however, expressions formulated in the 'abbreviated' syntax must be reducible to the conventional functor syntax.

For the purpose of defining your own operators, Prolog provides a predicate of arity 3 called *op*. Once you have seen how it works, it should be clear how the built-in functions work, i.e. how the system is capable of making such transformations as we indicated in the arithmetic expression above. Remember, it is only the conventional functor structure which can ultimately participate in the unification process.

As we have already seen, an operator is nothing more than a functor of arity 1 or 2 which does not necessarily have to be written before its arguments. For example, the logical negator **not** may simply be written in front of its argument, separated from it by a space (blank). Operations represented by special characters, like + or :- do not even have to be separated by blanks from their operands (arguments), although for the sake of readability blanks are sometimes used.

Operators fall into one of three classes:

(unary) prefix operators
> which appear in front of their operand, i.e. argument. For example,

> **not** p(X).

(binary) infix operators
> which appear between their operands. For example, a typical arithmetic operator,

> Z **is** X + Y.

(unary) postfix operators
> which follow their arguments. Normally such built-in operators do not exist in Prolog. However, we are familiar with such operators in our own written language. The question mark, for instance, converts a statement into a question:

> He is dead?

> And if you wanted to program a natural language interface, you could define a question mark operator with precisely this meaning.

> Because the operators eliminate the need for parentheses, Prolog must find a way to decide in what order it should evaluate a complex term such as

> Z **is** 4 * 5 − X + 3 * Y.

This brings us back to the *op* predicate. It not only defines the symbol(s) representing a given operator, but also establishes the *precedence* and *associativity* of the operator, in order to make complex expressions deterministically interpretable. The syntax of the *op* predicate is:

> op(Precedence,Associativity,SymbolicName).

Precedence is an integer, typically in the range 1 to 1200. The lower the value, the higher the precedence, i.e. the earlier the operator and its operands get evaluated with respect to other operations in a single expression.

If, for example, the built-in operators * and / have precedence 400, in contrast to 500 for + and −, then whenever a multiplicative operation occurs together with an additive one, the multiplication is done first.

The *associativity* describes the position as well as the arity of the newly defined operator. There are eight possible combinations:

fx, fy, xfx, xfy, yfx, yfy, xf and **yf.**

The interpretation is as follows: the **f** stands for the operator, i.e. the *functor* itself, and **x** and **y** stand for its operands, i.e. the arguments. Thus the different combinations indicate the position of the operator with respect to its operands: **fx** and **fy** defines a unary *prefix operator*, **xfx**, **xfy**, **yfx** and **yfy** a binary *infix operator*, and **xf** and **yf** a unary *postfix operator*.

The **x** and **y** are used to describe the actual associativity. Assuming no parentheses have been used in an expression to override the defined associativity, an **x** dictates that any further operators in the operand (argument) on the specified side of the operator (functor) being defined must have a *lower precedence* than the operator itself. A **y** on the other hand, allows operators with the *same precedence* as well, and only operators with higher precedence values mark the end of the argument to the operator under consideration.

Since this feature is foreign to most other languages, an example would certainly be helpful. In order to follow the explanation you must look at the definitions in Fig. 4.2, showing typical values for the precedence and associativity of some *built-in operators*. A complete list can be found in Appendix E. The definitions here for '+', '−', '*' and '/' all have the associativity **yfx**. Given the expression

$$5 * X + Y - Z / 3$$

and the lower precedence of the operators '*' and '/', they are evaluated first. The left argument to '/' ends at the '−', because it has a higher precedence value, and in Fig. 4.2 the *y* on the left side of the functor for '/' means that

```
:- op(900,fx,not).
:- op(700,xfx,is).
:- op(700,xfx,'=').
:- op(700,xfx,'\=').
:- op(700,xfx,'<').
:- op(700,xfx,'=<').
:- op(700,xfx,'>=').
:- op(700,xfx,'>').
:- op(700,xfx,'==').
:- op(700,xfx,'\==').
:- op(500,yfx,'+').
:- op(500,yfx,'-').
:- op(400,yfx,'*').
:- op(400,yfx,'/').
:- op(300,xfx,mod).
```

Fig. 4.2 *Precedence and associativity specification of a few of the built-in operators*

only operators of lesser or equal precedence could be included as part of the left, as it were, compound, argument.

How does the mechanism work for the additive operators in our example? Both have the same associativity specification **yfx**. This means that no operator of the same precedence, e.g. no additive operator, may be included as part of the *right* argument, but one is allowed in the *left* argument. Thus the argument to + ends at −, and the addition operation must be executed before the subtraction may be made. The − operator can (and does) by definition allow the incorporation of the result of an addition as its *left* argument.

Altogether, the evaluation occurs in the steps which we know from standard arithmetic, i.e. as if the expression had been explicitly parenthesized thus:

$$((5 * X) + Y) - (Z / 3)$$

Perhaps you should take the time now to examine the definitions in Appendix E of the operators :-,[2] '?−', ';' and ',' and consider how their respective precedence and associativity control the evaluation of a Prolog clause, and why they make the previously discussed rules for parenthesizing ; and , plausible whenever they appear in one and the same rule body.

One last word about the *op*-operator before we go on to the next topic. The predicate fulfills its task at that point in time at which the Prolog interpreter executes it as a goal. Thus, to define a new binary operator *loves* during a Prolog session, you merely have to enter the corresponding *op*-predicate as you would any other goal in response to the prompt:

?− op(100, xfx, loves).

yes
?− asserta(sasha loves nuts).

yes
?− sasha loves Steve.

Steve = nuts

yes
?−

As the dialog excerpt illustrates, the system no longer detects a syntax error in the case of *loves* once it has been defined as an operator. Try it with an undefined one to see that it does detect an error.

---

[2] The operator :- is defined both as unary and binary. The unary :- is identical with the '?−' prompt and is typically used in Prolog programs to cause the immediate execution of goals at the time of their being consulted. We have already seen examples of this. As a binary operator the meaning is that of *if* as explained earlier.

If you want to have new operators 'installed' merely by having them in a library file which you consult as needed then you must place the unary — operator in front of the *op*-predicate defining each new operator.

Thus the same effect illustrated in the above dialog could have been achieved by placing

    :- op (100, xfx, loves).

    sasha loves nuts.

in a file (let us call it *lovefile*). Then, instead of the original two interactions, you could merely enter:

    ?– **consult(lovefile).**

4.5   Strings and String Processing

In Chapter 1 we saw that any arbitrary sequence of characters is treated as an atom if we enclose them in *apostrophes*. Does that mean that we can manipulate such an atom as a string as well?

Unfortunately *not*! To be sure, atoms are also referred to as *names* when, for example, we want to display them as text output, as we shall see later on. Nonetheless, we cannot process such atoms directly as strings.

In order to facilitate string processing using the existing language constructs, Prolog uses a simple trick:

* an individual *character* is represented by its numeric *ASCII* value.

* A *character sequence*, or *string*, is treated as a *list* of the numeric equivalents of the individual constituent characters.

* Consequently, such a *list* can also be expressed as a string of characters enclosed in *quotation marks* (").

Thus, the Prolog term

    "this is a string!"

is synonymous with the list

    [116,104,105,115,32,105,115,32,96,32,115,116,114,105,110,103,33].

The advantage of this approach is that we can now apply all our list-processing predicates to string-processing problems. For instance, to concatenate two strings to create a new one, we can use the predicate

append(String1, String2, ResultString).

A small problem with the string-as-list solution is that texts in Prolog[3] frequently, indeed in most cases in practice, occur as names, i.e. atoms, and *not* as strings. Consequently, we need a conversion predicate to arbitrarily transform one representation into another. This function is fulfilled by the standard predicate

   name(Atom, String).

where either argument can serve as an input or output parameter.

Figure 4.3 illustrates the use of the *name* predicate, in the specification of a predicate which concatenates two names into one. *Concatenation* is the atom generated from the two atoms passed in. Note that the first two goals in the predicate use *name* to convert each atom passed in into an equivalent string. In the last goal the conversion is made in the opposite direction, i.e. the argument that served as input parameter by the first two invocations of *name* now serves as output parameter, and vice versa. The *Concatenation*

```
concat_atoms(Name1,Name2,Concatenation) :-
        name(Name1,String1),
        name(Name2,String2),
        append(String1,String2,ResultString),
        name(Concatenation,ResultString).
```

Fig. 4.3   *The predicate* concat_atoms *for concatenating two names (atoms)*

is generated from the string resulting from the *append* operation.

As defined in Fig. 4.3, however, *concat_atoms* assumes that both *Name1* and *Name2* are instantiated as atoms at the time of invocation. The arguments must not be variables or more complex terms. It would be a good exercise in the use of the classifying predicates discussed in Chapter 2 to try and eliminate this severe limitation.

One practical application of the *concat_atoms* predicate is in the definition of another predicate which takes a list containing the directory names in the path leading to a file (named as the last element in the list) and converts it into a (relative) *Unix-Pathname*, e.g.

   ['$HOME', prologbook, 'Chap04']

into

   '$HOME/prologbook/Chap04'.

Figure 4.4 contains a first approximation, i.e. one which assumes that the first argument, the path list, is the input parameter and, moreover, that all its elements are instantiated with legal Unix filenames.

[3] Many Prolog systems even permit the use of C language output control characters, like \t for tabulator and \n for newline, within *names*.

```
pathname( [BaseName], BaseName)
pathname( [Directory | RestPath], PathName) :-
        not RestPath == [ ],
        concat_atoms(Directory, '/', PathStart),
        pathname( RestPath, PathEnd),
        concat_atoms( PathStart, PathEnd, PathName).
```

**Fig. 4.4   The predicate pathname for generating a Unix-Pathname
by way of a list of constituent pathname elements**

The output parameter is always the second argument the *Pathname* generated. This is a direct consequence of the non-generalized *concat_atoms* predicate from Fig. 4.3 and the likewise limited *not* parameter. Eliminating the shortcoming is by no means a trivial task. Since the dissection of a Pathname into a list of its constituent elements is also a frequent need in practice, we suggest the reader make the effort to work out a solution to the problem.[4]

---

[4] *Hint:* note that every '/' in the second argument *PathName* separates the elements which are to appear in the path list, which is to be produced as first argument. (Why is this not sufficient to guarantee a solution for all pathnames passed in?)

5 FLOW OF CONTROL

In principle, flow of control in Prolog is quite simple. A predicate (or procedure, in the sense defined earlier) may be subject to resolution, sequential processing and recursion. If an invoked predicate ends as *true*, then the next predicate in the clause is called. If, however, it *fails*, then the interpreter returns to the previous choice point. With the *cut* operator such backtracking can be suppressed. These are the only basic control mechanisms. Nonetheless, since they can appear in complex combinations, confusing to the uninitiated, we introduce an interactive debugger, which allows you to observe the control flow.

5.1 Resolution

Gertrude Stein was born on February 3, 1874, in Allegheny, Pennsylvania and died July 27, 1946 in Paris. She was a poet, known among other things for her famous poem:

> A rose
> is a rose
> is a rose.

We will be taking a closer look at this poem ... not from a literary standpoint, but rather from that of flow of control in Prolog. We shall write a Prolog program which generates this and like poems.

We wish to develop this program *top-down*, using the method of *stepwise refinement*. We shall start with a general predicate, called *poem*, whose ultimate goal is to produce a poem. This will be repeatedly refined via subordinate predicates, until we have reached the level of built-in Prolog predicates and the output has been constrained to the 'Stein-like' structure.

During this development cycle we shall consider exactly how Prolog processes each of the predicates involved step by step. The strategy followed by the interpreter in evaluating or reaching a goal is called *resolution*. As we shall see, resolution is characterized by a successive approximation to a solution (overall goal), which observes all secondary constraints specified (sub-goals). Given this aspect of the interpretive process, it turns out that the *top-down* method and the Prolog language are quite well suited to each other. Indeed, our experience indicates that unless one has a very good reason to the contrary, this method is the one of choice when implementing solutions in Prolog.

Let us start at the highest-level predicate, with the *null* arity predicate *poem* in Fig. 5.1. What exactly happens,

```
poem :-
          opening(O),
          closing(C),
          concat_atoms(O,C,Poem),
          write(Poem).

opening('\nA rose\n').
```

Fig. 5.1   The predicate poem

when, in response to the prompt, we enter the goal

?– poem.

Prolog searches its database for a clause whose *head* can be unified with the predicate entered at the terminal, and discovers the rule in Fig. 5.1. If the clause were simply a fact, i.e.

```
poem.
```

then it would have trivially satisfied the goal and simply returned *yes*, followed by another prompt. Since it is a rule which associates with the requested structure, Prolog proceeds to interpret the request via resolution. It is as if the user had entered

?– opening(O),
   closing(C),
   concat_atoms(O,C,Poem),
   write(Poem).

as the goal.

Consequently, the first goal of the rule body, i.e. *opening(O)*, becomes the next goal to be processed. This causes the interpreter to search the database for a suitable match once again. In Fig. 5.1 we saw a clause which satisfies this goal. By instantiating the variable argument *O* as '\nA rose\n', the unification succeeds. Since the goal unifies with a fact, the resolution involves a mere substitution of the original goal by the matching fact, with its corresponding argument instantiation.

The first approximation or refinement yields

?– opening('\nA rose\n'),
   closing(C),

```
concat_atoms('\nA rose\n',C,Poem),
write(Poem).
```

Note how the instantiation of the variable is immediately 'known' to subsequent clauses sharing the internal variable. Now Prolog must process the second goal *closing*(C). Assuming that our database contains a rule which unifies with it, instantiating its argument C with

'\tis a rose\n\tis a rose\n'

then the next step or resolution leads to

```
?- opening('\nA rose\n'),
   closing('\tis a rose\n\tis a rose\n'C),
   concat_atoms('\nA rose \n',
       '\tis a rose\n\tis a rose\n',Poem),
   write(Poem).
```

as seen from the highest level. The *concat_atoms* predicate is the one you saw in the previous chapter. Its resolution unifies the variable *Poem* with the complete text of the poem, concatenated into a single atom. This atom contains *newline* and *tabulator control characters* coded as '\n' and '\t', respectively. You may discover that this manner of coding, which reflects a Unix convention, does not work on your system. Should this be the case, we must ask you to be patient (and work with a perhaps less elegant, non-indented version); in a later chapter we shall show you a different, albeit more complicated, way of formatting output in general.

The resolution of the last goal at the upper level invokes the built-in predicate *write*, which outputs the term passed in to it via the variable *Poem*, i.e. the test constructed by the previous goal predicates. A more detailed discussion of the internal workings of the *write* predicate can be found in the chapter on input and output.

5.2   Recursion and Backtracking

Utilizing the top-down approach, we now turn our attention to the second level of refinement, i.e. the definition of *closing*(C), as illustrated in Fig. 5.2.

```
closing(C) :-
        continuation(C).
closing(C) :-
        continuation(C1),
        closing(C2),
        concat_atoms(C1,C2,C).

continuation('\tis a rose\n').
```

Fig. 5.2   The predicate closing(C) *in refinement of Fig. 5.1*

The resolution of *closing*(*C*), as mentioned in the previous section, causes a substitution of the predicate by its rule body, i.e. in this case,

?– **continuation(C).**

This sub-goal, in turn, resolves to an instantiation of the variable argument *C* with '*tis a rose*\n'. This implies that our Prolog program's first response to the goal *poem* is not the desired version of Stein's famous work, but instead an entirely correct, yet literarily speaking, less profound statement:

?– **poem.**

A rose
     is a rose

;

Dissatisfied with this second-rate performance, we immediately enter a semicolon, requesting our poet to try again.

This input, as you already know, causes Prolog to *backtrack* in search of an alternative solution. This process unfolds as follows. First, the instantiation of the variable *C* via the unification of *continuation*(*C*) is undone, and the interpreter *resumes* its search of the database for an alternative unification of the *continuation*(*C*) predicate. Not finding any, the interpreter *backs up* a step in the resolution process, to the next previous *choice point* and searches for an alternative unification for the hierarchically higher situated goal *closing*(*C*) — with the concommitant *uninstantiation* of its *C* variable prior to any further processing.

The search resuming from this level, i.e. this choice point, is successful due to the occurrence, in the database, of the second, alternative *closing*(*C*) predicate. Since it too is a rule, resolution substitutes the predicate with the rule body, introducing the sub-goal *continuation*(*C1*) as the next resolution step. From our previous 'run', we know that the argument, this time referenced as *C1*, will be instantiated as '*tis a rose*\n'. This time, however, the rule body takes us a sub-goal further, i.e. invokes the predicate *continuation*.

This causes a *recursion*, since as you recall, the resolution of this rule body came about through a call to *closing*(*C*) in the first place. The recursive invocation, however, is made with a new variable named *C2*.

Recursion and backtracking are two fundamental control flow mechanisms in Prolog. *Recursion* simply means that a resolution carried out at a higher level is to be repeated at a lower level. Implicit in this process is that the search for unifiable clauses takes all possibilities into account and is *not* constrained by choice points established by previous invocations! Thus, the above recursion causes the first *closing* rule with the single sub-goal body rule body to be applied. The result is that *C2* gets instantiated with '*tis a rose*\n' via unification with the solitary fact *continuation*('*tis a rose*\n').

The third goal, *concat_atoms*(*C1, C2, C*), returns the two lines concatenated via *C*, and the second version of the poem is complete. As we see in Fig. 5.3 our poet has reached the stature of Gertrude Stein. Enter another semicolon and you will see a poem not even Ms Stein dared write!

> ?– **poem.**
>
> A rose
>> is a rose
>
> ;
>
> A rose
>> is a rose
>> is a rose
>
> ;
>
> A rose
>> is a rose
>> is a rose
>> is a rose
>
> yes
> ?–

Fig. 5.3   Recursive invocations of the **poem** *predicate*

Such a recursion presents some dangers. For one thing, it gets increasingly difficult to follow the flow of control as the number of unifications, instantiations and occurrences of backtracking accumulate as one moves from one level of resolution to another. This is particularly true when you consider that for *each* activation of the *same goal*, e.g. *closing* in our program, different 'current working sets' of clauses in the underlying database are subject to consideration. You should do a walk through with a manual trace, recording the respective choice point for each clause as it gets unified in the course of a recursion. You will find it most instructive!

The second danger, inherent in recursion in any language, is that of *non-termination*, i.e. the so-called *endless recursion*. This phenomenon is easily demonstrated. Instead of repeatedly entering a semicolon after each response to acquire an 'improved' poem, you could simply make the following request:

> ?– **poem, fail.**

Since *fail* never succeeds, backtracking will cause *poem* to be repeatedly activated. And since it *never* fails, the poet rages on! If you are lucky, Prolog will at some point put an end to the madness (and monotony) when some system resource is exhausted, e.g. a stack overflow.

Both problems are reason enough to finally introduce you to the debugging facilities available, using our little program as a test case.

5.3 The Box Model of a Procedure

Almost all debugging aids provided by the Prolog interpreter are based on one and the same graphic model of control flow in processing, i.e. the so-called *box model* of a procedure. The name box model derives from the depiction of a procedure and the flow of control through it as a box with four connections, or *ports*, as illustrated in Fig. 5.4.

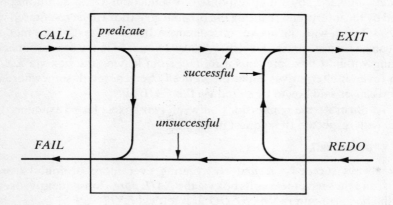

Fig. 5.4   The basic box model of a Prolog procedure

When a predicate is called, the box is entered via the *CALL port*, **after** the unification of the predicate arguments. If the procedure is *successful*, the control flow leaves the box via the *EXIT port*. Success generally implies the instantiation of heretofore uninstantiated variable arguments of the predicate invoked, representing, as it were, the values from the computation for which the procedure (predicate) is responsible. Should the procedure prove unsuccessful, control flow abandons the box via the *FAIL port*. This also causes any instantiations made within the context of the 'boxed' procedure, as well as those affected by the unification at the *CALL port*, as mentioned earlier, to become *uninstantiated*.

At the highest level, i.e. the user's request at the terminal, leaving the 'uppermost' box via the *EXIT port* signifies a successful resolution – a *yes* preceded perhaps by some value(s) generated, e.g. '*A rose...*'. A *no* implies an exit via the *FAIL port*.

The fourth and final port is the *REDO port*. This port is directly connected to the respective FAIL port of the (subordinate) procedures invoked from a given box. If such a *called* procedure, i.e. subgoal, *fails*, it leaves its box via the *FAIL port* and re-enters the *calling* procedure via its *REDO port*.

This characterizes *backtracking*. Should a box be re-entered via the *REDO port*, an attempt is made via *backtracking* in that procedure's context to find an alternative unification. If one is found, the calling procedure exits its box once again via the *EXIT port*, either to re-enter the box which had just failed, this time with *new arguments*, or to enter an altogether *new subprocedure*. If no viable alternative is found, then the calling procedure is exited permanently via its *FAIL port* and the process just described 'propagates' back up the calling hierarchy. At the highest level, the *failure* may be *explicitly 'induced'*, by a user response of a semicolon to the 'solution' presented by the interpreter, causing the original goal (box) to be re-entered via its *REDO port*, with the above consequences. In the context of this model, a *cut* can be seen as a barrier which, when encountered in the course of backtracking within a box, prevents a *REDO* from leaving the box via *EXIT* again (even if alternatives could theoretically be generated 'somewhere in it') and causes said box to be exited via the *FAIL port*.

To illustrate the connections between two boxes, let us examine the model with respect to the request in Fig. 5.5.

?– **poem, fail.**

poem always succeeds, *recursively* creating ever more profound 'rose' poems, and thus never leaves its box via the *FAIL port*. Consequently, every time the box is re-entered via *REDO*, it is left via *EXIT*.

The *fail* box, on the other hand, is, by definition, never successful. Its *EXIT* and *REDO ports* are as good as non-existent. Thus, after every poem, the *fail* box is entered via its *CALL port* and exited via the *FAIL port*, causing a re-entry of *poem*, ad nauseam (see Fig. 5.5).

And yet how is it that *poem* never fails? The answer to such a question is often crucial in the testing phase of program development — particularly when such an *unintentional endless loop* appears in a complex Prolog program.

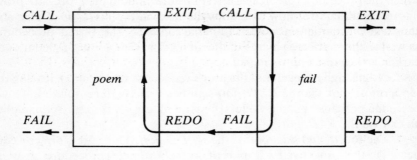

Fig. 5.5 The box model for the call poem, fail

The best way to detect the cause of such problems is to follow the flow of control. And this is best done by 'looking into the box', i.e. examining the structural context of the procedural dynamics. Figure 5.6 illustrates this for the predicate *poem*. The predicates *concat_atoms* and *write* offer no alternative path from *REDO* to the *EXIT port* when backtracking. On the other hand, *closing* does. Thus, *opening*, and consequently *poem*'s *FAIL port*, can never be reached!

Figure 5.7 illustrates the internal structure of *closing*; both (alternative) interpretations are shown using the box model. The first, *continuation*, contains no *REDO–EXIT* path. Consequently, it is successful only the first time it is activated, i.e. entered. A *REDO* leads directly to the *FAIL port* and from there control flows to the *START port* of the first goal of the second, alternative interpretation. Control passes through it and after the *EXIT port* of its last subgoal, *concat_atoms*, it leaves *closing* again via its *EXIT*.

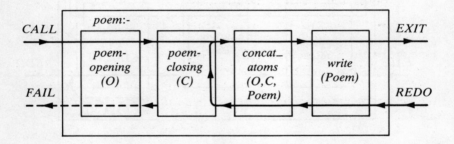

Fig. 5.6   Looking into the box for poem

A further *REDO* takes it through *concat_atoms* to the *REDO port* of the second goal of the second alternative — *closing* (again!), but this time *one level of recursion deeper*! We should have repeated Fig. 5.7 in that position in reduced size, but, as you hopefully now see, from that *REDO port* control again flows to the *EXIT port* and consequently into an endless loop.

5.4   Tracing a Run

Most Prolog interpreters permit you to *trace* the flow of control and the unifications made at the respective ports during the interpretation process. This facility is enabled with the request:

?– **trace.**

and disabled with:[1]

?– **notrace.**

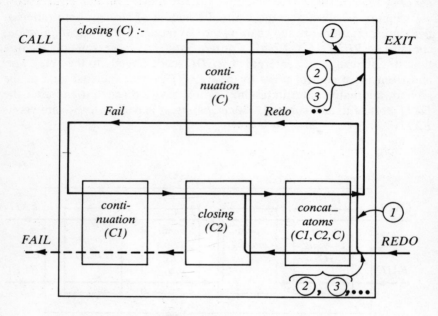

Fig. 5.7   Looking into the box for closing(C)

The trace protocol appears on the screen, one line for every pass through a port. Depending on how your terminal is configured, lines too long for the screen width are either continued on the next line or merely truncated. This has nothing to do with the interpreter itself! Both conditions are equally unsatisfactory. This form of tracing is, in practice, really useful only when you want to get a quick overview of the general program behavior, e.g. confirmation of the existence of an endless loop. The lack of control over the protocol produced — no scrollback, etc. — makes this form of trace virtually useless for a detailed examination of the interpretive process. You can remedy this problem by having the protocol written to an arbitrary file, e.g.

?– **trace**(ProtocolFile).

[1] If your version of Prolog does not have a screen-oriented *debugger*, the respective commands are likely to be *debug* and *nodebug*.

You can then examine the output with other system tools (editor, etc.) or
have it printed out. If you request a trace

?– **trace(protocol).**

yes
?– **poem, fail.**

you will find something resembling the following in the file named protocol.

```
(18)   CALL poem
(20)   CALL opening(_L178)
(20)   EXIT opening(
          A rose
          )
(20)   CALL closing(_L179)
(21)   CALL continuation(_G50)
(21)   EXIT continuation( is a rose
          )
(20)   EXIT closing(     is a rose
          )
(21)   CALL concat_atoms(
          A rose
          ,       is a rose
          ,_L180)
(22)   CALL name(
          A rose
          ,_L203)
(22)   EXIT name(
          A rose
          ,[10,65,32,114,111,115,101,10])
(22)   CALL name( is a rose
          ,_L204)
(22)   EXIT name( is a rose
          ,[9,105,115,32,97,32,114,111,115,101,10])
(22)   CALL append([10,...,10],[9,...,10],_L205)
(22)   REDO append([10,...,10],[9,...,10],_L205)
(22)   EXIT append([10,...,10],[9,...,10],[10,...,10,9,...,10])
(39)   CALL name(_G51,[10,...,10,9,...,10])
(39)   EXIT name(
          A rose
              is a rose
          ,[10,...,10,9,...,10])
(21)   EXIT concat_atoms(
          A rose
          ,    is a rose
          ,
          A rose
              is a rose
          )
```

```
(39)   CALL write(
          A rose
                  is a rose
          )
(39)   EXIT write(
          A rose
                  is a rose
          )
(18)   EXIT poem
(39)   CALL fail
(39)   FAIL fail
(20)   REDO closing(_L179)
(21)   CALL continuation(_L191)
                    •     •     •
```

While this is a somewhat abbreviated version, it does embody the
essential features of what you can expect to find.

We have shown you only the beginning and end of a *very* long listing,
where omissions on our part have been indicated by '...'. Also, we have
beautified the output by using indentation to make logically connected output appear as readable, distinct blocks, so that you may more easily follow
the sequence of control flow from port to port. Each such pass is marked by

- a box identification number, written in parentheses, and

- the name of the port through which the given box was entered or
  exited.

In addition, the affected predicate, along with the value of its arguments at
the given state of unification, is indicated. '*_Lnnn*' and '*_Gnnn*' are unique
internal identifiers of the respective local and global variables involved.

5.5   An Interactive Debugging Aid

If you made the effort to decipher the trace we showed you in the previous
section, or better yet, using your own trace at the terminal, then we should
not have any trouble convincing you that such traces are of limited value in
debugging. This is particularly true in those instances where you need such
help the most, i.e. when working on large, complex programs. Trying to
follow the interpreter's activity on the screen is a hopeless endeavour. A
printout of same is equally cumbersome, as the movements through the
various ports of a given box are typically distributed over several pages.
Furthermore, searching through and analysing complex trace expressions is
hardly the optimal method for debugging in a screen-oriented, interactive,
dialog system.

The essential shortcoming of the trace is that it supports only a *black-box* approach, i.e. only the events or states occurring at the call and exit ports of a procedure are recorded in the protocol. The view into the box, which in Figs. 5.6 and 5.7 enabled us to see the causes of the observed control-flow behavior, is not possible with the simple trace.

What we would prefer is a *white-box* approach, which would open a window into the respective active procedure box during the interpretation of a program and show us the control flow with the concomitant variable instantiations as they occur. That is the only way that we can get a feel for the process of resolution and certainly the only effective way in which we can detect errors.

Such a tool exists in the form of an interactive, screen-oriented debugger. The best way to illustrate its use is in a sample session. We can only present an excerpt, but it should illustrate the fundamental usage. A good debugger will provide many additional means to control the output and selectively search for possible errors, so after you have grasped the principle features in our example you should carefully read the documentation for your system to acquaint yourself with all its extensions.

To turn on the debugger you activate the pseudo-predicate *debug*. Then *nodebug* will turn it off. Thus we begin our session with

> ?– **debug.**

> yes
> ?– **poem, fail.**

In response the system creates a standard mask on your screen, representing the window into the box. Due to space constraints we shall show it in the illustrations (Figs. 5.8–18) in somewhat reduced size.

```
debugger_CALL_exit_redo_FAIL_LAST_____spy_____CREEPING
execute((poem, fail)) :-
CALL    poem,
        fail.




debug command ? _

yes
?– poem, fail.
```

Fig. 5.8

The first line of Fig. 5.8 contains status information. Following the string *debugger* is a list of ports at which the system can show the current status of the respective clause being processed during the execution of the program being debugged. Those shown in upper case are the ports at which the debugger will actually stop and display the information. As we see here, the default is *CALL, FAIL* and *LAST*, i.e. the last port of the last goal shown *before* leaving the clause. The debugger will not, however, stop at the other two ports, *redo* and *exit*. Naturally the user may change this setting in a manner which we shall explain to you in our sample session.

The entry *spy* enables you to instruct the debugger to display the selected information only for specific goals within the given program. This feature is turned off by default, as indicated by the fact that it is shown in lower case. We shall not be using this option in the following example, but will return to it at a more appropriate time in the book.

The last entry, *CREEPING* (enabled) means that the debugger will be single stepping through the program, i.e. it will automatically display the state of sub-goals activated as well, so long as these are not built-in predicates. This can be set to *LEAPING*, in which case the debugger suppresses the display of the descent into sub-goals and only displays the consequences with respect to the active goal, i.e. the debugger stays in the current box. In this context, stopping at the *LAST* port is significant in that it allows you to change from *LEAPING* to *CREEPING* at the end of the current goal, so that the system does not jump to a higher level in the calling hierarchy when it reaches the end of the procedure.

The next and largest section of the screen represents the actual window into the box. The clause presently being interpreted, including all its current variable instantiations, is displayed in it, as is illustrated in the subsequent examples. In addition, the port at which the debugger is stopped is indicated: in this case, at the very beginning, it is naturally the *CALL* port of the first clause, *poem*.

The last line of the screen displays the output which Prolog would normally produce. In our example you see the last entry prior to the commencement of the test run.

Preceding the standard output line you see a prompt *debug command ?*. As the cursor '_' located behind it should indicate, here is where the user enters her commands to control the debugging activity. The commands available to you can be found in the user's manual or you can request a brief summary via the help command:

debug mode ? **h**<*return*>

Hitting <*return*> without entering a command causes the debugger to take the next, pending step. We have done just that in our example and due to the *CREEPING* setting we get to look into the box of the predicate *poem* which was called (Fig. 5.9).

```
┌ ─ ─ ─ ─ ─ ─ ─ ─ ─ ─ ─ ─ ─ ─ ─ ┐
│  debugger_CALL_exit_redo_FAIL_LAST_____spy_____CREEPING      │
│  poem :-                                                     │
│  CALL   opening(_G63),                                       │
│         closing(_G68),                                       │
│         concat_atoms(_G63,_G68,_G75),                        │
│         write(_G75).                                         │
│                                                              │
│                                                              │
│  debug command ? _                                           │
│                                                              │
│  yes                                                         │
│  ?- poem, fail.                                              │
└ ─ ─ ─ ─ ─ ─ ─ ─ ─ ─ ─ ─ ─ ─ ─ ┘
```

Fig. 5.9

You will notice that all the variables involved are as yet uninstantiated and therefore we see only their unique, system-generated, internal names.

Hitting *<return>* again, we are shown the next box in the hierarchy, i.e. for the clause *opening* (Fig. 5.10).

```
┌ ─ ─ ─ ─ ─ ─ ─ ─ ─ ─ ─ ─ ─ ─ ─ ┐
│  debugger_CALL_exit_redo_FAIL_LAST_____spy_____CREEPING      │
│  opening('\nA rose\n') :-                                    │
│  CALL      true.                                             │
│                                                              │
│                                                              │
│                                                              │
│                                                              │
│  debug command ? _                                           │
│                                                              │
│  yes                                                         │
│  ?- poem, fail.                                              │
└ ─ ─ ─ ─ ─ ─ ─ ─ ─ ─ ─ ─ ─ ─ ─ ┘
```

Fig. 5.10

In this we see that the *global* variable _G63 from the previous box has been instantiated as the atom '\nA rose\n'. Furthermore, the debugger indicates that a *fact* is actually represented internally as a rule with a body consisting of the goal *true*. Thus when we once again press *<return>*, *true* is 'executed' — successfully of course! The *LAST* option being enabled, the debugger stops after evaluating the last goal of a given (sub-)procedure (Fig. 5.11).

```
┌ ─── ── ── ── ── ── ── ─── ── ── ── ── ── ── ── ── ── ┐
  debugger‗CALL‗exit‗redo‗FAIL‗LAST_____spy___CREEPING
│ opening('\nA rose\n') :-                                          │
  CALL      true.
│                                                                   │

│                                                                   │



│                                                                   │

  debug command ? Pl<return>
│                                                                   │

  yes
│ ?– poem, fail.                                                    │
└ ─── ── ── ── ── ── ── ─── ── ── ── ── ── ── ── ── ─ ─┘
```

Fig. 5.11

In our example, this has the effect of halting the debugger, following another <return> at the *EXIT* port of the *true* clause, despite the fact that this port is disabled (lower case) in the status line. Since this step is superfluous in our particular case, we disable the *LAST* option by issuing the command *Pl* and hitting <return>. In the status line we now see *last* and from now on the debugger will only stop at the last goal of a clause if it is exited via the *FAIL* port, since this is the only port still enabled besides *CALL*.

Another <return> takes us from *opening*'s *EXIT* port back up the hierarchy to the next goal, *closing*, in the still not fully evaluated predicate *poem* (Fig. 5.12).

```
┌ ─── ── ── ── ── ── ── ─── ─ ── ── ── ── ── ── ── ── ┐
  debugger‗CALL‗exit‗redo‗FAIL‗last_____spy___CREEPING
│ poem :-                                                          │
           opening('\nA rose\n'),
│ CALL     closing(_G68),                                          │
           concat‗atoms('\nA rose\n',_G68,_G75),
│          write(_G75).                                            │

│                                                                  │

  debug command ? _
│                                                                  │

  yes
│ ?– poem, fail.                                                   │
└ ─── ── ── ── ── ── ── ─── ── ── ── ── ── ── ── ─ ── ─┘
```

Fig. 5.12

We shall skip over the next two steps involving the clauses *closing* and *continue*, as they are essentially like the previous few steps. With <return>

we come back to the box for *poem* and find ourselves one unification and one goal further along (Fig. 5.13).

```
debugger_CALL_exit_redo_FAIL_last_____spy_____LEAPING
poem:-
          opening('\nA rose\n')
#         closing('\tis a rose\n'),
CALL      concat_atoms('\n...\n','\tis...\n',_G75),
          write(_G75).



debug command ? L<return>

yes
?- poem, fail.
```

Fig. 5.13

Since we are running out of space on our miniature screen, we have taken the liberty of using '**...**' in place of portions of text we have omitted. In reality the instantiated atoms in *concat_atoms* would indeed be shown in full. The following is of greater interest to us:

Not only has the *CALL* marker moved one goal further, but in its former position, at the previous goal, it has been replaced by a '#' symbol. This marks the *choice point* preceding the current call. If *concat_atoms* were to *fail*, then Prolog would return to that *choice point* when backtracking because there is an alternative clause for *closing* in the database.

Once you have gained some experience with the debugger you will probably consider this choice-point marker one of the most valuable features provided, since backtracking is usually the most difficult aspect of control flow in Prolog. The debugger simplifies things by keeping track of the choice points as they occur and shows you immediately, when you e.g. forget a cut or leave out a goal, etc., why the interpreter's response differs from your expectations. You will be surprised at how many unnecessary *repeats* you will find in published programs via this simple marker!

The other thing you likely noticed is the debugger command **L**. Since we are not interested in tracing the execution of the goal *concat_atoms* (too many screensful), we change to *LEAPING* mode by entering an *L*, causing the debugger to suppress display of the sub-goal activity, and thus remain, visually, in the *poem* box. The change in mode is displayed at the far right in the status line.

The *L* command is closed with a *<return>*, as are all debugger commands. In order to continue with the next step in the execution, we must therefore enter another *<return>*. The very next display immediately shows

us the result of the resolution of the *concat_atoms* predicate (Fig. 5.14).
Since our screen is so small, we again show an elided form of the instantiated
values for the predicate.

```
debugger_CALL_exit_redo_FAIL_last_____spy_____LEAPING
poem :-
          opening('\nA rose\n'),
          closing('\tis a rose\n'),
     [#]  concat_atoms('...','...','\nA...rose\n'),
CALL     write('\nA rose\n\tis a rose\n').



debug command ? _

yes
?- poem, fail.
```

Fig. 5.14

Should the output exceed the width of the screen, you should find that
the excess is continued on the following line, ad nauseam. In the case of
extremely long lists it becomes very difficult to read (try entering the *concat_atoms* box some time !), but this is hard to avoid, since the debugger does not
know and cannot know what information you are willing to do without.

We see a new symbol, '[#]' in the last display. The choice point marker
'#' in front of *closing* has disappeared, since the last step taken introduced
a newer and 'closer' choice point for backtracking from the current state.
This one no longer lies in the box displayed for the predicate *poem*, but

```
debugger_CALL_exit_redo_fail_last_____spy_____CREEPING
execute((poem , fail)):-
     [#]  poem,
CALL     fail.




debug command ? _

A rose
          is a rose
```

Fig. 5.15

rather in a *deeper* one, i.e. in the *concat_atoms* box. Thus, the square brackets indicate that the point lies hidden in a box not being displayed.

The argument of the *write* predicate is now instantiated with a complete, minimal version of the poem. Once activated it will cause the original *poem* goal in the output line at the bottom of the screen to be replaced by the text generated. Thus, when we hit *<return>* we leave the predicate *poem* and enter the next goal. No pause is made prior to leaving via *poem*'s *EXIT* port because we disabled the *LAST* option (Fig. 5.15). The *CALL* marker now appears in front of the *fail* goal and the current choice point lies deep within the *poem* predicate, as indicated by the '[#]'.

If you examine the status line at the head of the screen you also notice that we apparently issued two further debugger commands in the meantime. Since we know that *fail* by definition leaves via its *FAIL* port, we suppressed its display by entering

> debug command ? **Pf**<*return*>

changing *fail* to lower case in the status line. With

> debug command ? **C**<*return*>

we reselected the *CREEPING* mode so that the next *<return>* does not take us past the original request and thereby terminate its further execution. Instead execution resumes at the current viable choice point: the alternative clause for *closing* (Fig. 5.16).

```
debugger_CALL_exit_redo_fail_last_____spy_____CREEPING
closing(_G50):-
CALL    continuation(_G66),
        closing(_G71),
        concat_atoms(_G66,_G71,_G50).



debug command ? _

A rose
        is a rose
```

Fig. 5.16

You can now single-step through it. We skip over the effects of the next 10 <*return*>s and resume our discussion at the resulting view of the *poem* box (Fig. 5.17).

```
debugger_CALL_exit_redo_fail_last_____spy____LEAPING
poem:-
        opening('\nA rose\n'),
  [#]   closing('\tis a rose\n\tis...\n'),
CALL    concat_atoms('...','\t...\n\t...\n',_G212),
        write(_G212).



debug command ? L<return>

A rose
      is a rose
```

Fig. 5.17

The *closing* has grown correspondingly longer, as has the second argument of *concat_atoms* (they share the same global internal variable). Note that we have once again abbreviated the actual instantiated values for lack of space.

We skip over the concatenation predicate by changing to *LEAPING* mode, since the long character lists in the *name* predicate in it would otherwise flood even our 2000-character screen. Two more <*return*>s then lead us into the *write* predicate and out again (Fig. 5.18).

```
debugger_CALL_exit_redo_fail_last_____spy____LEAPING
execute((poem , fail)):-
    [#]   poem,
CALL    fail.




debug command ? N
A rose
      is a rose
      is a rose
```

Fig. 5.18

We are now back at the original request goal, i.e. *poem* has been unified, and the next version appears in the standard output line at the bottom of the screen. The window into the box looks identical to the one we saw after the first version had been output!

Since we now have a feel for how things get done internally, we enter the debugger command **N**, which is equivalent to the *nodebug* predicate, and turn the debugger off. The interpreter now runs freely and, due to the endless loop, proceeds to fill the screen with forever growing poems. At some point the message

```
GLOBAL STACK FULL

?-
```

appears, followed by the standard prompt '?-'. The system has aborted further interpretation as it has exhausted its allotted memory.

If you would rather not wait for this event, you can *interrupt*, i.e. terminate the loop explicity, by hitting the appropriate key at your terminal, e.g. *<DEL>*. Under Unix this can usually be achieved with *<control>C*. Your screen should then look something like:

```
        is a rose

A rose
        is a rose
        is a rose
        is a rose
INTERRUPT: a(abort),b(break),c(continue),d(debug) ?
```

As you see, you can now enter the corresponding letter to either terminate (*a*) or continue (*c*) or even reenter the debugger (*d*). The latter is particularly useful when you unexpectedly encounter an endless loop when running a program and want to quickly see roughly where the bug is.

The *break* option interrupts the program and places you in a sort of 'higher' state, i.e. you get a 'fresh' copy of the Prolog interpreter with the same database.

Now you can look at the rules and facts and perhaps (carefully) make modifications. Care is needed because when you return to the interrupted version, which is done with one of the usual 'stop' predicates, e.g. *halt* or *end_of_file*, the old interpreter may not find its way in the modified database and terminate with a *fail*. On the other hand, changing the database during the execution of a program is typically done only when you are fairly certain that the program as is would probably not make it to a successful conclusion anyway.

5.6 Iteration

Recursion is not always the most natural way of expressing repetition. Many programming languages do not even permit it. The more common method is *iteration*, expressed as a *do–while loop*. Prolog does not directly provide such a syntactic construct, but it can be derived from the *backtracking* mechanism built into the interpreter. The *fail* predicate serves this purpose, since it causes backtracking by definition. We used *fail* this way most recently to get our poem-generating predicate to iterate.

?– **poem, fail.**

As we saw in that example, however, you can often produce only endless loops in this fashion. This occurs whenever the predicate(s) preceding the *fail* are always *true*, as in the case of *poem*.

Thus, using *fail* to cause the iteration of the predicate(s) preceding it works in only two cases:

- when we really want an endless loop, e.g. in *interpreters* or for continuous polling of a measuring instrument in an automated laboratory, or

- when the iterating predicate(s) itself returns a *fail*.

The latter was true of the facts stored in our old database in Fig. 1.1. We could get a list of all of these facts without risking an endless loop using the simple query

?– **person(_,N,_,_),write(N),fail.**

Since Prolog repeatedly moves its internal search pointer in the database one fact further each time it backtracks, eventually there are no more *person*-facts to be had and the very first goal ends with *fail*, causing the query to fail and the loop to end.

How can we limit the number of iterations of a loop which would normally repeat endlessly? Some Prolog implementations provide a built-in predicate for such purposes, e.g. *for(Index, Increment, Limit)*, where the variable *Index* is incremented in *Increment* steps until *Limit* has been exceeded, at which time the predicate *fails*. Since this somewhat foreign language extension is not generally available, we shall not discuss it further.

To achieve the same with the standard features of Prolog we must learn a few other things beforehand. We will return to this problem a bit later.

Sometimes, however, we must solve the opposite problem: we want to repeat a predicate which is successful only once, i.e. when it is entered 'normally' from 'above', but not when reactivated due to backtracking. The I/O procedures, like *write(Term)*, represent this class of predicates. Backtracking over a *write* predicate does not cause it to repeat the last string output by it, as one might expect. This would certainly render it less useful!

But what if that is precisely what we want? We have been commissioned to write a program for meditation purposes, which is to endlessly repeat a *mantra*. Prolog provides the built-in predicate **repeat**, which is *always* successful, just for such special cases. Our mantra procedure could thus be written:

```
guru :-
        repeat,
        write('\nOm Mani Padme Hum'),
        fail.
```

Admittedly, you will seldom be called upon to write such programs and, therefore, you will find that you do not often use *repeat* in daily practice. You will, no doubt, be surprised at how often it is used *unnecessarily* in (sample) programs published in technical literature.

5.7 The *Cut* Built-in

There is another problem with the *fail* predicate. What do we do when we really mean it? When we do not want to specify an iteration with it, but simply want to say that the previous predicate, e.g. a test, was unsuccessful? It is annoying if Prolog attempts to find an alternative solution anyway, by backtracking.

The means we have for doing this has already been mentioned. It is known as the *cut* and is symbolized by an exclamation point (!).

We also mentioned that *cut* is a bit dangerous and many people would like to see it forbidden, much as the *go to* in traditional programming languages. Avoiding *cuts* completely in Prolog, however, is very difficult, because its meaning is virtually impossible to express otherwise: viz.

I really mean what I said!

(Perhaps this is why the exclamation point was selected to represent it?) Let's see how *cut* works in combination with *fail*.

Imagine we want a program for an automatic teller at the bank which implements the accessing of customer accounts. We must guarantee that a customer who has *no* right to access an account is refused permission regardless of how often she makes an attempt, i.e. that she does not acquire the right accidentally due to backtracking. The usual method of implementing the like involves the almost standard *cut* and *fail* combination:

```
accessacct(Customer,Acctnr) :-
            (       no_rights(Customer,Acctnr),
                    message('Not allowed'),
                    !, fail
            ;       services(Customer,Acctnr)
            ).
```

The scope of the *cut* is always restricted to the procedure immediately containing it. In this case, it implies

- we really mean the access attempt should *fail* altogether;

- no attempt should be made, via backtracking, to see if the customer might, under some other circumstances, be allowed to access the account; and

- the customer should not be offered any *services* as an alternative (!!) if she has been denied access.

Notice that precisely the latter would occur if a *cut* did not precede the fail: she would receive *services* because she had no access privilege.

A *cut* would also be useful when specifying the *services*; e.g.

```
services(Customer,Acctnr) :-
        (               overdrawn(Customer,Acctnr),
                        !, basic_service(Customer,Acctnr)
        ;               full_service(Customer,Acctnr)
        ).

basic_service(Customer,Acctnr) :-
        (               acct_balance(Customer,Acctnr)
        ;               deposit(Customer,Acctnr)
        ;               ...
        ).

full_service(Customer,Acctnr) :-
        (               basic_service(Customer,Acctnr)
        ;               withdrawal(Customer,Acctnr)
        ;               money_order(Customer,Acctnr)
        ;               ...
        ).
```

The *cut* in the clause *services* indicates once again that no alternatives are desired: if someone has overdrawn her account, then she should only have access to the 'basic' services.

5.8   Defining Logical Operators

Cut is especially important for defining new logical predicates. For instance *exclusive or*, i.e. *xor*:

```
:-  op(254, xfy, xor).

P xor Q :-
        P, not Q, !.
P xor Q :-
        Q, not P.
```

The *negation* operator, *not* should it be absent as a built-in:

```
:- op(60, fx, not).

not P :-
        P, !, fail.
not P.
```

or the *implication* operator 'if...then...', as

```
:- op(1100, xfy, '->').

P ->Q :- not P, !.
P ->Q :- Q.
```

The above definition of *implication* is somewhat tricky due to the precedence of 1100, which is equal to that of the semicolon, i.e. *or*. This was done intentionally, so that one could express the commonplace *if–then–else* construct as

$$(P-> Q ; R)$$

Beware, however: *like the semicolon,* -> *binds more weakly than and*, i.e. the comma. Thus, we recommend that you always use the *implication* operator in parentheses to indicate the scope explicitly.

Furthermore, when using the *not* operator, remember that its definition causes following the following problem: the *fail* in it causes all variable instantiations which the predicate using it had made to become *un*instantiated. Consequently,

```
not not member(X,[a,b,c])
```

is not equivalent to

```
member(X,[a,b,c]).
```

The predicate *member* instantiates the variable X with the element *a* when first called, and with every incidence of backtracking thereafter with the succeeding elements of the list. The double negation of *member*, however, has the effect that the first *not* already causes X to be *un*instantiated, i.e. to become a variable as it was before the call. Here the problem is relatively easy to see. Such unexpected effects, though, can be extremely difficult to recognize in more complex situations. This is a criticism leveled both at *cut* and *not* by many Prolog purists.

6 SPECIAL CONTROL STRUCTURES

In the last chapter we saw how Prolog controls the flow of execution with but a handful of simple constructs. And yet these are extremely powerful, as we now hope to demonstrate. We shall introduce you to several basic programming structures which you will encounter in other people's programs and also use yourself time and again. One in particular, the syntax-oriented processing of character strings or lists, is so important that most Prolog systems provide an abbreviated way of expressing and manipulating them. After introducing you to them, we will show you some typical control structures used in building expert systems and similar 'knowledge-based' applications.

6.1 The Syntax of Strings and Lists

We begin with the *syntax-oriented processing* of a data sequence. Within the context of Prolog, we can think of a data sequence as being a *list* of *atoms* exhibiting a structural organization which can be described by a fixed set of rules. These rules can be represented as a collection of *productions*. We will be explaining this notation in detail shortly.

Before doing so, however, we must remind you that a *string* in Prolog is represented merely as a *list* of the ASCII codes for the corresponding characters, e.g.

"1990" *is* [49,57,57,48]

or

"*MXM*" *is* [77,88,77],

and that the interpreter understands both representations.

Our sample applications concentrate on the processing of such character strings, but the principle applies to lists consisting of arbitrary constituent elements and you should feel free to experiment with those of your choice, e.g. lists of lists, etc. After all the *Jackson method* of structured programming is nothing other than a syntax-oriented technique.[1]

But now for the first example. The task involves translating roman numerals into their decimal equivalents.

As you know, specific numbers in the roman notation are represented by upper-case letters:

```
numeral(1)     — —>    "I".
numeral(5)     — —>    "V".
numeral(10)    — —>    "X".
numeral(50)    — —>    "L".
numeral(100)   — —>    "C".
numeral(500)   — —>    "D".
numeral(1000)  — —>    "M".
```

We have used the syntactic formalism of *productions*, which is inherent to Prolog, to express this knowledge. The production operator — —> can be read as 'is derived from'. Thus, the first production means that the (decimal) *numeral(l)* originates from the string "*I*", i.e. a list containing only the element corresponding to the roman numeral "1".

But what about all the other roman numbers, e.g. MCMLXXXVI, etc. They are constructed using the above 'primitives' according to the following rules:

1. If a lesser numeral precedes a greater one, then its value is to be *subtracted* from the greater.

2. If a numeral precedes one of lesser or equal value, then the values are to be *added* together.

3. Zero is not part of the roman numeric system, therefore the empty list is to be considered its equivalent.

The following productions embody these rules. The connecting operator (",") is to be read here as 'followed by':

```
roman(R) — —> numeral(X), numeral(Y),
                  { X < Y },
                roman(R1),
                  { R is Y − X + R1 }.
roman(R) — —> numeral(X), roman(R1),
                  { R is X + R1 }
roman(0) — —> [ ].
```

---

[1] You will find a reference in the bibliography to an article which deals with this in greater detail (*see* Logrippo and Skuce).

The expressions in curly brackets, i.e. {...} can be arbitrary Prolog *terms*.[2] They are bracketed because they describe not so much the actual *syntax*, but rather the *meaning* or *semantics* of the expression to be processed. Expressions such as those appearing in the curly brackets are often referred to as *attributes* and a collection of productions like the above, correspondingly, as an *attributed grammar* for the language produced by it — in our case the language of roman numerals.

These attributes are executed as soon as they are reached during the processing of the sub-goals from left to right.

Let us now read the first production clause for *roman(R)* in English:

> The roman numeral *R* is derived from
> > a numeral *X* followed by
> > a numeral *Y*,
> > where *X* less than *Y*,
> > followed by a roman numeral *R1*,
> > by subtracting *X* from *Y* and adding *R1*.

This is just what we had said informally in our rule (1) above, merely formulated somewhat more precisely and using the help of a recursion. The other two productions are even simpler. You should easily recognize them as being straightforward translations of the informal transformation rules (2) and (3).

Naturally, we must learn how to activate these productions in Prolog, since as they stand they represent Prolog *terms* but *not clauses*: the production operator ——> is *not* the same as :- and indeed has nothing to do with it!

Thus, we cannot simply call a production as we would a clause — of course not, because the only argument of *roman(R)* is precisely the decimal equivalent which we are looking for. How should the production know which roman numeral it is to produce the decimal value for?

6.2   The Translation and Processing of Productions

This problem is solved by a translator which is part of the input routine of the Prolog system and which transforms productions into clauses.

In order to explain how it works, we must first specify some of the terminology we will be using. Those *terms* representing the name of a given production and, consequently, something being produced, e.g. *roman(R)* or *numeral(X)*, we call *nonterminals*. The character strings or lists, on the other

---

[2] If you have ever worked with *yacc*, the Unix compiler–compiler, you will recognize this notation. It should consequently be clear that it would take little effort to implement all sorts of language processors in Prolog.

hand, directly represent the elements of the expression to be processed, e.g. "*I*" or "*M*", and are irreducible units called *terminals*.

The translator changes the productions it sees into clauses in the following manner:

- *Nonterminals* are supplemented with two variable arguments of the form *Sn*, which function as the input and output strings of the production. In the body of the production the input variable of any term is always the output variable of its immediate predecessor.

- *Terminals* are transformed into a *connect(Sx, Terminal, Sy)* predicate. Its job is to extract the respective terminal from its given position in the input string, should it exist, and insert it into the output string. If the terminal is not in the position designated by the production, then *connect* and thus the entire associated clause fails, since the production does not describe the input sequence encountered.

- *Attributes* are merely copied as goals, without the bracketing, into the body of the respective clause.

Let us see just how this would look in the case of our first production, *roman(R)*, and *numeral(1)* and *numeral(5)*:

```
roman(S0,S1,R) :-
        numeral(S0,S2,X), numeral(S2,S3,Y),
        X < Y,
        roman(S3,S1,R1),
        R is Y − X + R1.

numeral(S0,S1,1) :- connect(S0,"I",S1).
numeral(S0,S1,5) :- connect(S0,"V",S1).
```

Processing begins with the so-called *start* production, i.e. the one describing the entire string or character sequence to be processed. The clause derived from it is called as the initial goal, its input argument *S1* being the symbol sequence to be analyzed and its output argument set to the empty list (at the end there should be no more symbols remaining). Here is a sample clause, *c* for 'convert', which initiates this call:[3]

```
c(RNumeral,DNumeral) :-
        roman(RNumeral,[ ],DNumeral), !.
```

It is wise to include a *cut* following the *roman* goal. To see why, try it without

---

[3] Whether the supplemental arguments *Sn* get inserted at the beginning or the end of the argument lists depends on your implementation (no standards!), so if you have trouble with our examples on your system, try changing the order to see if that is the problem.

the cut on your own system. Backtracking causes incorrect alternatives to be generated whenever the roman numeral entered contains a symbol of lesser value followed directly by one of greater value. This is because the initial answer is based on the first production (using subtraction) whereas backtracking causes the second production (using addition) to be applied to generate the alternatives. With the *cut* this problem does not arise:

> ?– **c("MXM",D).**

> D = 1990 ;

> no
> ?– **c("MMMCMXLI",D).**

> D = 3941 ;

> no
> ?–

If you recall that 77 and 88 are the ASCII equivalents for the letters *M* and *X*, then you should be able to comprehend the processing of the string "*MMM*" without much trouble, at the very least by using the debugger.

6.3   Analysis and Evaluation of Arithmetic Expressions

A set of productions describing all possible, correct 'sentences' of a language is typically referred to as a *syntax* or *grammar*.

This form of notation can always be used, whenever you want to check the formal correctness of expressions and, at the same time, process them according to some given syntax. This abbreviated and easily understood formulation of the corresponding Prolog clauses is often used to implement interactive, natural language front-ends, as well as command and programming languages.

Consequently, our next example illustrates a simple desk-calculator program capable of evaluating expressions consisting of integers and the four basic arithmetic operators. It is to be called via the unary operator *how_ much_is Expression*, e.g.:

> ?– **how_much_is "12*(3+5)+−2".**

> 12*(3+5)+−2 = 94

> yes
> ?–

The predicate which does this can deal with negative numbers and parentheses. Figure 6.1 shows its implementation. With the exception of the clause *how_much_is Expression*, all the other predicates are written as productions. Based on your experience from the previous section, you should be able to follow the processing of a simple arithmetic expression relatively easily. If you cannot, examine the evaluation process using your debugger!

```
:- op(100,fx,how_much_is).

expr(Z) ——> term(X), "+", expr(Y),
                         { Z is X+Y }.
expr(Z) ——> term(X), "−", expr(Y),
                         { Z is X−Y }.
expr(Z) ——> term(Z).

term(Z) ——> number(X), "*", term(Y),
                         { Z is X*Y }.
term(Z) ——> number(X), "/", term(Y),
                         { Z is X/Y }.
term(Z) ——> "(", expr(Z), ")".
term(Z) ——> number(Z).

number(Z) ——> digits(Z,_).
number(Z) ——> "+", number(Z).
number(Z) ——> "−", number(X),
                     { Z is −X }.

digits(Z,P) ——> digit(X), digits(Y,PY),
                         { P is 10*PY, Z is P*X+Y }.
digits(Z,1) ——> digit(Z).

digit(0) ——> "0".
digit(1) ——> "1".
digit(2) ——> "2".
digit(3) ——> "3".
digit(4) ——> "4".
digit(5) ——> "5".
digit(6) ——> "6".
digit(7) ——> "7".
digit(8) ——> "8".
digit(9) ——> "9".

how_much_is Expression :-
            expr(Expression,[ ],Z),
            name(AN,Expression), nl, write(AN),
            write(' = '), write(Z), nl.
```

Fig. 6.1   A simple desk-calculator program

Note that in the clause *how_much_is* we use *name* to transform the expression entered into an atom before we output the actual result. If we had not, then *write* would display a list containing the individual characters constituting the string and, even worse, do so using the ASCII equivalents.

If you try using blanks in the expression to be evaluated, in order to improve readability, you will find that the *how_much_is* operator will fail, i.e. return *no* as its response. Now if you attempt to modify the syntax to allow optional blanks, you will find that this enormously increases the number of productions needed to define the grammar.

For this reason, compilers (translators) for programming languages typically apply two grammars, one after the other. The first one describes the *lexicographic units*, also referred to as the *symbols* or *tokens*, of the language to be analyzed. These are the meaningful elements of a source text, e.g. constants, identifiers, operators, keywords, etc., which often consist of more than one character, e.g. "**" for exponentiation. These are identified during the *lexical analysis*, during which such things as separating blanks and comments can be explicitly ignored and thus eliminated.

In Prolog the result of this first set of productions could be a *list* of the individual *tokens* found, each converted into an *atom* by the built-in predicate *name(Atom, TokenList)*. This preprocessed list is then passed to the 'actual' language processor, the *parser* or *syntax checker* as a data sequence. The parser itself consists of the clauses generated from the *higher-order productions*, as illustrated above. These no longer contain terminals defined as strings, but rather as lists of atoms — precisely those tokens which the lexical analysis extracted from the input stream.

If you wish to extend our simple example or, based on the principles demonstrated there, write your own language processor, we recommend you use such a two-step program architecture.

6.4 The Exhaustive Search

One of the most important application areas for Prolog is the development of *knowledge-based software*, often referred to as *expert systems*. These are software systems which manage facts and rules in a *knowledge base* and can derive 'new' knowledge, i.e. make inferences from it. In the first few chapters of the book we discussed some aspects of this, but restricted ourselves to simple search and access activities in the context of knowledge bases organized along essentially traditional database lines.

As the problems to be solved become logically more complex, knowledge is increasingly embodied as rules, i.e. in the body of the Prolog procedures, rather than as facts. Expert systems, however, differ from conventional, algorithmic programs in that the search process plays a major role in finding a solution. Searches are typically accelerated by *heuristics*, i.e. rule-of-thumb strategies derived from experience and used to optimize the process.

With respect to Prolog, a number of special, search-oriented organizational forms for control flow have proven useful in such applications. We shall examine these in the context of some logical puzzles, which exhibit traits characteristic of the problems experts solve, and offer concise examples of these classical solutions.

We beg your pardon should these problems appear to be of a less practical nature than usual.

The first and most primitive of these control-flow structures is the *exhaustive search*. As the name indicates, it simply involves attempting all possible solutions, until one or all actual solutions for a problem have been found. This is the 'knowledge-based' equivalent of the sequential search in a database and is practical only for problems of minimal complexity. If the task becomes more involved, then some heuristic must be found to better target the search.

Nonetheless, this basic structure is significant in Prolog programming, especially since *backtracking* is nothing less than the implementation of this search algorithm: it automatically searches the database for all permissible solutions. The programmer need not expend any effort to achieve this end: an exhaustive search is built in! On the contrary, she must devote her efforts more to streamlining the search, e.g. using cuts to avoid the unnecessary generation of undesirable solutions. Indeed she can concentrate more on the *heuristics* and need not waste time and code programming the trivial search.

6.5 A Crypt-arithmetic Problem

Let us look at a well known crypt-arithmetic puzzle which will help illustrate the exhaustive search. An arithmetic calculation is given, where the operands and results are encoded as letters, and we must derive a unique, one-to-one mapping of numbers to the letters which makes the calculation work.

Let us try it with the following addition:

```
  S E N D
  M O R E
_ _ _ _ _
M O N E Y
```

It is assumed that the encoded values contain *no leading zeroes*, i.e. it is certain that 'S' and 'M' are not zero. Under these circumstances, 'M' apparently represents a '1'.

We want to build both of these *constraints* into the program used to solve this puzzle. The 'no leading zeroes' constraint makes for unique solutions. (Leave it out and see how many alternative solutions can be generated where $S=0$.) The second constraint yields a primitive heuristic which, albeit minimally, limits the search.

Figures 6.2(a) and (b) show a solution based on an exhaustive search strategy: column for column all possible letter–number substitutions are tested until either a contradiction or a solution is found.

```
:- op(100,xfx,not_in).

send_more_money :-
            DigitList = [S,E,N,D,M,O,R,Y],
            M = 1,                  % constrain due to being
            digit(S), S \= 0,       % in column 1 and 2 !
            column(0,0,C2,M,0,DigitList),
            column(S,M,C3,0,C2,DigitList),
            column(E,0,C4,N,C3,DigitList),
            column(N,R,C5,E,C4,DigitList),
            column(D,E,0,Y,C5,DigitList),
            result(DigitList), fail.

column(Line1,Line2,Carry,Line3,NewCarry,DigitList) :-
            carry(Carry),
            (   var(Line1),
                digit(X1), X1 not_in DigitList,
                Line1 = X1
            ;   nonvar(Line1)
            ),
            (   var(Line2),
                digit(X2), X2 not_in DigitList,
                Line2 = X2
            ;   nonvar(Line2)
            ),
            Sum is Line1 + Line2 + Carry,
            NewCarry is Sum / 10,
            X3 is Sum mod 10,
            (   var(Line3),
                X3 not_in DigitList
            ;   nonvar(Line3)
            ),
            Line3 = X3.
```

(a)

Fig. 6.2(a)   **The solution to *SEND-MORE-MONEY* using an exhaustive search: (a) part 1;**

```
digit(0).
digit(1).
digit(2).
digit(3).
digit(4).
digit(5).
digit(6).
digit(7).
digit(8).
digit(9).

carry(0).
carry(1).

Digit not_in [ ].
Digit not_in [X|Rest] :-
        var(X),
        Digit not_in Rest.
Digit not_in [X|Rest] :-
        nonvar(X),
        Digit \= X,
        Digit not_in Rest.

result([S,E,N,D,M,O,R,Y]) :-
        write('\n S E N D\t'), out([' ',S,E,N,D]),
        write('\n M O R E\t'), out([' ',M,O,R,E]),
        write('\n---------\t'), write('---------'),
        write('\nM O N E Y\t'), out([M,O,N,E,Y]), nl, nl, ! .

out([ ]).
out([C|Rest]) :-
        write(C), write('   '), out(Rest).
```

(b)

**Fig. 6.2(b)   The solution to SEND-MORE-MONEY using an exhaustive
search: (a) part 1; (b) part 2.**

Before we begin discussing the Prolog text in Figs. 6.2(a) and (b), let
us glance at Fig. 6.3, where we see the solution returned by consulting the
program.

?– **send_more_money.**

```
    S E N D            9 5 6 7
    M O R E            1 0 8 5
    – – – –            – – – –
M O N E Y          1 0 6 5 2
no
?–
```

Fig. 6.3   The solution produced by the program in Figs. 6.2(a) and (b)

The *no* preceding the prompt is caused by the *fail* at the end of the *send_more_money* predicate in Fig. 6.2(a). The *fail* sends the flow of control back into the rule body in search of an alternative solution. That no others are found indicates the uniqueness of the given solution (at least so long as the leading zeroes are prohibited by the clause '$S \=\ 0$').

The essential data structure of the search program in Fig. 6.2(a) is the list *DigitList*, which is initialized with variables at the beginning of the *send_more_money* predicate. These individual variables get instantiated as digits during the search for a solution. At the same time, beginning in the leftmost column, the various *column* goals check that the addition operation for the respective column is not contradictory for the mapping thus far.

When a variable in *DigitList* is instantiated to some value, a test must also be made to insure that no two letters represent the same digit. This is done by the predicate

Digit not_in List,

which uses a defined infix operator to increase readability.

The predicate *column*, of arity 6, performs most of the work. Its first and second arguments are the respective operands in the column currently being processed and the fourth argument is the result. They all serve as either input or output parameters, depending on whether or not the respective letter, i.e. the placeholding variable in *DigitList*, has already been instantiated.

The third argument is the value being carried from the neighboring righthand column. Since the procedure works from the left column to the right, this value is unknown when *column* is called, except when the rightmost column is the one being examined. Consequently, in the following *column* goal both possible carry values, either 0 or 1, are tested.

In contrast, the fifth argument, *NewCarry*, is always already instantiated whenever a *column* goal gets called: with zero the first time and with the carry value from the previous *column* in the subsequent calls. It is conceivable, however, that this instantiation later proves to be contradictory. This is checked for by

NewCarry is Sum / 10

The operator *is* can of course be used as a logical test operator and not just for assignment.

The last argument to *column* is the *DigitList*. It is needed when one or both of the operands, i.e. the first and second arguments, still have not been assigned a value. They get instantiated by *digit*(*X*), whereby a check is immediately made that *X not in DigitList*. Notice that the act of instantiation automatically causes the value to be added to the *DigitList*. This is a consequence of variable sharing in *send_more_money*.

In the next step *column* calculates the digit for the result and, as mentioned above, for the carry value. If the result digit was not already instantiated, i.e. mapped, then it must be checked against the contents of *DigitList* to make sure that this digit has not already occurred.

With this information you should now be able to follow the exhaustive search mechanism in the program shown in Figs. 6.2(a) and (b). A brief comment regarding the output formatting done by the predicate *result* and illustrated in Fig. 6.3 may be useful. The auxiliary predicate *out* serves to output the digits passed to it, via the results list, in the proper position, separated by blanks. And the built-in predicate *nl*, which stands for newline, merely causes a *linefeed* in the output.

6.6 Generate and Test

The second basic control structure of importance in knowledge-based programming is the so-called *generate-and-test* sequence. The name describes rather clearly the basic scheme, as is illustrated in Fig. 6.4. In principle it too is a search process. But whereas in the *exhaustive search* both the main functions, i.e.

• the generation of solution candidates, and

• the testing of same for acceptability with respect to the relevant constraints,

are heavily intertwined, e.g. in our example in Fig. 6.2(a) the predicate *column* performs both duties, here they are well-defined, distinct tasks.

This has the advantage of being more modular and generally easier to comprehend: program development, debugging and adaptation to modified applications and specifications are simpler and more safely done.

To illustrate this structure we once again have chosen a brain twister as an example.[4]

There are three Widgets named *Redwidget, Bluewidget* and *Greenwidget*, each of which *kerpows* a Whatsit. Similarly, there are three Whatsits: *Blackwhatsit, Whitewhatsit* and *Pinkwhatsit*. Every Whatsit, in turn, *varooms*. Indeed, the first to do so varooms *back*, the second one varooms *in* and the third one varooms *over*.

Whenever the Whatsit varooming *over* gets kerpowed by either Bluewidget or Redwidget, then Blackwhatsit varooms *back*. Now Pinkwhatsit does *not* get kerpowed by Bluewidget

---

[4] Taken from Zweistein, *Neue Logeleien*, Hoffman & Campe, Hamburg, West Germany (1971).

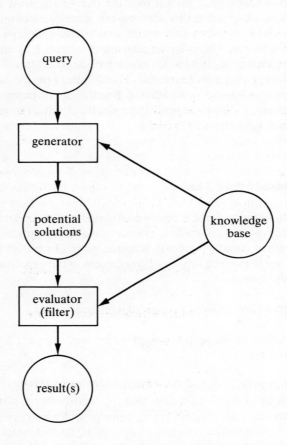

Fig. 6.4   Generate and Test, a basic structure for simple expert systems

and also does *not* varoom *over*. Furthermore, Redwidget does *not* kerpow Blackwhatsit and the Whatsit he does kerpow does *not* veroom *in*. And when Bluewidget kerpows Blackwhatsit, Whitewhatsit does *not* varoom *over*! Which Widget kerpows which Whatsit and how does each Whatsit varoom?

We would like to organize our system around a primitive dialog structure. The user should be able to ask questions about the habits of the Widgets and the Whatsits and receive appropriate answers from the system.

Figure 6.5 shows a sample dialog. The system responds with *no* to the question 'does Blackwhatsit varoom *back*? But if one asks *How* it varooms, then the variable is returned instantiated as *over*. One can also ask questions the other way around, e.g. which is the Whichwhatsit, i.e. the one that varooms back. The answer is pinkwhatsit. And lastly one can ask general questions, like which Widget kerpows which Whatsit? By entering a semi-colon after each response one can get the answer for all three 'kerpow-pairs' and convince oneself that the answers are unique: after the third ';', the response is *no*, i.e. there are no more solutions.

Our system is made up of three essential components: the knowledge base itself, the generator for producing possible solutions, and a component which tests if all constraints (conditions) are satisfied by a given solution. Figure 6.6 shows the knowledge base. The generator and test components are included via a consultation.

The knowledge base starts out by defining a few operators, namely the problem-specific 'verbs' *kerpows* and *varooms*, as well as the operator –> for the logical implication '*if … then*', which make it easier to formulate the problem description for the test component. The implication predicate is then defined as a rule.

?– **blackwhatsit varooms back.**

no
?– **blackwhatsit varooms How.**

How = over

yes
?– **Whichwhatsit varooms back.**

Whichwhatsit = pinkwhatsit

yes
?– **Widget kerpows Whatsit.**

Widget = greenwidget
Whatsit = blackwhatsit ;

Widget = bluewidget
Whatsit = whitewhatsit ;

Widget = redwidget
Whatsit = pinkwhatsit ;

no
?–

Fig. 6.5   *Sample dialog for querying the knowledge base about Widgets and Whatsits*

```
:– [generator, test].

/* operator definitions : */

:– op(70,xfx,kerpows).
:– op(70,xfx,varooms).
:– op(254, xfy, '–>').

P –> Q :– not P, !.
P –> Q :– Q.

/* Facts : */

is_a_widget(redwidget).
is_a_widget(bluewidget).
is_a_widget(greenwidget).

is_a_way_to_varoom(back).
is_a_way_to_varoom(in).
is_a_way_to_varoom(over).

/* rules : */

P kerpows L :–
        generate(Pop),
        test(Pop),
        member([L,P, _ ],Pop).

L varooms K :–
        generate(Pop),
        test(Pop),
        member([L, _ ,K],Pop).
```

Fig. 6.6   *The Widgets and Whatsits knowledge base*

The names of the Widgets and the different ways of kerpowing are included as facts. We could also have included the names of the Whatsits as facts, but it turns out that in our approach they need not be explicitly mentioned.

In the rules portion we see the definition of the new predicates kerpows and varooms. Their rule bodies mirror the structure indicated in Fig. 6.4 exactly: generate and test. First the predicate *generate* produces a possible 'Population' *Pop*, i.e. a data structure of the form

```
Pop = [ [blackwhatsit, widget1, VaroomStyle1],
        [whitewhatsit, widget2, VaroomStyle2],
        [pinkwhatsit, widget3, VaroomStyle3] ].
```

A specific Widget and way of kerpowing is suggested for each Whatsit.

test must then determine if the population *Pop* passed to it fulfills all the constraints described. If so, then the predicate *member* either checks or causes the desired instantiation of Widget, Whatsit and Varoomstyle in the respective three entries in *Pop*. Note that the operators kerpows and varooms are used as test, search or generator predicates, depending on which of their arguments are input and output parameters at the time they are called.

If *test* and *member* are successful, then the operators end with *true*; otherwise the interpreter backtracks to the predicate *generate*. As long as it can deliver a distinct, new combination for *Pop*, it does so.

Figure 6.7 shows how the generator actually functions. It simply instantiates its argument as the desired data structure, leaving the elements for Widgets and ways of kerpowing as variables. These are then instantiated with values by the predicates *are_widgets* and *are_ways_to_varoom*, which themselves access the facts *is_a_widget* and *is_a_way_to_varoom* in the knowledge base. The two predicates *are_...* merely see to it, via appropriate goals, that their three respective arguments always get instantiated with three distinct values. The generation of all possible permutations of them is provided for automatically by the backtracking mechanism!

Finally, in Fig. 6.8, we see the *test* predicate. The in-line comments should suffice for you to see that the individual goals are nothing more than a translation of the previously described constraints into formal logic.

```
generate(Pop) :-
        Pop = [ [blackwhatsit,P1,K1],
                [whitewhatsit,P2,K2],
                [pinkwatsit,P3,K3] ],
        are_widgets (P1, P2, P3),
        are_ways_to_varoom(K1,K2,K3).


are_widgets(X,Y,Z) :-
        is_a_widget(X),
        is_a_widget(Y), Y \= X,
        is_a_widget(Z), Z \= X, Z \= Y.


are_ways_to_varoom(X,Y,Z) :-
        is_a_way_to_varoom(X),
        is_a_way_to_varoom(Y), Y \= X,
        is_a_way_to_varoom(Z), Z \= X, Z \= Y.
```

Fig. 6.7   The Population generator

You should, however, note the use of parentheses in conjunction with the implication operator $->$. As we pointed out earlier, the parentheses should be used to define the scope of the operator with respect to the subsequent terms connected by *ands*, i.e. commas. The Whatsit program provides an excellent opportunity to see what happens if you leave out the parentheses. We recommend that you think about the effects, or better yet experiment with a thus modified version. You should find that *test* no longer functions correctly. For a query like

?– **redwidget kerpows Who.**

you will get many wrong solutions, if you repeatedly request alternatives by entering ';' after each response.

```
test(Pop) :–

% If the Whatsit varooming over gets
% kerpowed by either Redwidget or Bluewidget,
% then Blackwhatsit varooms back:

(            (            member([ _ ,bluewidget,over],Pop)
             ;            member([ _ ,redwidget,over],Pop)
             )
–>           member([blackwhatsit, _ ,back],Pop)
),

% Pinkwhatsit does not get kerpowed by Bluewidget:

not member([pinkwhatsit,bluewidget, _ ],Pop),

% and Pinkwhatsit does not varoom over:

not member([pinkwhatsit, _ ,over],Pop),

% Redwidget does not kerpow Blackwhatsit:

not member([blackwhatsit,redwidget, _ ],Pop),

% and the Whatsit kerpowed by Redwidget
% does not varoom in :

not member([ _ ,redwidget,in],Pop),

% If Blackwhatsit gets kerpowed by Bluewidget,
% then Whitewhatsit does not varoom over :

(            member([blackwhatsit,bluewidget, _ ], Pop)
–>           not member([whitewhatsit, _ ,over],Pop)
),
!.
```

Fig. 6.8   Testing the satisfaction of the constraints

7 DATA MANAGEMENT

Up until now you have only been able to fill the internal database by consulting Prolog text files. In practice, however, you will want to be able to modify it, adding and deleting facts and rules from within an executing program. In this chapter you are introduced to the predicates used to achieve this. Many of the examples you will encounter illustrate special forms of program control, e.g. state-dependent execution or one of the most important control mechanisms in expert systems, goal lists. With them, you can program control-flow strategies which diverge from the one built into Prolog.

7.1 Consulting

Prolog manages the facts and rules which you read in with the *consult* predicate or, in abbreviated form, with

$$?- [prologtext\_1, \ldots , prologtext\_n].$$

in an internal database. How it is physically organized need not concern us here. We can simply imagine that the clauses appear precisely in the order in which they were read and that this order is the one in which they are searched through for unification. If the unification is successful, then a pointer is set marking the selected clause. Should backtracking demand the next possible unification, then the search for it begins from the marked clause and proceeds towards the end of the database.

Clearly any given Prolog implementation tries to avoid a sequential inspection of all the clauses, and seeks to access only rules and facts which are in some way relevant to the current unification, i.e. those with matching functor and arity. Yet regardless of how the access mechanism has been implemented in a given Prolog system, the user of the system must be able to assume, for programming purposes, that the underlying data model is a sequential search. And, indeed, that is precisely what we will do in our examples and discussions below.

Should you consult a new Prolog text, either interactively from the terminal or from within a procedure, then the new clauses will be simply appended to the end of the active database. No check is made to see if perhaps the same clause already exists further up. Thus, if you should, presumably accidentally, consult the same file twice during the same session, then each clause will appear twice in the database.

This can lead to confusing errors: if every response appears twice, this may well be the cause!

Nonetheless it is not uncommon that one wishes to consult a Prolog text a second time. This is especially true when you are testing a program interactively: you have corrected a mistake in a file — just how you call the editor in the midst of an executing program will be shown later — and now you want to consult the modified version. Naturally, you want the old clauses to be disposed of.

This is precisely what the consulting predicate *reconsult* does for you. For example, with

> ?- **reconsult(***prologtext***).**

the clauses in prologtext are added to the database, *but* only after all the old clauses with the same functor and arity as those being added have been deleted from it. This, it is hoped, will bring your old version up to date.

We say 'it is hoped' because reconsulting has the potential side effect of causing other clauses, beyond those intended, to disappear. This does not occur without rhyme and reason. No, it occurs when you consult several files in the course of a session, or when you yourself write some additions into the database (we will show you how!), and there are some clauses among them which happen to have the same functor and arity as one of the clauses in the file you reconsulted. You see, reconsulting causes the *entire* internal database to be scrutinized!

Now such side effects are usually not wanted. Therefore one must reconsult with care. Make a habit of placing clauses with a particular functor all in a *single* file.[1] Furthermore, you should avoid using functor names which occur in Prolog texts you have consulted for those clauses which you create dynamically and enter into the database. If you observe these two simple rules, reconsulting should cause you no surprises.

If you use the abbreviated form for consultations, i.e. the filename list, then you can request a *re*consultation by preceding the respective filename with a minus sign:

> ?- **[–filename1, filename2, –filename3].**

causes files *filename1* and *filename3* to be reconsulted and *filename2* to be merely consulted.

---

[1] If you consider a Prolog text to be analogous to a *module* in a conventional language, then this will seem most natural: it would hardly ever occur to you to distribute the definition of a particular function over several modules!

There is one last thing you should watch out for whenever you write a consult — or for that matter any other predicate. It is trivial, but a stumbling block for even experienced Prolog programmers: filenames must, of course, be Prolog *atoms*. This means that a filename must begin with a lower-case letter and may not contain any special characters other than the underline ('_').

Now these restrictions hardly concur with the filename syntax of many, if not most operating systems. Under Unix, for instance, you might find filenames like

> *'directory/filename'*
> *'/tmp/00123xyz'*
> *'Makefile'*
> *'yaccscript.y'*
> *'.profile'*

Without apostrophes these names are not legal Prolog atoms, but *with* them they are. So set otherwise unacceptable filenames in quotes wherever you use them!

7.2 Consulting the User

In an interactive Prolog session, it is annoying to have to write one or a few clauses into a file, just so that one can then read them into the database via *consult*. Therefore, Prolog considers the user's terminal keyboard (*stdin* in Unix terminology) to be a file with the standard name *user*.

(Re)consulting *user* causes the system to read in clauses from the terminal until *end of file* is entered. Under Unix this is typically signaled by entering *<control>D*. Since this convention is not standard on all systems, most Prolog systems have a 'pseudo-predicate' *end_of_file* which, when entered (with the usual closing period), signals the end of direct user input to the database.

Figure 7.1 shows how you can enter new event or person data into the knowledge base constructed in Chapter 3 (see Fig. 3.6) during a dialog session using this method. Note that while the system is consulting the terminal the standard *prompt*, i.e. '?–' is replaced by a simple vertical bar '**|**'.

You can also *reconsult* the user by simply entering

?– [–user].

Beware of the risks though! In our example in Fig. 7.1 the reconsultation would cause all the other person and event facts to be deleted, leaving only the two new facts in the database.

All *consult* predicates can not only be used interactively, but also may be applied within procedures, e.g.:

```
register :–
        writer('Please enter new facts '),
        write('(End by entering "end_of_file.") :'),
        nl, nl, consult(user), nl, nl,
        write('New facts have been stored.'),
        nl, nl.
```

This predicate, *register*, prompts the user to enter new clauses, which it reads from the keyboard and installs in the internal database.

```
?– [user].

| p([ear,nose,throat,doctor],[dr,born],
|               [binghamton,murray,56],['607',7249861]).
| e([appointment,doctor],[6,18,1985],[14,15],
|               [murray,56],[dr,born]).
| end_of_file.

yes
?– event(doctor,[6,18,_],When,Where,Who).

When = [14,15]
Where = [murray,56]
Who = [dr,born]

yes
?–
```

Fig. 7.1   *Consulting the user's terminal*

7.3   Assertion Predicates

Usually you do not want to have the user change the database, but rather the program serving her should do it.

For example, your expert system has derived a new rule or fact through some logical manipulation of the existing knowledge base, and you wish to record the new clause for later reference.

Or you want to record a *program state* by writing a corresponding fact into the database, e.g. a *protocol*, to be used as a *switch* or *flag*. Other procedures could then test the switch and react accordingly, e.g.:

```
attendance(Employee,Hours) :–
        sum(attendancelist(Employee), Hours),
        (       not protocol, !
        ;       protocol(attendance(Employee,Hours))
        ).
```

We have assumed, in our example, that the arity 2 predicate *sum* adds up the entries in the list passed it via its first argument, and that *protocol* writes its argument out into a protocol file.

Or you may wish to remove such a switch, perhaps because the state which it indicates — here the recording of some results — has come to an end.

As you recall, consultations always cause the new clauses to be appended at the end of the database. When *storing* facts and rules from within the current program, it is necessary to have more control over where the information is recorded. It may be, for instance, that you absolutely must store a new clause *at the very beginning* of the database, before all the others with the same functor. This is how you implement a *stack*, from which you can then read the entries in the opposite order from which they were made. The stack is certainly as important a data structure in Prolog as in any traditional programming language. Its complement, the *list* or *queue*, requires that the new clause be stored *at the end* of the database.

Prolog provides for both of these actions in the form of two built-in *assertion predicates* for storing clauses in the internal database:

asserta(Clause)

>writes the argument *Clause* at the (logical) beginning of the database, making it the first to be accessed. Using *asserta* you can implement *stack*-like memory management.

assertz(Clause)

>writes its argument at the *end* of the database, making it the last to be accessed among clauses therein with the same functor. This is used to achieve *queue*-like behavior.

If it is all the same to you where a new clause gets placed in the database, then you can use either predicate.

It is often the case, particularly in knowledge-based systems, that a fact should only be added to the knowledge base when it cannot be derived from the clauses already present. This is readily achieved with a predicate *add_ fact*:

```
add_fact(Fact) :-
        not Fact,
        asserta(Fact).
```

Fact is added only if its activation fails.

We assume, here, that the fact's functor has already been defined, otherwise a good implementation of Prolog would refuse the call, producing an exception condition.

If you are not sure that there is already at least one clause with the same functor and arity in the database, you should first declare the predicate being tested for using

   is_predicate*(Functor,Arity)*.

This informs the interpreter that it should accept goals containing the declared functor, even if there is not a single clause by that name in the database. When the thus declared clause is encountered in a goal it merely *fails* rather than causing an exception condition.

7.4   Deleting Clauses

Prolog also offers two built-in predicates for removing clauses from the database. One is used to remove a single, specific clause, so that you can, for instance, delete each fact after it has been processed. The other one allows you to remove all clauses of a given functor name and arity in one fell swoop. A typical example might be the reinitialization of a program.

   The 'one-clause-at-a-time' deletion is done using

   retract*(Clause)*.

The argument *Clause* can be any arbitrary term. Prolog attempts to unify it with a clause in the database. The first one for which this is possible is then deleted. It is worth noting that, through the unification, any variables mentioned in *Clause* get instantiated as usual, so that this information can still be used for further processing.

   Thus, requesting

   retract(p(_,Name,Town,_)).

you would remove the first occurence of a *p*-clause from the knowledge base in Fig. 3.6. After the action had been taken, the variables *Name* and *Town* would be instantiated with the corresponding values of the clause just removed:

   retract(p(_,[carl,schulz],'new york',_)).

In our example above, with the switch for program states, the protocol mechanism which had been turned on with *asserta(protocol)* could be turned off with *retract(protocol)*. Naturally, you must be careful that you do not accidentally, e.g. due to a programming error, cause *asserta(protocol)* to be called more than once, because then the switch will appear several times in the database, and a single *retract* will not turn them all off! Those repeated assertions can easily occur during backtracking in an incorrectly specified program!

   If the unification necessary for a successful deletion cannot be made, then *retract* merely *fails*. This indicates that all clauses of the type specified by the argument have been removed from the database.

The combined use of *assert* and *retract* to record some current state of the process in the database, e.g. for counters, is quite common. The general scheme exploits the *fail* returned by *retract* to trigger the initialization mechanism: if no previous value for the state can be found, then the state is *asserted* with some initial value.

Let us look at an example of such usage. Remember the poem generator we stole from Gertrude Stein? We had a problem limiting the number of poems being automatically produced, due to our (assumed) lack of a counting loop control predicate, like *for*. With the combined use of *assert* and *retract* we easily construct our own. Indeed, speaking more generally, we can implement any arbitrary *finite-state automaton*.

You will recall: we had a predicate *poem* which we wanted to execute exactly *N* times in a row. In Fig. 7.2 we show you how to program a termination after *N* repetitions as a predicate *fail(N)* of arity 1 and how it would be used to limit the number of executions of *poem*. To start, *retract* checks if the database contains an arbitrary 'counter' fact, i.e. *count(C)*. If not, *retract fails* and the alternative action, i.e. the initialization of the counter to 1, is executed. Regardless of where the current counter value came from, the next step causes it to be incremented and recorded in the database by *asserta*, unless the limit has been reached.

If you want to use *fail(N)* as a kind of generalized, standard predicate, then you must exercise caution. It cannot be used in *nested counted loops*, because the initialization will no longer work correctly. Why?

```
:- op(100,xf,poems).

N poems :-
        poem,
        fail(N).

fail(N)    :-
           (        retract(count(C))
           ;        C = 1
           ),
           (        C >= N
           ;        C1 is C + 1,
                    asserta(count(C1)),
                    fail
           ).
```

Fig. 7.2   *Limiting the iterations of a loop*

Note, also, that we defined the unary predicate *N poems*, in Fig. 7.2, as a *postfix operator*, so that we could request five poems by merely entering

?– 5 poems.

Let us now move on to the second, usually built-in, predicate for deleting clauses from the database. It works globally, i.e. removes *all* facts or rules with a given functor name and arity: *abolish(F,A)* purges all clauses with the functor *F* and the arity *A*. It is understood that when it is called both arguments must be instantiated — *F* with an atom designating the functor name and *A* with an integer indicating the arity. Allowing the system to automatically unify the variable values would be much too dangerous in this case!

```
          abolish(F,A) :-
     atomic(F), integer(A),
     functor(Term,F,A),
     retract(Term :– _),
     fail.
          abolish(_,_).
```

Fig. 7.3   Implementation of the abolish predicate using retract

Should your system not provide a built-in *abolish* predicate it would be a good exercise to write your own version using *retract*. Figure 7.3 illustrates one possible implementation. Note that the argument passed to retract is specified using the operator ':–', describing, as it were, the general structure of a corresponding rule.[2] Why this unusual looking argument also unifies with facts, and why we consequently do not need a special abolish rule with the goal

```
     retract(Term)
```

to deal with them — this is something you should think about briefly, before reading any further.

The second clause in Fig. 7.3, essentially a 'null operation', merely guarantees that *abolish* always ends successfully (and why shouldn't it)! Actually this is important since the first clause uses an explicit *fail* to repeatedly send the flow of control back to the preceding *retract* goal, until all the facts and rules in question have been removed. At that point, the rule itself fails, causing backtracking to move to the ever successful, above-mentioned version. Now why do the facts get removed too? You might recall from our debugging discussion that facts in Prolog are treated internally as

---

[2] It is less than obvious that one can use a simple *anonymous variable* to represent the body of the rule retracted. This works, however, because ',' and ';' are themselves *operators*, and therefore a rule body '*Goal1,Goal2*' is, internal to Prolog, the same as the term ',(*Goal1,Goal2*)', where ',' is the functor.

rules whose body consists simply of the built-in predicate *true*. Indeed, you could run the above 'program' with the debugger and you would see that the anonymous variable gets instantiated with *true* whenever *Term* is a fact!

7.5 The Existence of Clauses

Besides adding and deleting clauses, we often want to determine if a specific clause is already present in the database, i.e. without having to remove it to find out!

This is possible with

clause*(Head,Body)*.

The arguments are the respective components of the clauses being tested for. When *clause* is called, its arguments must be terms in which variables, should there be any, are sufficiently instantiated for a fitting clause to be found in the database. To the extent that some variables are not bound to specific values, *clause* will return with these instantiated to the values in the database. Thus, the fewer uninstantiated variables there are when *clause* is called the more specific the test will be.

Now a *fact*, as mentioned above, is essentially a rule with *true* as its body. Thus, we could ask about a *person*-fact in our database of Fig. 1.1 with the query

?– **clause(person(Keyword,Name,Town,Telephone),true).**

If one is found, then the variables in the first term are instantiated to the fact's respective values; otherwise the predicate *fails*. When backtracking, initiated let us say by repeated input of ';' in response to the facts found, *clause* proceeds to search sequentially through the entire database, much like *retract* above, until no further unifications are possible, and it then *fails*, i.e. responds with 'no'.

Since a direct call of the fact itself, i.e.

?– **person(Keyword,Name,Town,Telephone).**

yields the same unifications and backtracking behavior, it might seem reasonable to dispense with *clause* altogether in such cases (with rules, since they 'do' things, this is obviously not an alternative). But there are problems! Good Prolog interpreters, as we already mentioned, respond to *un*defined predicates with error messages. Thus, should no clause of arity 4 and with the functor *person* happen to exist in the database, then if you do not use the *clause* test, the procedure in which it occurs will suddenly produce disturbing messages and unexpectedly terminate (from the user's point of view, at least!). You can 'intercept' the error, but that only gets more awkward and difficult to maintain.

7.6 Managing Program States

In our counting loop example we saw how the database is used to keep track of a current *program state* parameter. Now we would like to demonstrate how you can write a *random-number generator* in Prolog, since this is a very important, general function. It consists of a predicate *random(N)*, which instantiates its argument *N* to a new (pseudo) random number each time it is called. The number generated should be an integer which lies in the range 1 to *Limit*. We would like to be able to define the upper bound *Limit* as the fact *random_limit(Limit)* in the database, via an *asserta* or some clause in a Prolog text which gets consulted. If no such limit exists in the database a default value of 1000 should be taken.

Figure 7.4 shows the random-number generator. The binary predicate *random(N, Limit)* should, of course, be directly executable, in case the programmer wishes to fix the *Limit* explicitly at the time of calling.

The basis of most random-number generators is an *internal state*, represented by a *Number*, which changes with each execution according to some formula, and thereby produces as random a sequence of values as possible. A *mod*, i.e. modulo operation, is employed to keep the range of values from exceeding the maximum integer representable on a given machine; in our example in Fig. 7.4 this is the interval between 0 and 65 535. The state variable is used to generate the random number requested, by reducing the state indicator, *Number*, via another *mod* operation, to a value in the designated range.

Figure 7.4 shows how the first call to the predicate *random* initializes the generator's state, in the database, as the fact *random_state*. Its argument is the *Number* from which the respective 'next' random number is derived. After the initialization, every subsequent request for a random number causes the old state value to be *retract*ed and the new one to be recorded using *asserta*.

```
random(N) :-
        clause(random_limit(Limit),true), !,
        random(N,Limit).
random(N) :-
        random(N,1000).

random(N,Limit) :-
        (       retract(random_state(Number))
        ;       Number = 17
        ),
        RN is (25173 * Number + 13849) mod 65536,
        N is (RN mod Limit) + 1,
        asserta(random_state(RN)).
```

Fig. 7.4   The random-number generator random(N)

7.7 Stacking Intermediate Information

Not just current state information gets stored in the database. Intermediate information (states, values, frames, etc.), which must be collected and preserved during the evaluation of a predicate may also be kept there. Such information is *stacked* up, as the argument of facts with an agreed upon functor, by using *asserta*. Afterwards, they are fetched from the thus created *stack* by the predicate *retract*, in last-in–first-out order, for further processing.

This mechanism is illustrated by the predicate

findall*(Term,Predicate,ResultList),*

which is a built-in on many systems. Its job is to gather all *Terms* which satisfy the given *Predicate* into the list *ResultList*. For example, if applied to our personal database in Fig. 1.1, the request

```
findall( restaurant(Name,Town),
            place(restaurant,Name,Town,_),List).
```

would instantiate the third variable, *List*, with

```
[ restaurant(fridays,'new york'),
    restaurant(pier46,boston),
    restaurant(bigboy,berkeley) ]
```

As you can imagine, the predicate *findall* is very useful for generating the set of all solutions to a given predicate, when you intend to process these in a subsequent step. Should your system not provide *findall* as a built-in, you can easily program it yourself. Using the *fail* iteration mechanism, you must execute the *Predicate* repeatedly until it is no longer successful, i.e. until it has evaluated all applicable clauses in the database. For each *successful* execution, you must record the *Term*, with its respective variables instantiated just as they occur in the instance of the *Predicate* found, as a fact with some unique functor, e.g. *item_found*, into the 'result stack', using *asserta*.

The body of this first procedure would look like

```
Predicate,
asserta(item_found(Term)),
fail.
```

Once *Predicate* has *failed*, i.e. all *Terms* have been found, you must empty the result stack with

retract(item_found*(Term)*).

Each *Term* successfully *retracted* must, of course, be placed at the current head of the *ResultList* being produced.

This seems all quite simple, were it not for a very subtle problem! Take note of it, together with the standard solution — *mark*ing the stack – for use in similar situations.

A problem arises because *Predicate* can be instantiated to any arbitrary procedure and, consequently, we can never be sure that the one actually passed in does not itself call *findall* at some point. If it does, then that instance of *findall* will write the *Terms* it finds into the same kind of facts onto the same stack! How can we guarantee that the inner *findall* does not *retract* any *Terms* which might have been stacked by the outer one?

The trick used to avoid this is shown in Fig. 7.5. Every time a nested *findall* occurs in the *Predicate* of an outer one, it records a *mark* in the database, e.g.

item_found(mark)

before it begins its collecting activities.[3] This then separates the new stack from the old. Now every *findall* collects only those entries up to the first such mark it encounters. This leaves the stack in precisely the same state it was in when the respective inner *findall* was called.

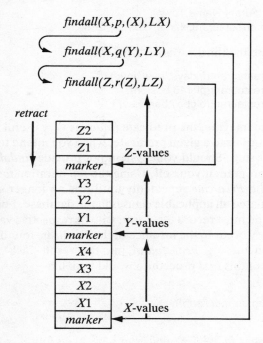

Fig. 7.5   The item_found *stack with markers by recursive calls to* findall

---

[3] This method will not work if one of the actual *terms* collected is coincidentally instantiated with the value *mark*. In practice one would, therefore, choose a more unusual marker, which virtually eliminates such unfortunate coincidences. For instance, Prolog itself uses names of special syntactic form for its system predicates, e.g. they always begin with '$'.

Fig. 7.6 shows the corresponding implementation of *findall*. If you read the in-line comments you should have no great trouble understanding it.

We must, however, briefly explain the function of the operator '==' used in the predicate *next*. It represents *strict equality* between two terms being compared. This means that it will not unify terms, i.e. 'assign' an uninstantiated, variable operand with the instantiated value of the other, in order to *produce* the equivalence, as does the less constrained, *simple equality* operator '='. Thus, had we used '=' instead of '==' in the predicate *next* in Fig. 7.6, then whenever *Term* had no value, it would be instantiated to *mark*. This is undesirable, because if by chance the *item_found* appearing on the stack were a variable which had satisfied the given *Predicate*, it should not be treated as being equivalent to a stack mark! By testing for *strict equality* this misinterpretation is avoided and we can be sure that variables found will properly end up in the *ResultList*.

```
findall( (Term,Predicate,_) :-
         % place marker in stack :
         asserta(item_found(mark)),
         % repeatedly execute Predicate
         % until no alternatives left "fail") :
         Predicate,
         asserta(item_found(Term)),
         fail.
findall( _,_,ResultList) :-
         collect([ ],ItemsFound),
         !, ResultList = ItemsFound.

collect( TillNow,List) :-
         % next stack entry up to mark :
         next(Term),
         !, collect([Term|TillNow],List).
collect( ResultList,ResultList).

next(Term) :-
         retract(item_found(Term)),
         % "fail", if Term is a stack mark :
         !, not (Term == mark).
```

Fig. 7.6   Implementation of the predicate findall
with stack marking feature

Finally, a brief remark regarding the binary predicate *collect*. It typifies predicates which you will often see in Prolog: The first of its two arguments stands for an initial value when the predicate is called – here the empty list – and the second for the desired result, in this case the list of the accumulated results. The rule body is effectively an iterative loop 'disguised' as a *tail recursion*. From the point of view of the logical process, one could replace the recursive call.

```
collect([Term|TillNow],List)
```

with a jump to the beginning of the same rule (indeed, good Prolog interpreters do precisely that). The initial list merely gets longer each time by the one element, *Term*, fetched from the stack.

The iteration goes on until the predicate *next* fails, because it encountered a *mark* indicating the end of the stack segment for the current *findall* call. The second *findall* clause is then activated, which causes its third argument, *ResultList*, to be instantiated with the second one from *collect*, i.e. *ItemsFound*, which has meanwhile become a list of all the 'items found' (except *marks*!) collected.

If the process is not immediately clear to you, we recommend that you walk through it once more and perhaps watch it at work via your debugger, because the principles involved will crop up frequently in your own programming endeavors.

7.8 Goal Stacks

Our last example, which uses the database as a receptacle for intermediate results, introduces a concept which is often used in the implementation of expert systems and similar, knowledge-based applications: the *goal stack*. Its use is particularly advantageous in areas where the problem to be solved can initially be formulated in terms of one or more (*sub-*)*goals*, which, when processed, may themselves generate further new goals. This process continues until either the original question has been answered or no more new goals emerge, and the information derivable from the knowledge base for the problem at hand is essentially exhausted.

The basic scheme is almost trivial: first the initial, or starting, goals are recorded as facts with a suitable functor name, e.g. *goals*, in the database. Once this is done, a small loop fetches the individual goals, one after the other with *retract*, until the *goal stack* is empty and *retract fails*. Whenever a new goal is generated by one being processed, it is merely added to the database, with either *asserta* or *assertz*, depending on which order of evaluation seems most sensible.

We would like to demonstrate this mechanism with a somewhat lengthy Prolog program. It solves a typical *allocation problem*, wherein objects are assigned to one another according to specific rules. Such tasks are often the subject of *operations research*, e.g. planning machine allocation in manufacturing, deciding where to insert advertisements in newspapers and magazines, determining the most appropriate assignment of retailing districts to agents or branches etc.

In our example, the allocation criterion is that of *lasting relationships*: N men and as many women are to be married to another, whereby couples should be optimally matched with regard to their respective notions about 'the ideal partner'.[4] Naturally, not everyone will be able to be paired with their ideal partner of choice. Therefore, the situation to be avoided is where one person prefers some stranger over his/her allotted mate, and that stranger likewise prefers said person to her/his life companion. In other words, two persons who are not married with one another should never feel the urge to disappear together and abandon their assigned companions.

Figure 7.7 shows the grouping of the men and women. The list of potential grooms is given in a list of *suitors*. A collection of facts enumerates the respective preferences of all the persons involved: the name of the individual is the functor, and the potential partners appear as arguments, where the order indicates the preference. Thus, *carol* is *steve*'s 'dreamboat', whereas *mary* is his 'last resort'.

```
suitor_list([steve,bruno,claus,michael,louis]).

% Preferences :

steve(carol,susan,annette,bonnie,mary).
bruno(annette,carol,bonnie,mary,susan).
claus(carol,bonnie,susan,mary,annette).
michael(annette,bonnie,carol,mary,susan).
louis(susan,bonnie,carol,annette,mary).

annette(louis,steve,michael,bruno,claus).
bonnie(steve,michael,bruno,claus,louis).
carol(michael,louis,bruno,steve,claus).
mary(claus,bruno,michael,steve,louis).
susan(michael,bruno,claus,louis,steve).
```

Fig. 7.7   Database for partner problem

The algorithm for solving such a problem has presumably been heavily influenced by the novels of the turn of the century: it is implemented with the help of marriage proposals by the gentleman followed by an official engagement (yes — the world is still in order here!). Each man proposes to the ladies, in his order of preference, until one accepts. A lady accepts a particular gentleman's proposal, either

- because she still has no partner, i.e. quite independent of her own

---

[4] This problem situation was drawn from R. Sedgewick's book *Algorithms*, Addison-Wesley, Reading (Mass.), 1983.

preferences ('better to have loved and lost, than never to have loved at all' — maybe? — see above),

- or, because she prefers the new fellow to the one with whom she is currently engaged (signs of hope for NOW!).

```
matches :-
        initialization,
        suitor_list(List),
        register_suitor(List,0),
        proposals,
        output.

initialization :-
        abolish(suitor,1),
        abolish(suitor_count,1),
        abolish(couple,2).

register_suitor([ ],N) :-
        new_fact(suitor_count(N)).
register_suitor([Suitor|Rest],N) :-
        new_fact(suitor(Suitor)),
        M is N + 1,
        register_suitor(Rest,M).

proposals :-
        repeat,
        propose.

propose :-                      % fail by Suitor !
        retract(suitor(B)),     % fail by propose = true
        propose(B,_),
        !, fail.
propose.

propose(Suitor,Fiance) :-
        suitor_count(N),
        functor(Choice,Suitor,N),
        clause(Choice,true),
        propose(Suitor,Choice,1,Fiance).

propose(Suitor,Choice,N,Fiance) :-
        arg(N,Choice,Lady),
        (       successful(Suitor,Lady),
                Fiance = Lady
        ;       Attempt is N + 1,
                propose(Suitor,Choice,Attempt,Fiance)
        ).
```

(a)

Fig. 7.8(a)   Programming the problem of lasting relationships for the database in Fig. 7.7: (a) Part 1; (b) Part 2

The abandoned groom is, once again, alone and resumes making his proposals. Or, to get to our Prolog program, his name will be added, as a fact with the functor *suitor*, to the *goal stack*.

No matter what you may have against the 'good old days': it can be demonstrated that this method always ends up with lasting relationships.

```
successful(Suitor,Lady) :-
        not clause(couple(_,Lady),true),
        new_fact(couple(Suitor,Lady)).
successful(Suitor,Lady) :-
        clause(couple(Rival,Lady),true),
        suitor_count(N),
        functor(LadiesChoice,Lady,N),
        clause(LadiesChoice, true),
        LadiesChoice =.. [Lady|PrefersList],
        favors(Suitor,Rival,PrefersList),
        retract(couple(Rival,Lady)),
        new_fact(suitor(Rival)),
        new_fact(couple(Suitor,Lady)).

favors(Suitor,Rival,[Suitor|_]) :- !.
favors(Suitor,Rival,[Rival|_]) :- !, fail.
favors(Suitor,Rival,[_|Rest]) :-
        favors(Suitor,Rival,Rest).

output :-
        nl, write('Lasting Relationships :'), nl, nl,
        retract(couple(X,Y)),
        write(X), write('\twill be forever happy with '),
        write(Y), nl,
        fail.
output :- nl.

new_fact(Fact) :-
        assertz(Fact),
        functor(Fact,Functor,A),
        debug_mode(Functor,A,_,off).

:-debug_mode(propose,2,_off).
:-debug_mode(propose,4,_off).
:-debug_mode(output,0,_off).
:-debug_mode(favors,3,_off).
:-debug_mode(register_suitor,2,_off).
:-debug_mode(suitor_list,1,_off).
:-debug_mode(successful,2,_off).
:-debug_mode(initialization,0,_off).
:-debug_mode(new_fact,1,_off).
```

(b)

*Fig. 7.8(b)   Programming the problem of lasting relationships
for the database in Fig. 7.7: (a) Part 1; (b) Part 2*

Figure 7.8(a) and (b) illustrate the automation of the Prolog process. The very first predicate, *couples*, when called upon, initiates the search for a solution to the entire problem (how noble!). Its very first action consists of reinitializing the database by using *abolish* to delete any temporary facts which may have been left over from a previous run.

Subsequently, the *suitor_list* is fetched from the database (see Fig. 7.7) and, for every man on the list, a unary predicate *suitor*, i.e. a fact with the respective suitor's name, is placed on the goal stack. The predicate responsible for this, *register_suitor*, has, in addition to the list of suitors, a counter as its second argument. It is initialized to *zero* and gets incremented during the recursive processing of the list of suitors. After the last suitor's name has been placed on the goal stack, the *suitor_count* is also written into the database as a fact. This is a state variable, which permits the program to terminate, independently of the number N of suitors and eligible women in the database.

matches then activates *proposals*. This is the core of the implementation of the aforementioned algorithm. The predicate *propose* is written such that it *fails* after it has fetched a *suitor* from the goal stack and processed his proposal. If, however, *no more* entries are found on the goal stack, then it *succeeds*. This somewhat unusual approach was selected so that the *loop* for processing the goal stack, implemented by *proposals*, could be formulated as compactly as possible. It consists, namely, of just two goals:

```
proposals :-
       repeat,
       propose.
```

repeat is always successful, so backtracking causes control flow to re-enter *propose* 'from above'. On the other hand, *propose*'s *fail* forces that very backtracking until an empty goal stack permits *proposals* to succeed.

This sort of loop structure is quite common. And it is not just used for processing goal stacks, i.e. for driving expert and similar dialog-oriented systems. Indeed, *interpreters* written in Prolog typically employ this technique — instead of *propose* there is merely a predicate *instruction*, which reads the next instruction in the text to be interpreted and executes it.

Just how *propose* evaluates the preferences of the suitors and the ladies and then respectively records the newly mated partners as the predicate *couple(Gent, Lady)* is best understood by walking through the text in Fig. 7.8(a) and (b) or watching it run with the debugger. Then you will see what happens when a suitor steals some other gent's fiance: the old *couple* entry gets deleted and the abandoned fellow joins the *suitors* on the goal stack once again.

The *output* of the lasting relationships, after all the *proposals* have been made, is implemented by a simple *fail* loop, which *retracts* the *couple* entries from the database and writes a protocol of this action. Figure 7.9

shows the resulting display. We introduced a bit of formatting into the *output* predicate in the clause

```
write('\twill be forever happy with ')
```

by including the Unix *tabulator* symbol '\t' in the atom to be printed. Your system may not interpret this the same way, so if need be just leave the tab symbol out.

?– **couples.**

Lasting relationships :

steve   will be forever happy with annette.
michael will be forever happy with bonnie.
claus   will be forever happy with susan.
louis   will be forever happy with carol.
bruno   will be forever happy with mary.

Fig. 7.9   Lasting relationships output by the program in
Figs. 7.8(a) and (b) for the database in Fig. 7.7.

7.9   The Debug Mode and the *spy* Predicate

When you examined Fig. 7.8(b), it may have surprised you to see that we did not use *assertz* directly to write new facts into the database, but instead employed the predicate *new_fact(Fact)*. The reason for this is that we wanted to be able to simplify running the program with the *debugger* by being able to inform it via the instruction

```
debug_mode(Functor,Arity,OldMode,NewMode)
```

that it should not display the specified fact each time it is registered, to avoid superfluous steps. To this end we set *NewMode* to *off*. We could inquire about the previous mode, *OldMode*, if we chose: *on* for displaying, *off* for suppression.

You will note that right from the start we suppressed the establishment of protocol for a number of predicates that were uninteresting for debugging purposes, as soon as our program is *consulted* by the user. This is done using precisely the *debug_mode* instruction just discussed. The ':–' operator appearing before the predicate causes the program loader to execute these predicates *immediately* upon encountering them.

So if you want to turn on the display of some suppressed predicate *during* a debugging session, then you need merely issue the command

?– **debug_mode(***Functor,Arity,_,***on).**

Yet even when we turn off the debugger for several predicates, it is still difficult to restrict the trace so that one can observe a specific unification, such as the interplay of the engagements and disengagements of the mating algorithm, which led to the results shown in Fig. 7.9.

For such finely focused observation the debugger itself has a feature which is available in some form or another on many Prolog systems: the *spy* predicate, of arity 2. Its first argument is a term specifying the head of the clause to be monitored. By furnishing it with appropriate variables, constants and structures one can specify the precise instance of the predicate call of interest. The second argument is an atom naming the *port* at which the *spy* mode should stop the processing of the predicate, assuming that the predicate has not been suppressed.

In our program in Fig. 7.8(a) and (b), we can see the respective pairs, as they get generated, if we simply monitor the predicate

   propose(Suitor,Fiance)

of arity 2 (and not the other versions!) at its *exit* port. We must inform the debugger of this, after we have consulted our Prolog program:

   ?– [user].

   | spy(propose(Suitor,Fiance),exit).
   | end_of_file.

   yes
   ?– debug.

   yes
   ?– matches.

On the other hand, if only Bruno's fate interests you, then you would merely have to change the description to restrict *spy* to corresponding instances of the predicate:[5]

   | spy(propose(bruno,Fiance),exit).

Upon calling *matches* the program executes under the control of the debugger. We then respond to the initial prompt for a *debug command* by entering an upper-case 'S' to turn on the *spy* mode (entering a lower case 's' turns the spying off again). Since the program should, with the exception of the *spy* points, run *unmonitored*, we would enter 'N' in response to the next prompt for a *debug command*.

We then could follow the selected predicate from *Exit* to *Exit* by merely entering the usual <*return*>s. And the debugger would produce a

---

[5] Unfortunately, many Prolog systems do not allow you to restrict the surveillance to a particular port, so that every call will be reported.

rather condensed version of the turn of the century tale of the heart:

```
propose(steve,carol)
propose(bruno,annette)
propose(claus,bonnie)
propose(michael,annette)        % poor bruno (authors' remark)
propose(louis,susan)
propose(bruno,carol)
propose(steve,annette)
propose(michael,bonnie)
propose(claus,susan)
propose(louis,carol)
propose(bruno,mary)
```

And they all lived happily ever after. So at least one chapter has truly a happy end!

8   MENU-DRIVEN INTERACTIVE INTERFACES

Menus are often the optimal way of managing the global flow of control in dialog-oriented user interfaces. To illustrate this we present a comprehensive example dealing with the use and maintenance of a database to administer a computer network. The inherent size of this model system offers an excellent opportunity to introduce the typical techniques of modularization in Prolog. Furthermore, since menu-driven interfaces and like tasks use character-oriented I/O, we introduce you to the built-in predicates employed in such contexts. Last, but not least, we will be demonstrating a number of useful programming techniques in the context of our example, such as the fundamentals of error detection in Prolog and the representation and analysis of networks or, mathematically speaking, graphs.

8.1   Menu-oriented Interfaces

In the last example in Chapter 6 (Figs. 6.5–6.8), the one about the Widgets and the Whatsits and their strange habits, we chose a rather primitive dialog structure as the basis for managing the interaction: the user poses a question (which the system hopefully can understand) and the system responds (with the correct answer, we hope).

Such an interface is not adequate for larger, i.e. more complex systems, simply because the normal user knows neither which questions she can ask, nor how they should be formulated. Thus, the user must be guided through the inquiry process.

The simplest, most popular and, for the *occasional user*, presumably best technique is using menus. We would like to show you how to program a *menu-driven* application in Prolog in this chapter. The technique is general enough, so that you can easily employ it in your own applications.

A menu-driven dialog only makes sense when your system is relatively large and complex, offering the user several different services. Therefore, we shall begin by developing the first stage of a typical, large dialog-oriented program, which, in its general function, embodies tasks which frequently occur in practical applications: a system which accepts messages from the terminal, records them in its database and, on demand, reports on information therein.

There are hundreds of variations on this theme, from simple data collection to complex optimization problems. We would like to tackle a task somewhere in the middle; our system should be non-trivial and yet not so extensive that we cannot deal with at least a minimal implementation within a single chapter. Naturally, our program will not offer all the utilities necessary for practical use, but it should serve as an adequate model for such a system, illustrating the user interface and some genuine practical functions.

Indeed, our sample system demonstrates one of the greatest strengths and most frequent applications of Prolog: its use in *rapid prototyping*. It shows how one can quickly, in a few pages of Prolog text, build a prototype system, which in many cases can be stepwise refined and developed into a production quality application.

8.2 The Problem: Monitoring a Network

Our application monitors a *computer network*, although it could easily be a transport network, e.g. pipelines.

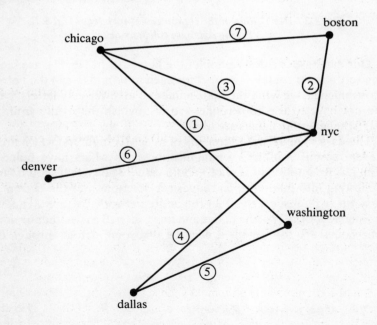

Fig. 8.1 Topology of a computer network

The network consists of a set of *node computers* connected by *communication lines*. In our example, we are concerned only with the connecting lines as such, and not their individual capacities and capabilities (full or half duplex, etc.). These are important parameters in a real network, but we have omitted these extensions because of space limitations. It would be a good exercise to consider how these factors might best be integrated.

Figure 8.1 shows a sample network topology. Each node is identified by the name of the city where the respective computer is located. The communication lines are simply labeled with unique numbers.

```
node(boston).
node(chicago).
node(nyc).
node(dallas).
node(denver).
node(washington).

line(1,chicago,washington).
line(2,boston,nyc).
line(3,chicago,nyc).
line(4,nyc,dallas).
line(5,dallas,washington).
line(6,nyc,denver).
line(7,boston,chicago).
```

**Fig. 8.2   *Description of the computer network from Fig. 8.1,
as a Prolog database (file network)***

Our database is a description of the network. In Fig. 8.1, we see that it is merely a table containing a fact for each *node* and *line* in the network. For convenience, we write the node names all in lower-case letters, so that we do not have to use apostrophes (to distinguish the names from variables!), whenever the names are used.

The data to be recorded consists of nodes (computers) which are, for whatever reasons, off-line, communication lines which have failed and repairs, i.e. resumption of service in both cases. The system should furnish the following information upon request: a description of the current network status, with respect to either the entire network, i.e. are all nodes up and connected, or to specific nodes and lines, as well as whether or not two specific nodes are connected, if need be, via some detour through other nodes?

8.3   The Menu-driven Dialog

We will present the menu-driven interaction for analyzing the network using a few excerpts from a typical dialog. Entering the goal *start* brings the user into the *main menu*, which offers her several alternatives:

```
?- start.
```

```
main menu :
                f  - register failure
                r  - register repair
                s  - network status
                b  - back to prolog
                e  - exit to operating system
```

```
choice please : x
choice please : f
```

The incorrect user input *x* causes the system merely to repeat its selection prompt. Notice that it is not necessary to follow the selection code letter with a period! The menu-driver program uses, as you will shortly see, a Prolog predicate, which reads in a single character.

The selection *f* calls for the sub-menu for component failures:

```
what is defective ?
```

```
                n - node failure
                l  - line failure
                s - network status
                b - back to main menu
```

```
choice please : n
```

```
which node (close with period) ? nyc
.
```

```
failure of nyc registered
```

The selection *n* causes a direct request for the name of the node which has failed. Since the menu-driver program reads the name of the node in, as an *atom*, via the built-in predicate *read(Term)*, the entry must be terminated with a period. Although the prompt mentions this, the user forgot it anyway, and so the program waits, despite the *<return>*, until a period is finally input (also followed by *<return>*). Only then is the failure of *nyc* recorded.

There is another unattractive side effect of using *read* as the input predicate for the node names: we would have to enclose all names in apostrophes, if we were to write them with a capital letter at the beginning, to avoid them from being interpreted as variables! This is the reason why we use lower-case letters everywhere, even in the menus.

Once you have mastered the programming of I/O in Prolog, you can then eliminate this limitation by writing some less finicky, hand-tailored predicates for the job. Indeed, we intend to do just that, but in the *next* chapter! For the time being let us overlook this blemish and concentrate on the original task.

After entering the defective node, the failure menu reappears, and we wish to report a defective line.

what is defective ?

          n - node failure
          l - line failure
          s - network status
          b - back to main menu

choice please : **l**

which line (close with period) ? **1.**

defect in line 1 from chicago
      to washington registered.

And now we examine the state of the network:

what is defective ?

          n - node failure
          l - line failure
          s - network status
          b - back to main menu

choice please : **s**

node boston on line
node chicago on line
node nyc off line
node dallas on line
node denver on line
node washington on line

line 1 from chicago to washington is defective
line 2 from boston to nyc is ok
line 3 from chicago to nyc is ok
line 4 from nyc to dallas is ok
line 5 from dallas to washington is ok
line 6 from nyc to denver is ok
line 7 from boston to chicago is ok

no connection between boston and denver
no connection between chicago and denver
no connection between dallas and denver
no connection between denver and washington

To report the fact that the node *nyc* has been repaired and brought back on line we go back to the *main menu* and from there into the second sub-menu:

```
what is defective ?

                    n - node failure
                    l  - line failure
                    s - network status
                    b - back to main menu


choice please : b

main menu :
                    f  - register failure
                    r  - register repair
                    s - network status
                    b - back to prolog
                    e - exit to operating system


choice please : r

which defect has been eliminated ?
                    n - node repaired
                    l  - line repaired
                    s - network status
                    b - back to main menu


choice please : n

which node (close with period) ? nyc.

node nyc back on-line

which defect has been eliminated ?
                    n - node repaired
                    l  - line repaired
                    s - network status
                    b - back to main menu


choice please : s

node boston on line
node chicago on line
node nyc on line
node dallas on line
node denver on line
node washington on line
```

line 1 from chicago to washington is defective
line 2 from boston to nyc is ok
line 3 from chicago to nyc is ok
line 4 from nyc to dallas is ok
line 5 from dallas to washington is ok
line 6 from nyc to denver is ok
line 7 from boston to chicago is ok

all nodes are connected

A new inquiry as to the state of the network indicates that, despite the defective line number 1, all nodes are again connected. After returning to the main menu we can then directly end our Prolog session.

main menu :
                    f - register failure
                    r - register repair
                    s - network status
                    b - back to prolog
                    e - exit to operating system

choice please : **e**

IF/Prolog session ended
$

The dollar sign is the prompt from the Unix operating system.

8.4 Modularization

The program implementing the above menu-driven dialog is, needless to say, not very small. Therefore, it is in everyone's interest to modularize it. As we have already mentioned, the way to *modularize* in Prolog is via *consulting*.

A 'driver' Prolog text, called *all* (or some other name which appears to be meaningful to you), should play the role of a main routine. It should essentially contain a *consult* instruction for all the modules making up the system. This serves two purposes:

●   it represents a sort of *table of contents* for the module structure and

●   makes it possible to load your system with a single *consult(all)* request.

```
:– [    menushell,       % Menu driver
        menus,           % problem-specific menus
        network,         % Database: facts
        node_failure     % Messages about nodes
        line_defect,     % Messages about lines
        computernet,     % "Knowledge Base": rules
        networkstatus,   % Total network status
        debugcontrol     % always the last module!
   ].

:–
        nl, nl
        write('network monitor: '),
        write('please enter "start." '), nl.
```

Fig. 8.3 *The file* all *describing the modularization*

Figure 8.3 shows the contents of the modularization file *all* for our planned network monitor system. The comments briefly describe the function of each individual module. *debugcontrol* contains the instructions to guide the interactive debugger. In the finished system, this file can be left out. If it is to be used, it must be consulted *last*, because all the predicates whose debugging output is to be in some way influenced by it must already exist in the database!

network is the description of the network topology, which we saw in Fig. 8.2 and discussed briefly. The remaining modules will be explained one after the other, but first a few closing remarks regarding the modularization file *all*.

If your Prolog implementation allows you to tell it which files should be consulted as soon as the interpreter has been loaded, i.e. as a parameter to the *system call*, then you can use this option to inform it about *all*:

$ ifprolog –c all

loads the application together with Prolog. Under Unix, you could use this to make Prolog virtually invisible to the user, embedding this command in a *shell script* or a *makefile*.

all is also a good place for all necessary *initialization* actions for your application, insofar as you do not have a module for such purposes. In our case, the initialization consists merely of displaying the prompt to start the system.

In very large systems, you can also set up a multi-level modularization hierarchy, wherein the files consulted by *all* themselves consult further sub-modules.

8.5 The Menus

Let us begin our discussion of the modules in *all* (see Fig. 8.3) with the one related to the main theme of this chapter, the *menus*. First, a look at the menu descriptions (Fig. 8.4) for our network monitor system. It defines three menus: a *main menu* called *start* and two sub-menus *failure* and *repair*.

```
start :–
        menu(start,'main menu :').

        m_line(start,f,'register failure',                    fail).
        m_line(start,r,'register repair',                     fail).
        m_line(start,s,'network status',                      fail).
        m_line(start,b,'back to prolog',                      true).
        m_line(start,e,'exit to operating system',            true).

'register failure' :–
        menu(defect,'what is defective ?').

        m_line(failure,n,'node failure',                      fail).
        m_line(failure,l,'line failure',                      fail).
        m_line(failure,s,'network status',                    fail).
        m_line(failure,b,'back to main menu',                 true).

'register repair' :–
        menu(repair,'which defect has been eliminated ?').

        m_line(repair,n,'node repaired',                      fail).
        m_line(repair,l,'line repaired',                      fail).
        m_line(repair,s,'network status',                     fail).
        m_line(repair,b,'back to main menu',                  true).

'back to main menu'.

'back to prolog'.

'exit to operating system' :– bye.
```

Fig. 8.4   *The menu description file* menus

The sub-menus are called by the procedures '*register failure*' and '*register repair*'. We enclose the names in single quotes because they serve, on the one hand, as *functors* for calling the respective menus, e.g.

```
'register repair' :–
        menu(repair,
                'which defect has been eliminated ?').
```

and on the other, as text to be displayed in the respective menu, explaining the meaning of a particular choice, e.g. the letter *r* in the following:

> m_line(start,r,'register repair',fail).

in the menu from which the call is made. See Fig. 8.3 and the session illustrated in Section 8.3 for more such examples.

It might surprise you, at first, that text expressed as an atom can be employed to name a procedure, i.e. a predicate. Nothing in the Prolog syntax definition, however, prohibits such usage! And, as you see in this example, such a naming convention can often make a program more compact and understandable.

You will note, in Fig. 8.4, that each menu description consists of two parts. The actual call, e.g.

> start :–
>   menu(failure,'what is defective ?').

activates the predicate *menu* in the *menushell*, a mini-interpreter of the menu descriptions, i.e. the *m_line* facts. The arguments of *menu* are

- the name of the menu just activated, *failure* in this case, which is used to select the corresponding *m_line* facts for display, and

- a title line for the menu, which in our example, consists of the prompting question for the given menu.

The second part of the menu description is made up of the four-valued predicate *m_line*, e.g.

> m_line(failure,n,'node failure',fail).

These predicates provide the menu interpreter with the choices to be displayed for each menu *in exactly the order in which they should appear*.

The first argument of each instance of *m_line* associates that line with a particular menu.

The second argument is an arbitrary symbol, which the user enters to select the associated action. Naturally, one should choose something meaningful, displayable and something available on the keyboards used.

The third argument, as already mentioned, is the explanatory text to be shown, in addition to the selection symbol, in the same line. It is also the name of the predicate/procedure to be activated as a consequence of the respective choice. This might be the activation of a sub-menu or, perhaps, another predicate. Indeed, some of the more trivial ones, like '*back to main menu*' can be found among the descriptions in Fig. 8.4. The others must be provided by the subsequent modules.

The fourth and final argument is a *state indicator* used to control the action taken by the menu interpreter *after* it has processed the given line. Only two values are permitted:

true means that, after the respective line of the menu has been processed, the current menu is no longer active and the interpreter should return either to the previous menu or to the system.

fail means that the interpreter should stay in the same menu, having processed the respective line, and prompt the user for a new choice with respect to same.

Based on the sample session discussed in Section 8.3, you should be able to follow the flow of execution in the menu dialog. The actual interpretation of the menu specifications by the *menushell* will be the next focus of our attention.

8.6   The Menu Interpreter

The menu descriptions, as shown in Fig. 8.4, are interpreted by the general-purpose *menushell* module listed in Fig. 8.5.[1] Please note that it is called respectively by the goal menu found in the descriptions in the *menus* module. It is defined here as a predicate of arity two.

This *direct interpretation* is unusual for interpreters implemented in conventional languages, but quite common in Prolog. Classical *interpreters* read one instruction after the other, analyze it syntactically and then carry it out. Prolog texts, as a rule, 'interpret themselves': the *term* to be interpreted activates a predicate with the same functor and arity, which is responsible for its interpretation. For the menus, this is the predicate *menu(Type, Title)* in the module *menushell*.

The logical organization is very simple. The *repeat* at the beginning causes the menu to display itself again, whenever the *m_line* selected by the user specifies a *State = fail* as its fourth argument, i.e. the last goal in the rule body of menu, State, initiates the backtracking. That the backtracking takes the interpreter all the way back to *repeat* before resuming its descent, and does not do so at one of the predicates lying in between, is the result of the strategically located *cuts* in those same predicates.

The local variable *Indent* merely embodies the number of columns from the left the menu should be indented on the screen. The menu itself is output by the predicate *display_menu*. Thereafter, *choice* prompts the user to select an action, i.e. one of the lines in the current menu, by entering a letter. This character, *Selection*, determines which corresponding second argument *Selection* for the menu *Type*, then the failure of this goal causes backtracking back to the *repeat* at the beginning of *choice* and, thus, a reiteration of the prompt to make a selection.

---

[1] The elegant basic scheme for the *menu shell* was discovered in the *Logic Programming Newsletter*, Winter 84/85, and was written by St. Greenwood.

If *m_line* did not fail, then this is the choice. *Option* and *State* are then instantiated to the corresponding values in *m_line*. *execute(Option)* calls the selected *Option* exactly once. The reason Option does not appear directly, as a goal, in the predicate *menu*, is the cut in *execute*, which insures that *Option* does not get repeated during backtracking!

```
menu(Type, Title) :-
        repeat,              % if State = fail
        Indent = 20,
        display_menu(Type, Indent, Title),
        choice(Type, Indent, Option, State), nl,
        execute(Option), State.

display_menu(Type, Indent, Title) :-
        new_menu,
        write(Title), nl,
        choice_list(Indent, Type).

choice(Type, Indent, Option, State) :-
        % Repeats when choice is unknown
        repeat,
        write('choice please : '),
        read_char(Selection),
        m_line(Type, Selection, Option, State), ! .

read_char(C) :-
        get0(Cn),
        name(C, [Cn]),
        skip(10), ! .

execute(Option) :-
        Option, ! .          % Execute option once

choice_list(Indent, Type) :-
        m_line(Type, Selection, Option, _),
        tab(Indent),
        write(Selection), write(' - '), write(Option), nl,
        fail.

choice_list(_,_) :-
        nl.

new_menu :-
        nl, nl.
```

Fig. 8.5   The general-purpose menu interpreter **menushell**

The function of *State* has already been mentioned. If its value is *fail*, then it builds a loop together with the *repeat* in *menu* to redisplay the contents of the menu. If it is *true*, then *menu* succeeds, and we end up back where the respective menu had been called from. In the case of a sub-menu, e.g. 'register failure' in the *menus* of Fig. 8.4, this is the predicate which activated the sub-menu. And since that predicate was itself an *Option* in the *menu* call preceding it, we end up in that menu, as it should be in such a hierarchy.

This explanation should suffice to allow you to work through the remaining predicates of the module *menushell* quite easily, with the exception, presumably, of the I/O predicates, which have yet to be dealt with. These predicates are character-oriented. Let us look at them in the next section.

8.7 Character-oriented Input and Output

Up until now we have essentially done all our I/O employing the *term*-oriented predicates *read* and *write*. For programs like the menu-driven dialog above, but for many other purposes as well, one needs *character*-oriented I/O predicates. Actually, we have been using one such predicate all along: **nl**, which outputs a '\n' character and places a *new line* into the output stream. Let us now look at some predicates for reading and writing one or more characters.

In *choice_list* the predicate *tab(CharCount)* is used to *Indent* the menu lines. The functor is something of a misnomer, as it has nothing to do with either the tabulator or the *tab* character. What it does is place as many *blanks* into the output as is indicated by the value of its numeric argument *Char-Count*. The fact that these make for an indentation in our output is caused by the *nl* predicate preceding it.

In *read_char* you find two more new input predicates. The behavior of the first one, *get0(Char)*, depends on whether its argument *Char* is a non-instantiated variable or a (numeric) value. In the first, more frequent case, the next character is read from the input stream and the variable is instantiated to its numeric *ASCII equivalent*. If the argument already has a value, however, then *get0* skips to the next occurrence of this value in the input stream, and the bytes in between are lost forever.[2] If the character value does not occur anymore, then it reads to the end of the stream and then *fails*.

Since one often wishes to omit control characters and only fetch the printable ones from the input, Prolog provides a related predicate,

---

[2] This is usually not the intention of the programmer, and a good place to start looking for bugs, should you discover that a program seems to arbitrarily swallow portions of the input!

get(Char). It only reads or searches for such characters; otherwise it behaves just like *get0*.

Our predicate *read_char* in the *menushell* module employs *get0(Cn)* in the usual fashion, i.e. it reads in a character via *Cn*. The *Selection* characters in the *m_line* facts, however, are not given as ASCII equivalents, but as atoms. Therefore, we transform the character in *Cn* immediately into an atom, with the familiar built-in predicate *name(C,[Cn])*, and the corresponding atom, not *Cn*, gets returned to the predicate *choice*.

Lastly, we must explain the second new predicate in *read_char*, *skip(Char)*. The predicate *skip* positions, in the input stream, to the next occurrence of the *Char*, whose *ASCII* equivalent is passed in as the argument. Thus, in contrast to *get* and *get0*, its argument is typically instantiated to a numerical value at the time it is called. You should use *skip* with care, however, since the input passed over in the process of jumping ahead in the input stream is lost forever, i.e. you cannot skip back!

So *skip(10)* moves up to the next character in the input equivalent to an ASCII'10'. That is a *newline* character, i.e. after reading the first character of the user's choice, any additional characters she may have entered are skipped, up to the closing *<return>*.

You may find the use of a numeric value '10' as the argument for *skip* somewhat irritating. Indeed, the rules of good programming prohibit such magic numbers: a reader who has perhaps only a superficial knowledge of Prolog and is, for instance, reviewing a Prolog text as a specification for a final implementation in a conventional language, like C or Pascal, might misconstrue this clause to be an instruction to skip over the next ten characters in the input.

With a bit more effort, but in the name of clarity and safety, one could (and should) improve the code by replacing the unadorned *skip* with:

```
is_newline(10).
    ...
predicate :-
    ...
    is_newline(NL),
    skip(NL),
    ...
    ...
```

Naturally, it would be best to include the fact *is_newline(10)* in a module just for declarations of character equivalents and other non-mnemonic values.[3]

We have reached the end of our discussion of the menu driver and will now consider the actual utility modules.

---

[3] Indeed, perhaps it would pay to define a standard module with just such declarations, which could be routinely used by yourself and other programmers in your group.

8.8   The Data-acquisition Module

Figures 8.6 and 8.7 list the two modules involved in registering the status of
the network: *node_failure* and *line_defect*. They are almost identical in their
logical structure and quite simple. Basically, they merely record the
reported breakdowns as facts:

```
node_failure :-
        node_name(NodeName),
        node_failure(NodeName).

node_failure(NodeName) :-
        node(NodeName),
        (       clause(failed(NodeName), true),
                write('\nnode failure already registered')
        ;       assertz( failed(NodeName)),
                write('failure of '), write(NodeName),
                write(' registered')
        ), ! .

node_failure(NodeName) :-
        no_such_node(NodeName).

'node repaired' :-
        node_name(NodeName),
        node_repaired(NodeName).

node_repaired(NodeName) :-
        node(NodeName),
        (       retract( failed(NodeName)),
                write('\nnode '),
                write(NodeName),
                write(' back on-line')
        ;
                write('\nfailure of '),
                write(NodeName),
                write(' was not registered')
        ), ! .

node_repaired(NodeName) :-
        no_such_node(NodeName).

node_name(NodeName) :-
        write('\nwhich node (close with period) ? '),
        read(NodeName).
```

Fig. 8.6
(cont. on next page)

```
no_such_node(NodeName) :-
    write('\nthere is no node named "'),
    write(NodeName), write('"').
```

Fig. 8.6   *The module* node_failure *for registering reports*
                 about the state of given nodes

failed*(NodeName)*

and

defective*(LineNo)*
in the database.

Consequently, we shall limit ourselves to a brief discussion of *node_failure*, i.e. the text in Fig. 8.6.

The predicates *node_failure* and *node_repaired*, both of arity 0, get called from the menus '*register failure*' and '*register repair*', respectively. Both request the effected node's name via the procedure *node_name(NodeName)*.

This procedure uses the built-in predicate *read(NodeName)*, which treats the input as a *term*. We have already mentioned the annoying consequences of using this predicate: the need to follow the input with a period and the interpretation of names beginning with upper-case letters as variables. The period is less of a problem should the user forget it, since the interpreter merely waits for it, and the user will soon enough remember to enter it. Should she unwittingly enter an upper-case node name, however, without enclosing it in single quotes, then the argument *NodeName* in the input procedure is instantiated to a variable.

This leads to an error, because the following predicates, *node_failure(NodeName)* and *node_repaired(NodeName)*, given a variable argument, would unify their respective first goal, *node(NodeName)* with the first node found in the network description in *network*, i.e. *boston* in our example (see Fig. 8.2).

Clearly our system does not fulfill the requirements of *defensive programming* here. Eliminating this problem would be a good exercise. Take a few moments break and think about how you would go about doing just that.

In any case, a check is made if the node named by the user does indeed exist; if not, an appropriate message is displayed. Corresponding messages also appear if the node failure was already reported or an attempt is made to register a repair for a node which has not yet been reported as being off line.

If the report passes this plausibility test, then the failure gets recorded

```
line_defect :–
        line_no(LineNo),
        line_defect(LineNo).

line_defect(LineNo) :–
        line(LineNo,From,To),
        (       clause(defective(LineNo), true),
                write('\nline defect already registered')
        ;       assertz( defective(LineNo)),
                write('\ndefect in line '), write(LineNo),
                write(' from '), write(From), write('\n\tto '),
                write(To), write(' registered')
        ), ! .

line_defect(LineNo) :–
        no_such_line(LineNo).

'line repaired' :–
        line_no(LineNo),
        line_repaired(LineNo).

line_repaired(LineNo) :–
        line(LineNo,_,_),
        (       retract( defective(LineNo)),
                write('\nline '),
                write(LineNo),
                write(' back on-line')
        ;

                write('\ndefect in '),
                write(LineNo),
                write(' was not registered')
        ), ! .

iine_repaired(LineNo) :–
        no_such_line(LineNo).

line_no(LineNo) :–
        write('\nwhich line (close with period) ? '),
        read(LineNo).

no_such_line(LineNo) :–
        write('\nthere is no line number "'),
        write(LineNo), write('"').
```

Fig. 8.7   The module line_defect *for registering reports*
about the state of given lines

as the fact *failed(NodeName)* in the database. Repair reports, naturally, cause the corresponding facts to be removed.

Note the different ways in which the various erroneous reports are recognized:

The non-existence of a given node
> is tested by simply calling the fact *node(NodeName)*. This works because we can assume the existence of at least one fact with the single-valued functor *node*.

A node failure which has already been registered
> cannot be tested in the same simple fashion, because it is conceivable that no fact with the functor *failed* as yet exists in the database. Doing so under such circumstances would cause a good Prolog system to produce an exception condition. Consequently, we make our test using the familiar binary *clause* predicate.

The repair of a node not known to be offline
> is recognized by the fact that the *retract* predicate activated to remove the alleged reported fact *failed(NodeName)* from the database is unsuccessful, i.e. *fails*.

If you were to modify the program to test for an 'unwanted' *NodeName* entry variable, i.e. upper-case input for *NodeName*, by testing the entry with *var* or *nonvar*, then you would have a complete set of typical error-checking mechanisms used in Prolog, except one: the means to catch *exception conditions*.

We will not be dealing with that, however, because unfortunately it is not available on most implementations of Prolog. But check your handbook to see if your system is an exception, and if so, try integrating exception handling into our example.

Exception handling is useful for many purposes, and in at least *one* application absolutely indispensable: when you use Prolog as a *specification language* for complex systems. In that case, you must define the systems error and exception behavior *explicitly*. And as you have just seen, these typical Prolog error-handling methods occur *implicitly* or 'in passing', so to speak. Therefore they are not of much use in describing how an exception condition should be dealt with.

8.9   The Network Analysis

The third utility provided in all three menus of our interactive network

monitor system is the analysis and display of the current state of the network.
Figures 8.8 and 8.9 list the contents of the modules providing this service.

```
connection(Node1,Node2) :-
        (       line(Number,Node1,Node2)
        ;       line(Number,Node2,Node1)
        ),
        not clause(defective(Number),true).

reachable(OriginNode,DestinationNode) :-
        % the nodes already visited are
        % collected in the third argument
        reachable(OriginNode,DestinationNode,
                [OriginNode]), !.

reachable(OriginNode,DestinationNode,_) :-
        connection(OriginNode,DestinationNode).

reachable(OriginNode,DestinationNode,NodesVisited) :-
        connection(OriginNode,Node),
        not member(Node,NodesVisited),
        not clause(failed(Node),true),
        reachable(Node,DestinationNode,[Node|NodesVisited]).
```

Fig. 8.8   *The module* computernet, *the knowledge base*
for the reachability of nodes

The short Prolog text in Fig. 8.8, *computernet*, turns the database of Fig. 8.2
into a knowledge base by extending it with the definition of the concepts of
connectedness and *reachability*.

A *connection* exists between two nodes when a direct communication
line exists from one to the other, i.e. from *A* to *B* or *B* to *A*, since we assume
bidirectionality. And a node is *reachable* from another one if either a direct
connection exists, or the *OriginNode* has a direct *connection* to an intermediate *Node* from which the *DestinationNode* is *reachable*.

In theory we could write our specification of the concept of *reachability*
exactly as described. But only in theory! The above-defined recursion
encounters a practical, not theoretical, problem in the implementation of
the Prolog interpreter: the repeated calling of the predicate *connection* by
reachable possibly leads back to a node which has already been visited; for
instance, the very first *OriginNode*. This would describe a loop in the graph
and cause its endless repetition with respect to execution!

To prevent this the predicate *reachable* of arity 2 calls a predicate of the
same name, but of arity 3. Its third argument is a list of *NodesVisited*, which
starts out empty on the first call but accumulates the name of each intermediate node on the subsequent ones. For each *Node* with a *connection* to

the current *OriginNode* a check is made to see if that *Node* is perhaps a *member* of the *NodesVisited* list. Only when this is not the case is *reachable* called again, taking the recursion a level deeper.

This causes the search to terminate for certain, since either the *DestinationNode* is found (first *reachable* rule of arity 3) or all *Nodes reachable* from the *OriginNode* have been collected in the *NodesVisited* list (second rule of same arity).

In Fig. 8.9, the module *networkstatus* employs the predicate *reachable* in the third, alternative rule for '*network status*'. The first two are fairly trivial. They merely check if the individual nodes and lines registered in the database have *failed*, i.e. are *defective*. The third rule uses the procedure *findall*, which we discussed in an earlier chapter, to gather all the *DefectiveLines* into a list. Naturally, in doing so it only considers those nodes which have not *failed* anyway.

In the end, the *DefectiveLines* are output by the procedure *defects_ report* — itself not terribly original, but a typical example of the routine processing of a list in Prolog.

We should, however, examine the binary operator *precedes*, which has been defined as an infix predicate. It fulfills a rather trivial need: *findall*, in the procedure '*network status*', fetches two arbitrary nodes from the database by calling the predicate *node(Nx)* twice. Now, as it stands, nothing would guarantee that these two nodes, *N1* and *N2*, were not in fact one and the same. And even if they are not, every pair of nodes would certainly be found twice — the second time around merely in reverse order, e.g. [*a,b*] and [*b,a*]!

```
:- op(100, xfx, precedes).
:- op(100, xfx, precedes_list).

'network status' :-
        node(N), write('node '), write(N),
        (       clause(failed(N),true),
                write(' off line'), fail
        ;       not clause(failed(N), true),
                write(' on line'), fail
        ).

'network status' :-
        nl, line(L,From,To),
        write('line '), write(L),
        write(' from '), write(From),
        write(' to '), write(To),
        (
```

Fig. 8.9
(cont. on next page)

```
                    clause(defective(L),true),
                    write(' is defective')
         ;          not clause(defective(L),true),
                    write(' is ok')
         ).

    'network status' :-
         findall( [N1,N2],
              (        node(N1), node(N2),
                       not clause(failed(N1),true),
                       not clause(failed(N2),true),
                       N1 precedes N2,
                       not reachable(N1,N2)
              ),
              DefectiveLines),
         defects_report(DefectiveLines).

    defects_report( [ ] ) :-
         write('\n\nall nodes are connected\n\n').
    defects_report( [ [A,B] ] ) :-
         write('\nno connection between '),
         write(A), write(' and '), write(B).
    defects_report( [C1,C2|Rest] ) :-
         defects_report( [C1] ),
         defects_report( [C2|Rest] ).

    Name1 precedes Name2 :-
         name(Name1,L1), name(Name2,L2),
         L1 precedes_list L2.

    [_,_] precedes_list [ ] :- !.
    [X|Rest1] precedes_list [X|Rest2] :-
         Rest1 precedes_list Rest2.
    [X|_] precedes_list [Y|_] :-
         X < Y.
```

Fig. 8.9 *The module* networkstatus *for network analysis*

These two possibilities must be eliminated. This is best achieved by introducing some (arbitrary) order among the nodes and then permitting only those node pairs where the first node *precedes* the second one (whatever the meaning of *precedes* may be in the ordering relation).

We chose a *lexicographic ordering* here: one node *precedes* another if its name would occur before that of the other in a dictionary of node names organized according to the order of the characters of the standard ASCII code.

The predicate *precedes* checks this. And since lexicographic order is commonly used in many practical applications, either of convenience or due to standards involved in manipulating names, texts, etc., you are likely to find sufficient use for this mechanism, as well as encountering it in the Prolog texts of others.

8.10   Controlled Debugging

In closing, we turn our attention to the module used to control the scope of debugger actions. For the working production system it is unnecessary, but for getting out the bugs it is a great help.

When a system has grown quite large, it gets increasingly difficult, even with a good interactive debugger, to keep track of what is happening in the program. Every call and exit of even the most trivial procedure is displayed, rather than just those truly of interest to you, as you hunt down specific bugs. Things can get easily bogged down in voluminous detail.

Therefore your debugger will presumably provide some means of influencing the debugger's standard behaviour, such as the predicate *debug_ mode*, which we encountered in the previous chapter. Needless to say, explicitly turning off every predicate whose display you wish to have suppresssed before starting a debugging session is laborious. Therefore it is a good idea to write a module *debugcontrol*, similar to the one illustrated in Fig. 8.10 in abbreviated form. This contains all the necessary instructions to suppress the display of those predicates which are not of interest to you during debugging.

Remember that the *debug_mode* instructions must be preceded by the ':–' operator, since they are to be executed immediately upon being consulted. Also, the *debugcontrol* module should always be the last to be consulted, since if a predicate is not yet present in the internal database, then the *debug_mode* predicate has *no effect* upon it!

```
:– debug_mode(choice,4,_,off).
:– debug_mode(choice_list,2,_,off).
        . . .
:– debug_mode('node repaired'),0,_,off).
        . . .
:– debug_mode(precedes_list,2,_,off).
:– debug_mode(read_char,1,_,off).
```

Fig. 8.10   The module debugcontrol *(excerpt)*

Should you change your mind about the suppression of one or the other predicate, you can always interactively turn it back on, e.g.

:– **debug_mode(***Functor,Arity,_,***on).**

Should you see the need to do so before you have consulted *all*, then you could, of course, modify the *debugcontrol* module, placing the corresponding *debug_mode* instructions in comment delimiters /* ... */, causing them to be ignored. This is usually easier than actually deleting them, since you then have less work (and room for error) when you decide to turn them off again.

9 INPUT AND OUTPUT

In the previous chapters we introduced most of the built-in I/O predicates in Prolog as the need arose. But, as we saw in the last chapter, for example, a predicate like *read* has some serious drawbacks. It forced us to accept substantial limitations in our user interface. Furthermore, we have yet to deal with the problem of accessing files in external storage. This chapter will take us into the details of I/O in Prolog, with sample programs and common applications to illustrate their usage.

9.1 The Model of Prolog's Environment

So far, we have always limited I/O in our programs almost exclusively to communications with the user at her terminal. The only non-interactive I/O done has been the consulting of Prolog texts. That fairly non-discriminating, broad file access, however, is inadequate for even the most modest of practical applications. Any user of the network monitor system developed in the last chapter would presumably express the wish to be able to save the current status of the network, so that the *network* description is up to date when consulted at the next session.

This calls for the ability to access arbitrary files in Prolog. Let us begin by looking at how Prolog 'views' its environment.

Figure 9.1 shows the model of the environment upon which implementations of Prolog are based. It fits the Unix view of the world quite well, since Prolog also views all files as sequential byte streams. The keyboard and terminal, *stdin* and *stdout* in Unix terminology, are both referred to here as *user*, and are treated as normal files (as in Unix). Mix-ups between the input and output *user* files cannot occur, because the predicates for input are distinct from those for output.

Internally, the Prolog interpreter knows of only one input and one output stream. When the interpreter is loaded, both are initialized, associated with the two *user* files. Thus, every I/O command automatically refers to the user terminal, or, on a Unix system, to *stdin* and *stdout*. Thus, if you redirect these two streams, using the means available in Unix or your operating system, into other files or *pipes*, then you can use your Prolog programs just as you would any other Unix tool, e.g. as a *filter* or in the *background*, etc. Normally, though, Prolog programs are dialog oriented; typical batch jobs are better dealt with using traditional programming languages. This explains why the I/O for the interpreter is attached to the terminal by default.

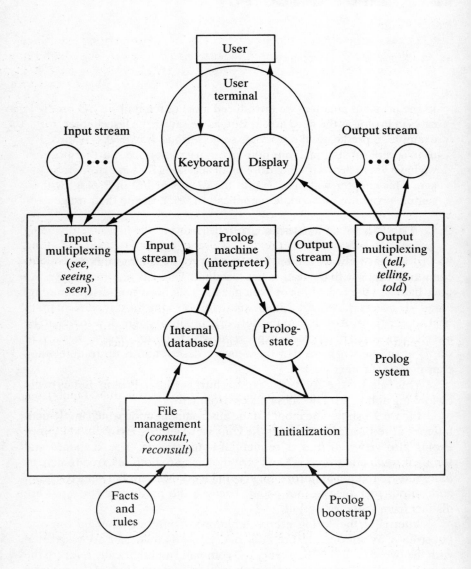

Fig. 9.1   The Prolog Model of the I/O Environment

9.2 Opening and Closing Files

If you wish to read or write to files other than the (pseudo-file) terminal, then you must redirect the standard I/O from/to the respective files for the duration of the I/O activity. There are two groups of built-in predicates for doing just that:

tell(FileName)

> opens (creates) the file given by *FileName* for writing; starting, initially, at the beginning and deleting its current contents should it already exist. *FileName* must be instantiated with an atom indicating a legal file name. Names beginning with upper-case letters or special characters (e.g. '/' in Unix *pathnames*) must be enclosed in single quotes to make atoms (versus variables) out of them, just as was the case with *consult*. Once *tell* has succeeded, all built-in output predicates will write to the file opened automatically, until *FileName* has been closed. If *tell* is called again with the same *FileName* in the context of the same process, then the output is written beginning where the last write operation left off, positionally speaking.

telling(FileName)

> instantiates a *variable* argument to the name of the file currently being used for output. If the argument is already instantiated with an atom, then the predicate checks if that is, in fact, the name of the current output file, failing if not.

told

> closes the current output file. Note that this does *not* cause the output to automatically revert to some other standard output stream; this must be done explicitly, using a subsequent *tell* instruction.

see(FileName)

> opens the file *FileName* for reading, starting from the beginning. Thereafter, all built-in 'reading' predicates fetch their input from *FileName*. Subsequent calls to *see*, from the same Prolog process, cause input to be gotten from wherever the last read action ended in the *FileName*.

seeing(FileName)

> behaves like *telling*, except that the file must have been opened for reading, if *seeing* is to succeed.

seen

> closes the current input stream. A new input source must be explicitly (*re-*)*opened* using *see*.

> Figure 9.2 illustrates a standard programming scheme for temporarily switching input files (or output files, if one *tells* rather than *sees*).

```
read_from(NewInputFile) :-
        seeing(OldInputFile),
        see(NewInputFile),
        ..., % From here on
        ..., % fetch input from
        ..., % NewInputFile until
        seen, % explicitly closed!
        see(OldInputFile).
```

Fig. 9.2   Switching the input stream temporarily to another file

The predicate *seeing* is used here to *note* the name of the original file, so that input can be switched *back* to it later, i.e. reopened using *see*.

Notice, in Fig. 9.2, that we *closed* the *NewInputFile* again in our scheme. This would cause a later call of *see*, in this program, using the same *NewInputFile* name to reopen the file for reading from the *beginning* again. If you wish to have the reading continue where it had last left off, then you must leave out the *seen* preceding *see(OldInputFile)*.

Naturally, it is conceivable that a predicate called in the body of *read_from* likewise changes its input source file. As long as such predicates abide by the same convention of switching back to the former source, before returning, there should be no problems.

There are both character-oriented and term-oriented I/O predicates built into Prolog. They are essentially complementary, so that they can be learned rather quickly and, more important, output from one program can be read by another without any fundamental problems.

9.3   Term-oriented I/O Predicates

Let us begin with the *term-oriented I/O predicates*.

We have already seen *read(Term)* for reading a term from the current input stream. It is called with an *uninstantiated* argument, *Term*, which gets instantiated to the next term found in the input stream. This term *must* be terminated by a period. If the term found is not syntactically correct, then the interpreter issues an error message to that effect.

Thus, *read* is typically used only when one wants to read in terms which were written out to a file by a corresponding term-oriented output predicate. The problems arising when one uses it for other purposes, as we did in our menu-driven network-monitoring system, should be familiar to you by now.

A number of predicates are provided for outputting terms, each differing from the others, essentially in the format which the output assumes.

Perhaps the most commonly used of them all is the predicate *write(Term)*. It writes its term argument into the output stream as is, omitting only the closing period. If you wanted to read this term back in again *as a term*, then you would have to add the period and newline-carriage return yourself, e.g. with *write('.\n')*.

The predicate *display(Term)* serves a function similar to *write*, except that *write* observes any defined operators when formatting the output, and *display* does *not*:

> ?– **op(100,xfx,sells).**
>
> yes
> ?– **op(90,xf,sea).**
>
> yes
> ?– **write('She' sells sea shells).**
> She sells sea shells
>
> yes
> ?– **display('She' sells sea shells).**
> sells(She,sea(shells))
>
> yes
> ?–

As you see in the example, both *write* and *display* omit the single quotes, which are used to enclose terms, i.e. atoms beginning with upper-case letters or containing blanks. If the output is going to the user's terminal, this is usually desirable. But should the term be written out to a file from which it is to be read in again, at some later date, then we usually wish to preserve the quoting. And the two built-ins *writeq(Term)* and *displayq(Term)* do just that:

> ?– **writeq('She' sells sea shells).**
> 'She' sells sea shells

Getting back to the problem we mentioned at the very beginning of this chapter: updating the *network* file of our sample program in Chapter 8 is really quite simple. We merely open the file up for writing, i.e. *tell(network)*, and proceed to enter all the *node, line, defective* and *failed* facts into it, using *writeq*. The best way to gather these facts would be a combination of appropriate *clause* goals and a *fail* at the end of the output procedure for each predicate type. The next time the network monitor is activated, *consult* would load the latest state of the *network*.

Despite the relative ease with which it is accomplished, switching from file to file gets particularly annoying when, while writing large quantities of data out to a file or exchanging them with another installation, one wishes to occasionally communicate with the interactive *user*, i.e. *stdout* and *stderr*. Prolog implementations under Unix should provide a *write_user(Term)* and *write_err(Term)* for just such situations. They write to the terminal *regardless* of where *tell* is having other data be sent to.

9.4 Character-oriented Predicates

Section 8.7 covered almost all the character-oriented I/O predicates available, so we shall keep our discussion here brief and concentrate simply on a few more illustrative examples.

With *put(C)* we can write a single character to the current output stream, and to read one from the input we can use *get(C)* and *get0(C)*. The argument *C* either is instantiated to some value (for *put* this is a must) or it is instantiated by the implied action. *get* ignores non-printing characters, i.e. those with ASCII values less than 32, in contrast to *get0*. We also saw *skip(Ae)*, which causes the characters up to the next occurrence of the ASCII equivalent of *Ae* to be read from the input stream and *ignored*, as well as the predicates for producing *white space*, i.e. *nl* for placing new lines and *tab(N)* for *N* blanks into the output stream.

Of special significance with respect to all these predicates is that they *do not get executed* again during backtracking. This is only reasonable, since otherwise it would be very difficult to employ them in recursive or iterative structures. Therefore, when you do indeed wish to have a repetitive output you must specify it explicitly by embedding the I/O predicate(s) in a *repeat ... fail* loop.

In practice, these I/O predicates get used mostly as primitives, with which higher-order I/O procedures are defined. For instance, not every Prolog system permits the inclusion of the tabulator symbol '\t' in atoms which you intend to use as output strings for *write*. In this case, it is possible to define a predicate *horizontal tab (ht)*, analogous to *nl* for *new lines*:

    ht :– put(9).

The number 9 is the numeric equivalent, in ASCII, for the non-printable character *TAB* on your keyboard.

A more complex example is the unary predicate *puttext*, in Fig. 9.3, which takes the string or list passed to it and writes it as a text to the current output stream. It is implemented as a recursive procedure, where the terminating boundary condition, as usual, is the empty list. Numeric atoms are treated as characters and written using *put*. If the head of the list to be output is itself a list, then a recursion is initiated. The latter enables the inclusion of substrings, e.g. for *text substitution*. Every other nonvariable term appearing as an element of the list to output is simply passed to *write*. This essentially takes care of non-numeric atoms. Variable terms are simply suppressed, which helps when specifying substitute text: text segments

```
                    puttext([ ]).
                    puttext([H|T]) :-
                        integer(H), !,
                        put(H), puttext(T).
                    puttext([[H|T1]|T2]) :- !,
                        puttext([H|T1]), puttext(T2).
                    puttext([H|T]) :-
                        nonvar(H),
                        write(H), puttext(T).
                    puttext([H|T]) :-
                        var(H),
                        puttext(T).
```

Fig. 9.3   The procedure puttext for writing a text to the output stream

which are not to be included are simply not instantiated and thus never
appear in the output.

9.5   ASCII Character Equivalents and Special Characters

The character-oriented I/O is *not* limited to only those symbols which can be
printed on the screen or are directly available on the keyboard. On the contrary, Prolog accepts every symbol of the ASCII character set in the form of
its numeric equivalent. We exploited this fact to define the *horizontal tab*
predicate above.

Likewise, the value 7 represents the acoustic signal which is a beep on
most contemporary terminals, but is called *bel*, i.e. bell, in reference to the
margin bell of mechanical typewriters. In Prolog, we could cause this
historical bell to ring, with the following predicate:

```
bel :- put(7).
```

But it is a bit annoying to have to always provide the character-oriented
predicates with the corresponding numeric value. Therefore, it would be
more functional to define a generalized procedure which, when given an
atom identifying the desired character, returns the equivalent ASCII value.

Figure 9.4 shows the definition of just such a predicate, which we call
ascii. Its first argument, *CharAtom*, represents the character requested and
the second argument, *CharValue*, represents the corresponding numeric
ASCII value.

Now in addition to all the printable characters, the predicate also
'knows' the conventional abbreviation for all the non-printing characters 0–
32 and 127. These are stored in a table, whereas the printing character atoms
are matched to their ASCII numeric equivalents by mere application of the
built-in predicate *name*.

Whenever we need the ASCII equivalent of a given character, or vice versa, then we need only call *ascii* with the proper argument instantiated. And of course, in the case of upper-case letters or special characters, as input arguments, we must remember to enclose them in apostrophes. Figure 9.5 illustrates a little dialog using *ascii*. Please note that when a digit is used as the first argument it too must be set in single quotes; otherwise Prolog treats it as an integer and not the printable character '1', leading to an exception error.

```
ascii(nul,0).
ascii(soh,1).
ascii(stx,2).
ascii(etx,3).
ascii(eot,4).
ascii(enq,5).
ascii(ack,6).
ascii(bel,7).
ascii(bs,8).
ascii(ht,9).
ascii(nl,10).
ascii(vt,11).
ascii(np,12).
ascii(cr,13).
ascii(so,14).
ascii(si,15).
ascii(dle,16).
ascii(dc1,17).
ascii(dc2,18).
ascii(dc3,19).
ascii(dc4,20).
ascii(nak,21).
ascii(syn,22).
ascii(etb,23).
ascii(can,24).
ascii(em,25).
ascii(sub,26).
ascii(esc,27).
ascii(fs,28).
ascii(gs,29).
ascii(rs,30).
ascii(us,31).
ascii(sp,32).
ascii(del,127).
ascii(CharAtom,CharValue) :-
        name(CharAtom,[CharValue]).
```

Fig. 9.4 *The procedure* ascii(CharAtom,CharValue)
for transforming atoms into ASCII equivalents

It was with the help of this *ascii* predicate that we produced the ASCII character set table which you can find in Appendix F of this book. In Fig. 9.6 you can see the entire procedure used. We define *two* predicates called *ascii_table* of arity 0 and 1 respectively. The unary predicate's argument is *OutputStream*, i.e. the file into which the table produced should be written. The zero arity *ascii_table* writes to the standard output file *user*; it demonstrates the conventional method in Prolog for achieving *default values*, e.g. it merely calls the parameterized version of *ascii_table* with a predefined value. This takes advantage of the fact that predicates with the same functor name but different arity are as functionally distinct as two with entirely different functor names!

?– **ascii(C,7).**

C = bel

yes
?– **ascii(nl,N).**

N = 10

yes
?– **ascii('7',N).**

N = 55

yes
?– **ascii('A',70).**

no
?– **ascii('A',N).**

N = 65

yes
?– **ascii(C,95).**

C = _

Fig. 9.5   Sample dialog using the predicate ascii *from Fig. 9.4*

Since the table is to be printed in four-column format and there are 128 ASCII characters, the predicate must output 32 lines. These get numbered with the number *N1*, the value of the respective first character in the respective line.

Thus the line numbers run from 0 to 31. The predicate *tb_line*, which actually outputs the line, is therefore passed the line number value 0 (zero) when activated by the table generator *ascii_table*. Each time it calls itself with the goal *tb_line(Next)*, *Next* has been instantiated to the current value of *N1* incremented by 1. This recursion terminates with the call *tb_line*(32).

The individual ASCII values are output by the predicate *put_ascii*. Notice how the alignment problem in the output of numbers of varying length has been solved. A general solution is, however, by no means as simple as that; it typically requires some more involved field-length calculations. Thus, it is useful to write yourself a set of procedures for formatted output. We recommend that you undertake this task as a very instructive exercise, whose results should prove of great practical use.

```
:- consult(ascii).

ascii_table :-
        ascii_table(user).

ascii_table(OutputStream) :-
        telling(OldOutStream), tell(OutputStream),
        tb_line(0),
        told, tell(OldOutStream).

tb_line(32) :- nl, !.
tb_line(N1) :-
        nl, put_ascii(N1),
        N2 is N1 + 32,
        ht, put_ascii(N2),
        N3 is N2 + 32,
        ht, put_ascii(N3),
        N4 is N3 + 32,
        ht, put_ascii(N4),
        Next is N1 + 1,
        tb_line(Next).

put_ascii(X) :-
        ascii(Z,X), tab(3), write(Z), ht,
        (       X > 99
        ;       X > 9, tab(1)
        ;       tab(2)
        ),
        !, write(X).

ht :-   put(9).
```

Fig. 9.6   Producing an ASCII character-set table

If you try the *ascii_table* predicate of arity 0, then it will no doubt bother you that several of the lines at the top of the table will be scrolled off the screen, i.e. assuming you have a standard 24–25 line display. A more professional version would recognize that the output is being sent to the screen and not a storage file, and thus stop the output after say the 16th line, displaying the remaining ones only when requested, by pressing an arbitrary key. The implementation of the necessary predicate, e.g. *stop(Condition)*, is relatively simple:

```
stop(Condition) :-
        Condition, !,
        get0(_).
stop(_).
```

Now we need only add a second argument to the predicate used to output the lines, i.e.

```
tb_line(N1,OutputStream).
```

and insert the goal *stop* just before the recursive call in *tb_line*:

```
stop( (OutputStream = user, N1 = 15 ) ),
```

and we have a solution. Perhaps you would like to inform the user of the situation by issuing a message such as

```
hit any key for remainder of output.
```

We will leave the modification up to you. You may even want to elaborate it so that you can switch the message on or off via a second argument to *stop*.

9.6   Reading a Word at a Time

You will still find that the predicates for I/O discussed thus far are not optimally suited for most applications. Reading *terms* is too strongly bound to Prolog syntax and fetching the input character by character usually does not correspond to the logical unit to be processed.

The solution typically lies therein, that one develops some 'hand-tailored' I/O procedures for the purpose, or better yet, one makes a library of standard modules covering the most important common I/O tasks, which are then consulted by the programs needing them. Let us take a look at just such a module. This one implements reading a line or a (short) file into a list, *one word at a time*.

If the list, or its individual words, are in a not yet directly interpretable form, a description of the *syntax* of the input text, for example, could serve as a basis for further processing. In Chapter 6 we showed you the notation and method for defining such a *grammar* in Prolog, albeit character and not word oriented. At the same time, we also mentioned that such *syntax-driven processing* is best divided into two steps, i.e. with a *lexical analysis*, transforming the original stream of characters into a corresponding list of higher-level, typically more compact *lexical units*, preceding the actual application process.

```
words_in_line(WordList) :-
        read_in(WordList,till_nl),!.

words_in_file(WordList) :-
        read_in(WordList,till_EOF),!.

read_in(WordList,End) :-
        get0(C), read_word(C,Word,C1,End),
        word_in_list(Word,C1,WordList,End).

word_in_list(char(end),_,[  ],_) :- !.
word_in_list(char(whitespace),C,WordList,End) :-
        /* suppress "whitespace" words : */
        read_word(C,Word,C1,End), !,
        word_in_list(Word,C1,WordList,End).
word_in_list(Word,C,[Word|WordList],End) :-
        read_word(C,Word1,C1,End),
        word_in_list(Word1,C1,WordList,End).

/* termination criteria : */
read_word(4,char(end),_,_) :- !.
read_word(10,char(end),_,till_nl) :- !.
/* "whitespace" Words : */
read_word(9,char(whitespace),C,_) :- get0(C), !.
read_word(10,char(whitespace),C,till_EOF) :- get0(C), !.
read_word(32,char(whitespace),C,_) :- get0(C), !.
/* legal words : */
read_word(C,Word,C2,_) :-
        in_word(C), !, get0(C1),
        rest_of_word(C1,String,C2),
        name(Word,[C|String]).
/* special characters : */
read_word(C,char(C),C1,_) :- get0(C1).

rest_of_word(C,[C|String],C2) :-
        in_word(C), !, get0(C1),
        rest_of_word(C1,String,C2).
rest_of_word(C,[  ],C).

/*      The definitions for    */
/*          in-word(C)         */
/*      must be added here.    */
```

Fig. 9.7   Predicates for reading word by word from the input line or files

The predicates for reading 'words', illustrated in Fig. 9.7, perform a lexical analysis directly on the input file. In this case, the major lexical unit recognized is the rather simply defined 'word'. Drawing on a definition common to the Unix system, a word is essentially a contiguous string of non-

whitespace characters. Thus, words are primarily separated by *blank, tabulator* and *newline* characters. Occurrences of these characters in the input stream will therefore *not appear* in the list of words delivered by the predicates.

Secondary word separators are also recognized, these being simply any non-whitespace characters which are *not* among the characters permitted in words, as defined by the predicate *in_word(C)*. These differ from the primary separators in that the secondary separators *do appear* in the word list produced; not as themselves, but rather as the logical function *char(CharValue)*, whereby the argument *CharValue* represents the ASCII equivalent of the character read.

Both the predicate *words_in_line(WordList)*, used to read words of an input line up to its closing *newline* (ASCII 10), and *words_in_file(WordList)*, used to read the contents of a file up to the end of file (ASCII 4), employ the same binary predicate *read_in*, merely with different values for the argument *End*, i.e. the termination criterion. If instantiated as *till_nl* then a *newline* is recognized as the end of the input; if it is *till_EOF* then the *end-of-file* condition is recognized. In either case, the *WordList* returned is terminated with a logical marker *char(end)*.

The occurrence of a *char(end)* in the input is the terminating condition for the recursive procedure *word_in_list*, generating an empty *WordList* for that respective call. With the exception of 'white-space words', which get suppressed, every call in the recursion sequence places its *Word* at the head of the *WordList* it receives from the call which followed it (recall that a recursion causes a stacking of the previous calls, so that the last recursion returns first).

Each word is fetched from the input by the sub-predicate *read_word*, which must always *read ahead* one character in order to recognize the end of a word. Since this character must itself be processed (due to the definition of word and whitespace), it is passed by *read_word*, through its third argument, into *word_in_list* via the latter's second argument, the variable *C*.

In the predicate *word_in_list* this character, which was fetched in the read ahead, then gets passed back to *read_word*, but this time as its *first argument*.

read_word takes its first argument to be the first letter of the next word to be read, unless it recognizes it to be *whitespace*, the *termination character* or a character rejected by the predicate *in_word(C)* as being a 'non-word' character. All such exceptions cause *read_word* to generate a corresponding 'special word' *char(C)*.

If the initial character is permitted in a word, then *rest_of_word(C,String,C1)* proceeds to produce a list of characters, *String*, out of the uninterrupted sequence of legal 'word' characters following it. *rest_of_word* employs the same technique as *word_in_list*: its first argument, *C*, is always instantiated with the value of the next character, i.e. the one read by some *get0(Char)* as part of the look-ahead strategy. If this character passes the *in_word(C)* test, then — as in *word_in_list* — it is placed at the head of the *String* assembled in the recursion from letters following it, respectively. And therein lies the trick: each recursive call represents the next character in the word, which is to be placed at the head of the result variable *String*. But this pasting together can be carried out only when the end of the string has been found, i.e. when the *String* which the letter is waiting to be pasted onto, has been generated. And the pasted version resulting at one level of recursion becomes the *String* of the previous level, causing the *String* to evolve backwards, i.e. from the end to the beginning. This is, by the way, typical for most recursive procedures in Prolog!

So the critical recursion is the one that discovers the end of the word, and this can actually instantiate *String* with a value, so that the pending 'pasters' can get to work. This occurs when the look-ahead character passed in to *rest_of_word* via its first argument, *C*, proves to be a character *not in_word*. Backtracking then activates the second version of *rest_of_word*, which instantiates *String* to an empty list, i.e. the end of the word found and, of course, passes the first argument back via the third argument, since this look-ahead character is not included in the word just ended and must still be processed.

When the *rest_of_word* originally called is complete, *String* contains all the characters constituting the word to be read, *starting from the second one*. Now *read_word* must merely append this *String* to the initial letter of the word, which it has received from its caller, and the complete word now exists as a *list* of characters. This is then converted into an atom, called *Word*, by the predicate *name*.

The verbal explanation may sound somewhat complicated. The process should become much clearer, however, once one has grasped the function of the look-ahead characters and the recursion-induced reverse generation of the word strings and lists. These factors ultimately explain the role of the arguments in the respective predicates, and the values passed through them. Be sure to take the time to fully grasp the techniques used here, as they are of great practical application in a variety of problem areas.

9.7 Lexical Units

Which sequence of characters in the input stream is to be considered a word, i.e. a *lexical unit* or *token*, naturally depends on the problem at hand. For this very reason, we chose to specify this crucial criterion in a separate test predicate for evaluating the individual characters read, i.e. *in_word(C)*. In Figs. 9.8 and 9.9 we illustrate two common definitions, the version in Fig. 9.8 being suitable for many text-processing applications involving the analysis of natural and formal languages.

```
in_word(C) :-
        /* uppercase letters : */
        C > 64, C < 91.
in_word(C) :-
        /* lowercase letters : */
        C > 96, C < 123.
in_word(C) :-
        /* digits : */
        C > 47, C < 58.
```

Fig. 9.8   Predicate* in_word(C) *for text analysis

The predicate *in_word* accepts all upper- and lower-case letters and digits as legal characters in a word. Characters specific to non-English alphabets, as well as special symbols, e.g. '$' etc., are not accepted. Should they be accepted, then you must supplement the predicate accordingly.

Numbers and word symbols can be distinguished from one another by using the classifying predicate *integer(Atom)*. If the language being analyzed permits specific special characters in words, such as the underline character, '_', or the hyphen, '-', or a decimal point in numbers, these *compound words* can be easily assembled from the *Words* and *char(X)* elements found in the *WordList*. In many applications, however, e.g. the processing of floating-point values or compound words, this is not even desirable, since the decomposition into primitive elements often simplifies the analysis.

```
in_word(C) :-
        /* all printable characters */
        C > 32, C < 127.
```

Fig. 9.9   The predicate* in_word(C) *for Unix words

Figure 9.9 shows another extreme, which is useful, for example in the analysis of Unix command lines. Here all printable characters are defined as legal. Technically speaking, the Unix convention allows even non-printable characters and only excludes the three whitespace characters mentioned above.

But since the appearance of a non-printable character in a Unix word, e.g. in a filename, is not particularly desirable, and usually the result of a typo on the user's part, it is probably better to separate these characters using our *char(X)* convention, and thus call attention to their occurrence.

This convention, incidentally, is a good example of an important, basic programming technique in Prolog, i.e. the introduction of a *Skolem function* for naming objects uniquely. Therefore, we shall return to this theme later, discussing it in greater detail.

10   THE SYSTEM ENVIRONMENT

A good Prolog system not only provides access to the file-handling facilities of the underlying operating system, but, at least under Unix, also offers simple, yet powerful means to make use of all the operating-system utilities otherwise available. Because of this, Prolog is able to dispense with the complex, dedicated embedding in the host system, so typical of its main competitor, Lisp, without any loss of comfort. On the contrary, most users find it far more agreeable, when the familiar tools and utilities, e.g. their favorite editor, are available just as usual. In this chapter we shall show you how you access these system utilities, under the assumption that your Prolog implementation also provides similar, if not identical, mechanisms. Be sure to check the handbook for your implementation to see precisely how these have been realised. Most of the predicates and techniques illustrated in this chapter inevitably depend upon the operating-system environment and certain details of the Prolog implementation upon which the examples were run.

10.1   System Calls

Most Prolog systems have a predicate for making *system calls*; indeed, usually in several different forms. The simplest is the predicate of arity 0, e.g. under Unix the predicate *sh*. This predicate is primarily intended for interactive users of the Prolog system. After activating the predicate in response to the Prolog prompt, e.g.

```
?– sh.
$ : a Unix shell command follows
$ who am i
hps     tty08     Aug     5     08:47
$ : back to Prolog with <control>D
$

yes
?–
```

162

the Unix prompt '*$*' indicates that you are now in the operating system or, to be more exact, in an interactive *sub-shell* subordinate to your Prolog interpreter process. Now any input is interpreted by the system command interpreter, *not* your Prolog interpreter. The command ':' is a sort of 'no-op' command; we use it here to introduce explanatory comments — a typical use of it, by the way. Entering the *EOF*, i.e. *<control>D*, at most Unix installations causes the sub-shell process to terminate, bringing you back to your Prolog interpreter. This is indicated by the familiar 'yes' and the subsequent Prolog prompt.

Whatever actions you took with the help of the Unix commands issued in the *sub-shell* have, as a rule, no influence on the Prolog process temporarily suspended. As you perhaps know, there is normally no direct communication between a sub-process and its parent.

Consequently, the second version of the *system call* is usually of more practical use in the programming of Prolog applications. It is the unary system call predicate, which passes its argument, a command (line) to the operating system for execution. Under Unix, this predicate has the form *sh(Command)*. Under other operating systems there should be a corresponding predicate, e.g. *ms_dos(Command)*. The function of the predicate itself, however, remains the same.

The argument *Command* is an atom. It is passed directly to the operating system, which interprets it as a command string. Thus, the power of this predicate is limited only by that of the command language and the utilities of the underlying operating system. In the case of Unix, where a command can represent an arbitrary *shell script*, this automatically integrates not only the *shell* command language, but the sub-languages like *awk* and *sed* into Prolog too!

The following simple application shows the predicate *cat(TextFile)*. It imports the Unix command of the same name, to be used in displaying the contents of the file *TextFile* on the standard output — typically the user's terminal:

```
cat(TextFile) :-
        concat_atoms('cat ',TextFile,Command),
        sh(Command).
```

The file name, passed in via the argument *TextFile*, is treated as an atom and must under given, now familiar, circumstances be enclosed in single quotes. Furthermore, we employ the *concat_atoms* predicate introduced in Chapter 4 to concatenate two atoms into a single *Command* atom, i.e. the *cat filename* used in Unix. This *Command* is then passed, via *sh*, to the operating system.

This *cat* predicate is very useful, if a Prolog program must frequently display longer texts, e.g. 'help' information or *operating instructions*. It is not only more convenient in terms of system development and maintenance, when one can simply take a text editor and produce the corresponding text files in exactly the desired format. It also reduces the demands on main memory considerably, when such texts are not stored there, in the form of atoms, but rather fetched, as needed, from some file and sent directly to the terminal. Indeed, in the above solution, by using the *sh* predicate, such output actually bypasses the Prolog interpreter altogether!

For *documentation* and *information-retrieval* applications, such a direct output predicate is indispensable, since the volume of information typically dealt with prohibits storing it completely in the internal Prolog database. Thus, it is more practical to store the information in the file structure administered by the operating system, and the search and access mechanisms programmed in Prolog need only use and manipulate the names of the respective files involved. Then when a text requested is to be output, the Prolog program need only call upon the operating system to carry this out.

Following the same scheme, one can integrate numerous other system services into Prolog. Frequently, however, one wants the system commands to have some effect on the calling Prolog program, either by modifying it or returning some data to it, etc. Typical, practical examples of it are the interactive calling of an editor, the reading of a Unix directory, incremental data collection, or fetching the current date and time for further processing.

10.2 Calling an Editor Interactively

When developing a program interactively, it is very important that the programmer be able to call *her* editor, to modify a module — correcting errors, adding new predicates, etc. — without having to terminate her Prolog session. We say *her* editor, by the way, intentionally, because a professional programmer, who develops software in a number of different languages, should not have to learn a different editor for each language, just because the implementor of that language thought that editor X was a particularly 'nice environment' for her system. Now because the Unix editor *vi* is *our* editor, that is the one which gets *interactively activated* by the predicate shown in Fig. 10.1, when we enter the following instruction at any time during a Prolog session:

> ?– **vi** *ModuleName*.

We must be sure to close the instruction with a period, and if the *Module-Name* begins with an upper-case letter or special character it must be enclosed in quotes.

ModuleName is the name of an arbitrary Prolog text file. It is read into

```
:– op(70,fx,vi).

vi ModuleName :–
        name(ModuleName,FileName),
        append("vi ",FileName,CommandString),
        name(Command, CommandString),
        sh(Command),
        reconsult(ModuleName).
```

**Fig. 10.1   Predicate vi for calling editor interactively
during a Prolog session**

the editor's workspace and we can modify it accordingly. When we leave the editor, the next goal in the predicate *vi* causes the file to be automatically *reconsulted*. This causes all the modifications made to become part of the 'new' Prolog database. And thus we can immediately use and test the new version.

The predicate does everything that one expects in terms of editorial support for *interactive program development*. Moreover, it can do this for *any* editor. You merely have to change the name used in the predicate from *vi* to *ed* or *emacs* or *hit* or whatever it may be called on your system.

We recommend that you always consult this predicate at the beginning of each session, if you develop your programs interactively. If your Prolog interpreter allows you to specify files to be loaded together with the interpreter, then the best solution, under Unix, would be to write a small script which calls Prolog accordingly for you. You could then place this in one of the directories in your search path *$PATH* in a command file named, let us say *testprolog*. Assuming the predicate *vi* is in the file *$HOME/prolog/vi*, then your *shell* procedure should look something like:

```
: procedure "testprolog" for loading the
: interactive editor predicate with Prolog

ifprolog –c $HOME/prolog/vi $*
```

By issuing the command

```
testprolog –c program1 –c program2
```

you then automatically get the interactive editor predicate, as well as *program1* and *program2*, loaded into the database.

In the case of bigger program development projects, it pays to automate things even more, by using *make* and placing the configuration commands for your different project phases and modules in respective *makefiles*. This is not the place for more details, however, and we refer you to the literature on Unix for more information.

It is, of course, possible to include a predicate like *vi* as a goal in some other predicate, if you would like to provide your intended *end-user* with an editor to process some given text. In this case, however, it would presumably make sense to use some predicate other than *reconsult* to deal with the text resulting from the user's editing session. Perhaps a word-oriented read, using the predicate *word_in_file(WordList)* from the previous chapter, followed by some syntax-driven processing of *WordList*?

10.3   Exchanging Data with System Processes

You can always communicate with a system process activated by *sh* using intermediate files, i.e. the *sh* process writes its data into a (pre)defined file, which is then read by the Prolog program using *reconsult* or some other reading procedure. This method, however, will certainly only seem elegant and natural in situations such as the editor-calling predicate illustrated in Fig. 10.1.

If the process called produces data according to some particular algorithm, or if it must be fed some input data or instructions by the calling Prolog program, then the use of intermediate files is neither elegant nor efficient. Unix solves this problem much better with *pipes*. For example, if a C program spawns another process with which it wishes to exchange information, then it merely defines an output *pipe* attached to the spawned process' standard input, i.e. *stdin* and an input *pipe* attached to its standard output, i.e. *stdout*. Now when the original, parent process performs a read or a write with the normal file-access functions, the information is received from, i.e. passed to the child process.

Now what C can do should also be possible with your Prolog system. The predicate used to establish the communication *pipes* is a ternary version of the *system call sh*:

    sh(*Command,Stdin,Stdout*)

activates a *shell*, just like the unary version, and this starts a process to execute the *Command*. Furthermore, it installs *pipes* connected to the executing process' *stdin* and *stdout*, which are accessible via the names assigned by the values in the second and third arguments to *sh*, i.e. the variables *Stdin* and *Stdout*. Your Prolog procedure need only open the streams identified by *Stdin* and *Stdout* as usual, and then it can use the reading and writing predicates to exchange information.

Just how that looks in practice can be seen in the example in Fig. 10.2. The predicate *ls(Dir,FileList)* reads the file names in the directory named by *Dir* into the list *FileList*. It should be fairly self-explanatory at this stage. As when reading from a normal file, we save the name of the current input stream in *OldInput*, open the *stdout* of the *Unix ls* command as the *new input stream* and read the file names output by the *Unix ls* command into *FileList* using our old friend *words_in_file*. When this is done we close the *pipe* and (re)open the input stream *OldInput*.

Naturally, we must take care that the reading predicate, *words_in_file* is provided with the proper, Unix-oriented predicate *in_word(C)*, which only recognizes *whitespace* as the word separator. That was the one in Fig. 9.9, if you recall.

```
ls(Dir,FileList) :-
        concat_atoms('ls ',Dir,Command),
        sh(Command,_,_stdout),
        seeing(OldInput), see(stdout),
        words_in_file(FileList),
        seen, see(OldInput).
```

Fig. 10.2   A predicate for reading a Unix directory (uses Unix version of predicate in_word(C)*!)*

10.4   Incremental Data Collection

One often wants to store data produced or gathered by a Prolog program in a file, without destroying its previous contents. The *tell* predicate is poorly suited for this, because it always (re)positions to the beginning of a file which has been (re)opened for writing. Thus, we need an alternative predicate for *reopening* files. Let us call it *retell(FileName)*, to draw the functional analogy to *tell*. After calling it, all data written with the customary predicates for standard output should appear *appended* to the previous contents of the file identified by *FileName*. Fig. 10.3 illustrates the predicate.

```
retell(FileName) :-
        concat_atoms('cat >>',FileName,Command),
        sh(Command,cat_input,_),
        tell(cat_input).

retold :-
        put(4),   % EOF character for "cat"
        told.
```

Fig. 10.3   The predicate retell *for reopening write files*

retell also uses the Unix *cat* command. Since *cat* must be informed when the *end of file* has been reached, so that it will terminate normally, we need, in addition to *retell*, a corresponding *retold* predicate for closing the reopened file. This is also found in Fig. 10.3.

It is understood, that when using the predicates for reopening files for writing, we must also note the original output file name for reconnection of it after we are finished *retelling*, just as we did with *tell* and *told*.

A sample data collection application using these predicates will be presented in the next chapter. We will show you a useful programming trick there, which, however, does not have anything to do with our current topic, Prolog and the system environment.

10.5   Fetching the Date and Time from the System

Figure 10.4 illustrates another application for the ternary *sh* predicate. *date(TimeStamp)* allows you to fetch the current date and time from the system, using the Unix command of the same name.

```
date([Year,Month,Day,
      Hour,Minute,Second,DayOfWeek]) :-
         sh(date,_,datum),
         seeing(OldInput), see(datum),
         words_in_file([DayOfWeek,Month,Day,
                        Hour,char(58),Minute,
                        char(58),Second,_,Year]),
         seen, see(OldInput).
```

Fig. 10.4   A predicate for fetching the Unix system time
(uses 'text version' of in_word(C) and might have to be adapted
to the output format of your system's date command.)

The procedure in Fig. 10.4 assumes that the system command *date* returns the timestamp in the following form:

Thu Aug 1 09:14:08 GMT 1985

If this is not the case on your system, you must make some minor changes to the procedure illustrated before it will perform correctly.

Since the output from the Unix command *date* is not optimal for further processing by Prolog, we use the predicate *words_in_file* to isolate its individual information elements. The character *char*(58) is the colon. If *date* has an altogether different format on your system, then chances are good that you will not simply get an incorrect result, but that the predicate *date* will draw your attention to the problem encountered via its failure.

The argument *TimeStamp* for *date* is a list. Typically, it will be used as an output variable, except if you want to use the predicate to check if it happens to be a particular day of the week or a specific month, etc. You can do that too, of course: the following example returns *true* only on Mondays in the month of December.

?– **date([_,12,_,_,_,_,'Mon']).**

The elements of *TimeStamp* have been arranged such that you can easily define an operator which makes a *time comparison* between two *TimeStamps*, e.g. *Time1* after *Time2*.

```
:– op(700,xfx,after).

[X|Rest1] after [Y|Rest2] :–
        integer(X),
        (        X > Y, !
        ;        Rest1 after Rest2
        ).
```

**Fig. 10.5   The operator after for comparing lists
of the form TimeStamp from Fig. 10.4**

Figure 10.5 is an example of such an operator. For the priority of the operator *after* we selected a value comparable to the comparison operators '<' and '>'. Should their priorities be different on your system, then you should modify the operator definition shown in Fig. 10.5 accordingly.

10.6   Interfacing with other Programming Languages

If your Prolog implementation provides a set of predicates for system calls, these should give you sufficient access to the system utilities for solving many problems. But in some cases this will not do, for at least the following two reasons:

1.   The predicate *sh* spawns a separate process to execute the command you request. This is costly: should you request such services in quick succession, e.g. in an inner loop of some procedure, you will rapidly reach the performance limits of your system, and intolerable degradation of response time.

2.   There are cases where the set of built-in predicates of even the best Prolog system is not comprehensive enough. You must then supplement these built-ins with new predicates, which, like those already present in your interpreter, are written in the *programming language* of your *basic system*, e.g. most likely C on a Unix-based system.

Many implementors of Prolog systems will dispute the second reason given above, claiming that *their* system offers so many built-in predicates that the need to supplement them is unthinkable. If the creator of your system should happen to make such a claim, then tell her simply (and chances are it is true anyway) that you already have a database management system in use, and important business data of yours is stored in it. You must be able to access this data via Prolog, since, after all, you intend to do serious data processing with it. In principle, there are only two possibilities: either the implementor of your Prolog system delivers the necessary access predicates for this database management system or you must write them yourself.[1]

Just how (and if!) your Prolog system provides interfaces for integrating procedures written in other programming languages, will depend on the internal structure of your interpreter. Therefore we will discuss the implementation of a built-in Prolog predicate in general, conceptual terms, which should reflect the overall features to be found in just about every interpreter. In the subsequent section, we will then introduce a small example, which by necessity will exhibit characteristics peculiar to our specific IF/Prolog system.

As you have already seen, Prolog differs radically from most other languages, with respect to the flow of control and the passing of parameters. Naturally, it is essential that a predicate which you custom build into your Prolog abides by the same conventions used by the implementor of your system. To help you better understand the general model, let us summarize the critical points briefly:

- Variables must be *typeless*, i.e. they must be capable of being instantiated with arbitrary Prolog terms. In the case of a database connection, this implies that a variable could be instantiated with either an atom or a character string, a number, a list of data or even an entire relation (a structure in Prolog terminology), all depending on the information found in response to a given query.

- Conversely, we must be able to *evaluate* constants passed in. If an argument is instantiated with an atom, then we must be able to access its name as a character string without any trouble.

- Each argument of a procedure call must be able to function both as an input, as well as an output parameter. As is customary in Prolog, we should only have to write a single predicate for accessing database information. Those arguments which are given constant values should serve as the search keys and the variables should get instantiated with the respective data from the record in the database found to have satisfied the query.

---

[1] If you want to be sure that she does not just proceed to sell you an expensive extension package for connecting to database system *XYZ*, tell her that your database system was developed in-house, and you are not prepared to simply reveal the interface definitions to her — after all, she does not publish her internal Prolog interface definitions either!

- The predicate must fit into Prolog's standard flow of control. In particular, it should behave normally with respect to *backtracking*. Should the arguments given as search keys match more than one record in the database, then backtracking should deliver the respective variable values in each record, one after the other, as alternative selections.

- Above all, it must be assured that each time the interpreter backtracks over the predicate, all variables instantiated by it become uninstantiated. Otherwise Prolog has no way of processing and returning alternative solutions.

- Lastly, the predicate must observe *cuts*. If a *cut* was encountered somewhere *before* the predicate as a goal, then backtracking must be prohibited from directing control flow back into it for purposes of resatisfaction. On the other hand, in the event of such a cut it must still perform any cleaning up necessary for proper, further execution. In the case of the database, the databank must be properly closed, or the locked segment freed for use by others, as soon as it is clear that it will no longer be accessed by the predicate.

As you can see, the requirements are by no means trivial. You should check your handbook against this list and see if the interface provided for integrating procedures really permits you to build in new predicates. Any open questions should be cleared up *before* acquiring the Prolog interpreter of your choice, since it is most exasperating when you discover that you cannot properly implement a connection to your database, your menu system or your communications package, etc.

Let us now examine the general model for a Prolog procedure. You will recall the *box model* of Chapter 5. In our discussion there, built-in predicates remained *black boxes* into which neither we nor the debugger could look.

Now we shall open up the *black box*: Fig. 10.6 illustrates the control flow for a Prolog procedure implemented in a conventional programming language. The scheme shown is very general; in practice, however, the internal *REDO* loop may be more complex and/or there may actually be several *DETACH–RESUME* blocks.

As you see in the figure, the predicate is defined by its *semantic function*. When you implement your own such predicate, then you must essentially write this function, in C or some other language, corresponding to the conventions observed by your Prolog interpreter. We shall show you a sample function in the next section.

In order to be able to deal with *backtracking* the semantic function must be implemented as a *coroutine*. This means that the flow of control normally does *not* exit via the 'end' of the routine, i.e. the *EPILOG* in our illustration. That only happens when the function is about to be left for good, via the *fail* port.

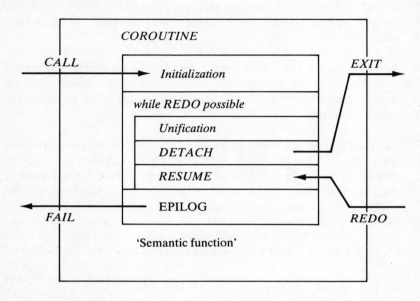

Fig. 10.6   Internal flow of control of a simple built-in predicate

Let us follow the flow of control through the box in Fig. 10.6, starting from the very beginning. The first activation through the *CALL* port causes an initialization of the predicate according to explicit instructions coded into the function by the programmer, e.g. perhaps opening the database.

A substantial part of the initialization, however, is often taken care of by the interpreter, in accordance with various instructions which are specified in an agreed upon way, e.g. via macros. For instance, the declaration of all the internal variables of the procedure, which are needed in the event of re-entry into the predicate via the *REDO* port, as a result of backtracking, is typically handled by the interpreter. In our case, this might be the access identification of the databank, which was returned to us as a result of opening it during the initialization process, and is needed by the actual access instructions.

These variables cannot merely be kept in *static* storage, because Prolog permits recursive calls to the predicate. Each recursive call would, under such circumstances, overwrite the previous value with each new instantiation. If the interpreter then attempts to backtrack, the older values are no longer available.

The set of all such variable values, which must be saved each time prior to leaving the predicate via the *EXIT* port, is called the *state of the predicate*. It is the interpreter's job to save this *state information* on the predicate activation frame stack administered by it, each time the predicate is about to leave its box via the *EXIT* port. The general purpose macro *DETACH*, in Fig. 10.6, does just that. In addition, it also records the *continuation address* of the *coroutine*, i.e. the address of the *RESUME* block immediately following the respective *DETACH* block, as this is where execution is to resume should the box be re-entered via the *REDO* port.

In the event of such a *REDO*, the interpreter fetches the activation record from the stack and (re)instantiates the respective variables to the values in it, before jumping to the corresponding *RESUME* block. Thus, the former state of the predicate is reconstructed and the semantic function continues executing as if it had never been interrupted.

The interpreter also sees to it that for each call, regardless of whether it be the first *CALL* or a *REDO*, all the arguments to the predicate are initialized just as they were passed in. Thus, by *RESUME* the arguments are instantiated exactly as they were by the original *CALL*.

The actual function defined by the predicate is specified in the block denoted *Unification*. It would, in our proposed predicate, read the next record satisfying the query out of the databank and instantiate the variable arguments of the predicate accordingly. The implementor of the Prolog system should provide us with the necessary macros for reading the already instantiated values and recognizing the variable arguments. These are presumably the same ones which she used to write her own built-in predicates. The same is true of the macros needed to unify the variable arguments with the values received as a result of the function's semantic action, in our case, the values in the record fetched from the databank.

If the unification block cannot find any more alternatives, i.e. it has seen all the relative records in the database, then the *REDO* loop ends and flow of control goes to the end of the procedure. The interpreter then executes the *EPILOG* defined by the programmer of the new built-in predicate. This is done regardless of whether the procedure ends *internally*, i.e. by virtue of its completing its programmed task, or *externally*, e.g. due to a *cut*. The interpreter must therefore be able to locate the jump address of the *EPILOG* just as it had for *RESUME*.

In our hypothetical predicate, the *EPILOG* would close the databank. Since such clean-up actions are not always necessary, it is quite possible that a built-in predicate has no *EPILOG*. The routine measures to be taken before a predicate finally terminates, i.e. the removal of its activation record from the stack and the departure from the box via *FAIL*, are all dispatched automatically by the interpreter, without any help from the programmer of the semantic function.

10.7   A C-Predicate for Interfacing with a Databank

Our choice of the databank problem above was not purely hypothetical. Since Prolog normally stores its entire database in main memory, practical applications make the possibility of communicating with a databank virtually indispensable. Just as in conventional programming languages, you want to fetch the *facts* relating to your programming task from the external database *as you need them*.

Main memory should be used primarily for storing the *rules*. These typically take up far less space, so that even without virtual memory you are no more likely to run short of this resource, than if you were programming in a conventional language. The knowledge stored in the *rules*, after all, would be embodied in the procedures of the programming language, and these too are always in main memory. And compared with the space requirements of object code for the same task, the internal representation of Prolog rules is relatively compact.

So we should like to program a predicate in C to access a (small) database. To be sure, such a predicate for practical applications would tend to be more complex, but the overall approach will certainly serve as a basis for your own efforts, particularly if your system provides the same or similar interface macros for this purpose as ours does.

For the purpose of our example, we assume that our databank stores ternary relations with the following fields:

Object   Attribute   Value

All three fields of a relation may contain a string consisting of any printable characters, including blanks, but *excluding tabs and newlines*.[2] Any of the three fields, i.e. its contents, may be used in the search expression. The only limitation is that the string given as search word from a given field must match exactly and entirely with the contents in the record being searched for; matching via substrings is not possible.

To make things a bit more realistic, and at the same time, we hope, more pleasant, let us assume that the user of our databank is the proprietor of a restaurant. In the database she has stored different meals so that she can produce menus, bids for parties and ethnic events and similar business-related materials quickly and easily, as well as being able to tailor these to the current quality and cost of the available foodstuffs.

The objects are the different menu entry names themselves, e.g. 'continental breakfast', 'american breakfast', 'kiddie menu', 'italian menu', 'brunch', etc., the attributes are the components, e.g. 'appetizer', 'soup',

---

[2] The reason for this restriction is that our databank simulator, which we present to you in Appendix A, for purposes of testing the predicate to be developed, uses these two characters as field and record separators, respectively. Thus, it has nothing whatsoever to do with Prolog or the implementation of the unification.

'main course', 'beverage', 'dessert', etc. and the values are the names of the actual dishes like 'carpaccio', 'pea soup', 'cordon bleu', or 'apple pie'. Since larger meals may have several appetizers or main courses, it is quite possible that even when the search expression is a unique combination of object and attribute, several relations will be returned from the databank. This is especially true, if only the object, i.e. the name of the meal, or only the value, i.e. a specific dish, is given as the search string. In such cases, the access function returns the records found one after the other, i.e. for each call the next combination of *Object, AttrName* and *AttrValue* for which the given search expression matches.

For this databank application we should like to have a ternary access predicate:

```
attribut(Object,AttrName,AttrValue).
```

The predicate should make the read call to the databank accessible to Prolog in a manner corresponding to the C-function:

```
getattr(db,object,attribute,value)
DB     *db;
char   *object, *attribute, *value;
```

where *db* is a pointer to the databank, returned by the following function, used to open an arbitrary databank for reading:

```
DB *
db_open(dbname,"r")
char   *dbname;
```

The pointer is also used by the function for closing the databank:

```
db_clos(db)
DB     *db;
```

The Prolog predicate should implicitly open and close the databank, so that this argument is not necessary when employing the built-in predicate.

The remaining three arguments of the access function *getattr*, namely *object, attribute* and *value*, are pointers to character strings, which specify the search expression for the three fields of the relation. If a field is not involved in the search expression, then the pointer for the corresponding argument contains a null address. Thus, to fetch those meals with 'carpaccio' as an 'appetizer' one would call the C-function as follows:

```
getattr(db,NULL,"appetizer","carpaccio");
```

The Prolog predicate with the same semantic function is

```
attribut(Menu,appetizer,carpaccio).
```

The latter has its first argument uninstantiated, the former has the corresponding argument set to *NULL*.

Each time (call) the C-function finds a (new) record satisfying the search expression, *getattr* returns a boolean value *TRUE*. The contents of the fields of the respective record are then accessible as strings via pointers with the predefined, global names *objp*, *attrp* and *valuep*. The new predicate's semantic function must then transform into Prolog atoms the strings corresponding to the arguments which were uninstantiated when the predicate was called, and unify them with the arguments. Following that, a *DETACH* must be executed, so that the interpreter puts the predicate to rest for the time being and leaves via the *EXIT* port to activate the next goal.

If *getattr* cannot find a(nother) fitting record, it returns the boolean value *FALSE*. This implies that the corresponding Prolog predicate must abandon its box for good, via the *FAIL* port.

In Appendix A you will find a C-module, which simulates the database access functions *db_open*, *getattr* and *db_close*. The database itself consists of a normal Unix text file named *databank*.

If you wish to experiment with the C-predicate, which we are about to show you, then you must copy the module into a file named *db.c* and have it included in your compiled semantic function with the help of the C-preprocessor, via the instruction *#include "db.c"*, which must appear *before* the actual source code in your function's source file.

Figure 10.7 illustrates the complete C-program for the new predicate, including the above instruction for the preprocessor. Before we go on to discuss the formulation of the semantic function, we must first explain some of the less interesting, yet necessary statements appearing in the figure. The first preprocessor instruction

```
#include <cpred.h>
```

loads, on our system, a Unix *header* file, containing certain conventional statements and macros required for the C-Prolog interface. The small *Cboot*( ) procedure at the end is obligatory and has a predefined format. It is used by the Prolog interpreter to link our new predicate into the Prolog system, under the given name "*attribut*", with arity 3, in the same way as the standard built-in predicates, at load (*boot*) time.

But now to the actual predicate itself. The first instruction after the *#includes* declares a data structure for storing the *state* of the predicate, i.e. those variables which must survive the *EXITs* from the procedure. In our case, this is merely the reference to the databank, returned by *db_open*. The *COROUTINE* macro, which initiates the semantic function, ensures that we can always reference this data structure of type *ATTSTATE*, in the functions *get_attr* and *db_close*, via the pointer variable *state*, whenever we wish to manipulate the respective databank.

The actual procedure body is enclosed in the macros *BEGIN* and *END*. If you compare it with the structure chart in Fig. 10.6, you will presumably note only one difference: *RESUME* is not located immediately

```
               #include <cpred.h>
               #include "db.c"

               typedef struct { DB *db ; } ATTSTATE ;

               COROUTINE(attribut, ATTSTATE, state)
                    RESUME(1, redo1) ;
                    HASEPILOG;
               BEGIN
                    if ( ! ( (state->db) = db_open(dbname, "r") ) )
                         EXCEPTION("cannot open db") ;
                    while ( getattr(state->db,
                              ( IsVar(Arg(1)) ? NULL
                                             : AtStr(Arg(1)) ),
                              ( IsVar(Arg(2)) ? NULL
                                             : AtStr(Arg(2)) ),
                              ( IsVar(Arg(3)) ? NULL
                                             : AtStr(Arg(3)) ) ) ) {
                      if ( IsVar(Arg(1)) ) {
                         UnifyArg(1,StrAt(objp)) ;
                      }
                      if ( IsVar(Arg(2)) ) {
                         UnifyArg(2,StrAt(attrp)) ;
                      }
                      if ( IsVar(Arg(3)) ) {
                         UnifyArg(3,StrAt(wertp)) ;
                      }
                      DETACH(1, redo1) ;
                    }
                    EPILOG :
                      db_close(state->db) ;
               END

               Cboot( )
                    { Cpred("attribut",3,attribut,sizeof(ATTSTATE)) ; }
```

Fig. 10.7   The C-predicate attribut(Object,AttrName,AttrValue)

behind *DETACH*, but instead is declared just after the introductory
COROUTINE macro.

This is a consequence of the technique used to implement coroutines
in C. In C, as in most other programming languages, procedures have only
a single entry point, i.e. at the top, or beginning. Thus, the desired point of
continuation, just behind *DETACH*, must be reached via an explicit jump,
located immediately at the standard point of entry. Actually, *RESUME* gets
expanded to a *case* statement, implicitly specifying the necessary branching.
In the case of several possible *DETACH*s, the correct respective continua-

tion address is encoded in the identification of the *DETACH*, here "1", which gets saved as part of the predicate state, and the associated jump marker set by it when evaluated, here *redo1*. From the point of view of the procedure's *dynamics*, i.e. its behavior, it is as if *RESUME* were indeed physically located immediately behind its respective *DETACH* point.

Since our predicate has an *EPILOG*, which closes the databank before the predicate exits via its *FAIL* port, this fact is declared following the *RESUME* macro (recall that *EPILOG*s are optional). This declaration is necessary, as the case structure must also provide a branch for the *EPILOG*, e.g. the clean up, or whatever other action might be involved.

Looking at the body of the function, the first thing to be seen is the initialization. As might be expected, it is merely the opening of the databank for reading, using *db_open*. If this cannot be done, the error-handling mechanism of the system is called. In our system, this is simply a general *exception handling*, which is realized here as the macro *EXCEPTION*. It normally aborts program execution, but the Prolog programmer can suppress termination by trapping the exception error, with the predicate *exception*. We shall not discuss this aspect any further, since as already mentioned, this feature is not terribly common in this form. Check your Prolog handbook if you are interested in pursuing this possibility.

After the initialization (Fig. 10.7), control flows immediately into the *while* loop. The looping criterion is the *getattr* call itself, which returns *FALSE* if it cannot find any more records fitting the search expression. It is interesting to see how values are bound to its arguments. The first argument is simply a reference to the databank via the pointer value returned by the *db_open* call in the initialization section, i.e. *state->db*. The arguments two, three and four must be either *NULL*, if the corresponding argument to the predicate *attribut* is uninstantiated, or it must reference the Prolog atom, to which the respective argument has been instantiated, as a C-character string.

For each such case, a conditional expression, employing macros provided by the implementor of the Prolog system in the library *"cpred.h"*, has been used.

Arg(n)	references the *n*th argument of the Prolog predicate.
IsVar(Arg(n))	checks if the given argument is an uninstantiated variable.
AtStr(Arg(n))	converts the Prolog atom passed in via argument *n* into a character string.

If *getattr* finds a record satisfying the query, the field contents can be referenced via the global pointer variables *objp, attrp* and *valuep*. Now we only have to unify the uninstantiated predicate arguments, accordingly, with these values. In addition to the above macros, we have, for this purpose, the following at our disposal:

StrAts(s)   converts the C-character string addressed by *s* into a Prolog atom.

UnifyArg(n, Term)   instantiates the *n*th argument of the current predicate with *Term*.

Once the unification has been made one can then *DETACH*, i.e. safely exit the predicate to call another or itself.

As you see, with a little support from the Prolog system you can easily define your own Prolog built-ins in C — more easily, at least, than is often the case between two conventional programming languages. This is, of course, partly due to various characteristics of C, which are often missing from other high-level languages:

- It supports recursion in the same way as Prolog.

- It has a powerful preprocessor, providing a simple *#include* mechanism and extensive macro expansion facilities.

- It supports a variety of data *types*; moreover, it allows programmable extensions to the standard types via the comfortable *typedef* statement.

Needless to say, if the underlying language for your Prolog system does not exhibit similar characteristics, then you should not be surprised if writing semantic functions is more difficult. On the other hand, you will no doubt find that most computers which run Prolog will also offer the C language.

It should be understood that once you have compiled your newly written predicates into object modules, they must then be *built into* your Prolog system. This is done with your linkage editor, which links the object modules into the existing Prolog system, i.e. produces a new Prolog interpreter in the form of an executable object. If you wish to have the supplemental predicates be a permanent part of your system, then you can replace, i.e. overwrite the old version with the newly generated one. If that is not the case, then merely give the new system a new name, e.g. *extprolog*, or, under Unix, you could store the new version in one of the directories in your private command search path, *$PATH*, which comes before the one in which the standard Prolog version is stored.

In closing this chapter we now show a brief dialog in which the *attribut* predicate is employed to query our restaurateur's databank:

```
?– attribut('Thanksgiving',dessert,'fortune cookie').

no
?– attribut(Menu,'main course',MC).
```

```
Menu = 'Italian'
MC = 'chicken cacciatore' ;

Menu = 'Greek'
MC = calamares ;

Menu = 'Thanksgiving'
MC = turkey ;

Menu = 'Chinese'
MC = 'lobster cantonese' ;

Menu = 'American'
MC = 'southern fried chicken' ;

Menu = 'American'
MC = 'prime rib' ;

no
?– attribut(Menu,Course,spinach).

Menu = 'Italian'
Course = 'side order' ;

Menu = 'American'
Course = 'side order' ;

no
?–
```

We hope we have stimulated your appetite sufficiently! The Unix file with which the databank was simulated can be found in Appendix A.

11 PROGRAMMING TECHNIQUES

Prolog, like every other programming language, has its 'idioms', i.e. common ways of formulating things or methods which every experienced user of the language has at her command. We have tried to introduce as many of these as possible, in the previous chapters, calling your attention to those which we have found to be particularly useful. To be sure that we leave you with an adequate supply of such idioms for your daily practice, we shall discuss a few more typical ones in this chapter. In particular, we should like to show you how to deal with *sets of objects*, which, as you have already seen, are represented by *lists* in Prolog. A common problem, in this context, is how to designate an object whose (unique) name is not known to you? For instance, the 'end of a text' or a 'special character'? At the end of this chapter, we shall show you a general solution to this problem. It is a Prolog idiom for which you are not likely to find a counterpart in any other language — the *Skolem function*.

11.1 Lists in Lisp and Prolog

We have already mentioned the major competitor of Prolog in the area of non-numerical data processing several times: *Lisp*. Its name is derived from '*Lis*t processing'. As the name implies, the basic data structure in Lisp is the *list*. All other structures used in Lisp are derived from it and represented internally ultimately as lists.

Lisp is a much older programming language than Prolog. Indeed, along with Fortran, it is the oldest higher-order programming language still in use: it was developed by McCarthy at MIT and implemented by his co-workers in the late 1950s.

Consequently, Lisp is the mother tongue of most computer scientists who have been working in the field of non-numerical data processing for many years now. For almost an entire generation this has been the language spoken and the one in whose categories much conceptual work has been grounded. On the other hand, it is likely that this book is your first real contact with Prolog. Keep that in mind when you read certain comments being made about the 'upstart in town'.

●   For instance, that Prolog is a dialect of Lisp and is best implemented on Lisp systems. Precisely the opposite happens to be true. The underlying data model for Prolog is the *structure*, i.e. *logical functions*. Lists, however, are not primitive structures. Since Prolog, from the point of view of Lisp, has the 'top' and the 'bottom' in precisely the opposite places, any implementation of Prolog based on Lisp is inevitably inefficient.

●   Programmers convinced that Prolog is a dialect of Lisp, and that lists are therefore the data structure to be used universally, tend to write 'Lisp programs' in Prolog. That is to say, they construct complex data structures out of lists. Indeed, they often merely translate their Lisp programs into Prolog by making some minor syntactic modifications therein. This is harmless, as long as they do not then publish their results as examples of Prolog programs or, even worse, run *benchmarks* against the original Lisp programs. It should be clear that Prolog programs of such origin will invariably be less efficient than their carefully programmed Lisp predecessors.

Thus, you should be a little suspicious of Prolog programs in which lists have been excessively, if not exclusively, used. Ask yourself, in each instance, if it would not be possible to employ a structure instead. If so, and that is usually the case, when the number of arguments in the list does not vary, then you should consider whether it would not be better to rewrite the list as a structure. This is, as a rule, a more efficient form, because you can *directly* access each argument of a structure with the predicate *arg(Nth, Struct, ArgValue)*, which is not true of elements of a list.

11.2   Using Lists to Process Sets

Nonetheless, *list processing* and the associated predicates and techniques for it do play an important role in Prolog. Their primary function is the representation and manipulation of ordered and unordered *sets* of objects, as well as *character strings*. The latter, as we have already discussed, are nothing more than ordered sets of the ASCII equivalents of the corresponding characters.

The *findall* predicate of Section 7.7 and Fig. 7.6 is representative of the philosophy: it generates, in the form of a list, the *set* of all objects satisfying a particular predicate.

We shall present a number of other useful predicates for manipulating sets represented by lists below.

It should be noted that we define *set* such that the same element may occur more than once: *character strings*, representing text, are a trivial example. Indeed, in the literature a distinction is often made between *sets*, where an element may occur only once, and *bags*, where this restriction (as in *our* definition) does not hold. In this more narrow sense, *findall* does not return a *set*, but rather a *bag*. If we wish to enforce the uniqueness condition, then we would have to further process the resulting *bag* with a predicate like *uniq(Set, Bag)*:

```
uniq([ ],[ ]).
uniq(Set,[X|Bag]) :-
        uniq(RestSet,Bag),
        (       member(X,RestSet),
                Set = RestSet, !
        ;       Set = [X|RestSet]
        ).
```

An important attribute of a set is its *cardinality*, i.e. the number, C, of elements in it. Since a string is treated as a list, the cardinality is useful for determining the *length* of an atom. Figure 11.1 illustrates the predicate *card(S, C)* for calculating the cardinality C of a list representing a set S, as well as *length(Atom, L)*, which determines the length of the atom's name.

```
card([ ],0).
card([X|Rest],C) :-
        card(Rest,C1), C is C1+1.

length(Atom,L) :-
        name(Atom,Name),card(Name,L).
```

Fig. 11.1   The predicates card and length

One often wants to process all the elements of a set with a given predicate. For this purpose we have two predicates borrowed from Lisp: *applist(P, List)* applies the predicate *P* to all the elements of the given List and *maplist(P, OldList, NewList)* applies the predicate *P* to all the elements of *OldList* to produce *NewList*. This is illustrated in Fig. 11.2. In Fig. 11.3 you can then see how we used all these predicates to produce a telephone list from the personal database we introduced in the very first chapter of this book (see Fig. 1.1).

The predicate *phonelist* uses *findall* to produce the list *L1*, made up of elements containing the *Name, Town* and *Telephone* for each *person* in the database. Since the *AreaCode* is missing from the entries, we have written a predicate *add_areacode* using the *maplist* predicate. Once the list is ready, we want to give the information to the display a line at a time. To do this, we apply the predicate *printline* to each entry in the list, using *applist*.

The predicate *printline* employs the predicate *length(Atom,L)* to calculate the number of blanks needed to pad the respective *Name* and *Town* information in each output line, so that we get orderly columns displayed. Admittedly, we assumed that both *Name* and *Town* are each less than 20 characters long. Perhaps you should consider how one could do away with this restrictive and rather arbitrary assumption.

One possibility employs *applist* again: applying a predicate, which leaves two facts in the internal database indicating the longest *name* and *town*, i.e. *maxl(name,X)* and *maxl(town,Y)*, to all the entries.

```
applist(_,[]).
applist(P,[X|Rest]) :-
        CallPred =.. [P,X],
        CallPred,
        applist(P,Rest).

maplist(_,[],[]).
maplist(P,[X|Rest],[Y|NewRest]) :-
        CallPred =.. [P,X,Y],
        CallPred,
        maplist(P,Rest,NewRest).
```

Fig. 11.2   *The procedures* **applist** *and* **maplist** *for applying a predicate* **P** *to all the elements of a set*

```
phonelist :-
        findall([Name,Town,Telephone],
                person(_,Name,Town,Telephone),
                L1),
        maplist(add_areacode,L1,L2),
        applist(printline,L2), nl, nl.

add_areacode([Name,Town,Telephone],
        [Name,Town,AreaCode,Telephone]) :-
        areacode(Town,Areacode).

printline([Name,Town,AreaCode,Telephone]) :-
        nl, write(Name), length(Name,LN),
        Pad1 is 20-LN, tab(Pad1),
        write(Town), length(Town,LO),
        Pad2 is 20-LO, tab(Pad2),
        write(AreaCode), write('/'), write(Telephone).
```

Fig. 11.3   *Producing a telephone list from a personal database (see Fig. 1.1)*

11.3 Sorting

There is one slight problem with the output produced by our procedure *phonelist* (see Fig. 11.3): it is not sorted, unless the *person* entries in your database happened to have been made in some particular order. But assuming that that is not the case, we must learn how to sort lists.

A *sort* predicate is, in theory, quite simple in Prolog. We only have to translate a definition of what we mean by sorted into Prolog, e.g.:

A sorted list is *the* permutation of a given list in which no element is smaller (less than) than the element preceding it.

Figure 11.4 shows the formal specification of such a sorted list in Prolog.

```
:- op(700,xfx,less_than).

:- [less_than, perm].

slowsort(Unsorted, Sorted) :-
        perm(Unsorted, Sorted),
        is_sorted(Sorted).

is_sorted([]).
is_sorted([_]).
is_sorted([A,B|Rest]) :-
        not ( B less_than A ),
        is_sorted(B|Rest).
```

Fig. 11.4   The sort predicate slowsort

The predicate central to this specification is *perm(List, PermutedList)*, illustrated in Fig. 11.5. It exploits backtracking to produce all the possible permutations of the list passed in. You often find this predicate as a built-in of the Prolog system, but we wish to show it to you anyway, as it is a perfect example of Prolog programming; indeed, probably the shortest and most elegant permutation generator in any language. You should be sure to take the time to carefully analyze it. And if you have trouble understanding the basic idea, you should watch it in action, using the debugger.

In addition, our *slowsort* predicate also uses an operator *less_than* in the sub-goal *is_sorted*. This operator must, naturally, be defined according to the particular sort criterion being employed, i.e. exactly what *kind* of order is sought (alphabetic, numerical, etc.). We shall look at this operator more closely later.

For the time being, we can ignore it, since, without even executing *slowsort* you might notice that it is not particularly efficient for practical use. We presented you the above *slowsort* only to keep a promise made earlier: to show you a Prolog procedure illustrating the fact that unfortunately, even in Prolog, one cannot always merely specify the *What* of a problem, and leave the *How* to the interpreter. This does not mean *slowsort* will not work – it does, but only *very slowly*.

```
perm([],[]).
perm(List,[Element1|RestPerm]) :-
        delete(Element1,List,Rest),
        perm(Rest,RestPerm).

delete(X,[X|Rest],Rest) :- !.
delete(X,[Y|Rest],[Y|Rest1]) :-
        delete(X,Rest,Rest1).
```

Fig. 11.5   The list-permuting predicate perm

Before we show you how the sort predicate can be made more efficient, let us take a brief look at the comparison operator *less_than*. Since it defines the order to be imposed on the elements in accordance with the problem at hand, you would typically write this yourself, corresponding to the given requirements. If you wish to spare yourself the trouble, you could, of course, often define it using the built-in Prolog predicate *compare(Op, Term1, Term2)*. It merely compares *Term1* with *Term2* and then instantiates its first argument, *Op*, with either '<', '=' or '>', depending on how the two terms relate, according to Prolog's internal ordering criterion.

If *Op* is already instantiated when the predicate is activated, then *compare* simply tests if the relation applies with respect to the two terms in

```
quicksort(Unsorted,Sorted) :-
        quicksort(Unsorted,Sorted,[ ]).

quicksort([],AuxiliaryList,AuxiliaryList).
quicksort([Element|Rest],Sorted,AuxiliaryList) :-
        split_up(Element,Rest,ListA,ListB),
        quicksort(ListB,ListC,AuxiliaryList),
        quicksort(ListA,Sorted,[Element|ListC]).

split_up(_,[],[],[]) :- !.
split_up(Element,[Head|Rest],[Head|RestA],RestB) :-
        Head less_than Element, !,
        split_up(Element,Rest,RestA,RestB).
split_up(Element,[Head|Rest],RestA,[Head|RestB]) :-
        split_up(Element,Rest,RestA,RestB).
```

Fig. 11.6   Quicksort

the second and third arguments. Thus, using *compare* we could define the operator *less_than* as

```
:- op(700,xfx,less_than).
```

```
X less_than Y :- compare(<,X,Y).
```

Let us now look at a faster version of the sort predicate. Figure 11.6 illustrates the perhaps most elegant and in most, if not all cases, most efficient procedure for *sorting a list*. It is an implementation of C. A. R. Hoare's *Quicksort*. It is based on the repeated breaking down of the list to be sorted into two sub-lists, one containing all the elements 'less' than a particular one and the other containing all those 'greater than or equal to' it. It is *recursive* by definition, and thus very simple and compact in Prolog.

To best understand exactly how *quicksort* works, you should observe it in action using the debugger.

11.4 Variables as the Primitive Units of Data Structures

One of the most important predicates for processing *sets*, which are represented by *lists*, is the built-in *member*. Up to now we have always employed it either to *test* if a particular element (value) is present in a given set (list) or to extract the individual elements of a list, one after the other, as in

```
member(X,[a,b,c,d,e]).
```

It can, however, also be used to *generate lists*, i.e. *sets*. This somewhat surprising application is achieved in the following manner: we instantiate the second argument to *member* as a list, whose *last* element is a variable, preferably an *anonymous* one, since we are not going to reference it directly. In the simplest case, we start with a list consisting of *two* variable elements:

```
build_list(List) :-
        List = [_|_],
        next_element_in( List ).
```

```
next_element_in( List ) :-
        create(X),
        (       end_marker(X)
        ;       member(X,List),
                next_element_in( List )
        ).
```

next_element_in(List) is a recursive procedure, which uses *create(X)* to somehow spawn successive elements of a list, e.g. by reading words from a file, until an *end_marker* is encountered. Each element is gathered into the *set* represented by *List*, whereby elements which already exist in the set are automatically ignored, i.e. a *set, not a bag* is the result.

The reason for this can be found in definition of the predicate *member*:

```
member(X,[X|_]).
member(X,[_|Rest]) :- member(X,Rest).
```

If the current value of the argument X is already in the list, then the first *member* clause will terminate the recursion, returning *true*, i.e. it will have served its test function. If the value of X does not occur, then at the *end of the list* the *second version of member* activates the *first* and it ends up instantiating *Rest* with the value in X followed by the (anonymous) closing element. X is now (temporarily) the last entry in the list.

The initialization of this 'growing' list occurs when the *first* variable in the 'result' list gets instantiated with the value passed into *member* (see first clause) via X, when it gets called the very first time.

Let us illustrate the use of this 'trick' in a practical example. It is a simple system for *incremental data capture* employing the *retell* and *retold* predicates of Section 10.4.

The unary predicate *register* in Fig. 11.7 assumes that data records are being received from a terminal (or perhaps a laboratory measuring instrument; it really is essentially all the same). Each record is terminated by a *newline*. The first 'word' of a record identifies or labels the data that follows, also in word units, while at the same time it represents the name of the file into which the data should be stored. Entering a '*q*' as the first word of a record indicates that data capture is to be ended at this point.

The recursive procedure *lines* implements the data capture process, using our old predicate *words_in_line*. First, however, *output* is called, which in turn opens the file named by the first word of the current record. The *Rest*, i.e. the actual data to be recorded, is then written to the now (re)opened file. The individual words thus saved are separated from one another by blanks.

Before it begins reading any data, *register* initially instantiates *FileList* with a list [_|_] consisting of two elements which are anonymous variables. Thereafter *output(FileList)* uses *member(File,FileList)* in its 'generating' capacity, as described above, to collect the file identifiers occurring in each record into the *FileList*. As we have already seen, *member* ensures that each file name occurs only once. *FileList* thus serves as a protocol of all the files updated, and can subsequently be used to control output or for further preparation and evaluation of the data captured.

In a like fashion, you can have a variety of different data structures 'emerge' from variables. Clocksin and Mellish's standard text (see Bibliography) presents an example for producing *trees* from variables; the predicate *lookup* is worth taking a look at, although it is, oddly enough, not even listed in the index!

```
:- [-retell, -words_in_line].

register(FileList) :-
        FileList = [_|_],
        lines(FileList).

lines(FileList) :-
        read_line([Word1|Rest]),
        (       Word1 = q
        ;       output(Word1,Rest,FileList),
                lines(FileList)
        ).

read_line(Line) :-
        words_in_line(WordList),
        (       WordList = [],
                /* skip empty lines : */
                read_line(Line)
        ;       Line = WordList
        ).

output(File,WordList,FileList) :-
        retell(File),
        print_lines(WordList),
        retold,
        member(File,FileList).

print_lines([]) :-
        nl.
print_lines([Word|Rest]) :-
        write(Word),
        put(32),
        print_lines(Rest).
```

Fig. 11.7   A program for incremental data capture

11.5   The Problem with the Built-in Predicate *not*

In our discussion of the built-in predicate *not*, in Section 5.8, we mentioned that it must be used with caution. The problem with *not* is that it appears, on the surface, to simply implement the negation of a logical statement. Yet experienced Prolog programmers know that, in practice, this is not always the case, i.e. that a 'logical discontinuity' arises when *not* is involved in back-tracking.

In more mundane terms, Prolog *forgets* what exactly was 'not' the case, once it has applied the predicate. This can lead to rather unpleasant errors, as we shall show you shortly. Before we do, however, let us take the following rule to heart: wherever possible, couch your statements in 'positive' terms; not out of optimism, but rather as a matter of caution.

Now to our example. Let us assume that you have a business in which you employ a large number of representatives. Naturally, it is preferable that a given customer always be taken care of by the same representative. This is indeed usually the case, but due to errors, changes of address and other events it sometimes happens that a client is assigned *two* different representatives. So you decide to write a little program, which checks your list of customers against your list of representatives. You run this occasionally to make sure things are all right; if you have a Unix system, perhaps once a month at midnight, with the help of the *at*-command.

Just how you fetch your customer list from your database and how you frame your program so that via backtracking each customer list is compared with the others for duplicates will not be dealt with here. But it should not cause you any difficulty at this point anyway.

We prefer to focus our interest on the comparison of any two arbitrary customer lists. The solution is really quite elegant:

```
different(CList1,CList2) :-
        not ( member(C,CList1),
            member(C,CList2)
            ).
```

The predicate *different* is successful only if the two customer lists *CList1* and *CList2* have no customers in common. This is a typical case of *declarative* or *non-procedural programming*: the *what* and not the *how* is specified. In conventional programming, we would have to define the *algorithm* for attaining our objective. In our Prolog solution, we leave it up to the interpreter to organize a reasonable approach for searching for a given element *C*.[1]

But elegance has its price! Perhaps you not only wish to know *that* a customer is registered in the lists of two different representatives, but also want to know *who* that customer is! Many an unsuspecting programmer might then decide to implement this in the following manner:

```
different(CList1,CList2) :-
        (       not ( member(C,CList1),
        (               member(C,Clist2)
        ), !
        ;       write('Customer '),
                write(C),        % won't work !!!
                write(' in two lists\n')
        ).
```

---

[1] If the mechanics interest you: the first goal *member* unifies *C* with the next element in *CList1* every time backtracking occurs. And the second *member* goal initiates the backtracking every time it cannot find the value unified with *C* in its respective list. When the first *member* has exhausted its *CList1*, i.e. no more alternative members, then it fails. This implies all *C* in *Clist1* differ from those in *CList2*. And the failure is negated by *not*, thus yielding a *true* for the predicate *different*!

Unfortunately, this does not do what she expects! This is because the variable *C* has been *uninstantiated* by the time you go to print out her name with *write(C)*. If you think about it for a moment, you should discover why. As soon as the second *member* clause determines that the customer *C* also occurs in the second rep's *CList2*, the parenthesized, compound clause returns *true*, which is then evaluated by *not*, yielding false, i.e. *fail*, and before backtracking to the alternative section of the predicate, following the ';', *C* gets uninstantiated. Thus, in order to backtrack, the clause must forget what it was that initiated the backtracking in the first place!

Due to this inexorable series of events associated with the backtracking mechanism, it is difficult to ascertain which true fact or circumstance caused a *not* to *fail*. This rather unsavory feature will probably be the source of program bugs even after you have been using Prolog for quite a long time! But do not despair, as you will recognize the symptoms more and more quickly and, as we shall see, there are some simple remedies.

The best one, as already emphasized earlier, is to specify the predicate in 'positive' terms, e.g.:

```
common_customer(Clist1,Clist2) :-
        member(C,CList1), member(C,Clist2),
        write('Customer '), write(C),
        write(' in two lists\n').
```

common_customer will *fail*, if there are no customers common to both representatives' customer lists. On the other hand, if a customer is found in both, then *C* contains her name after successfully exiting the second *member* goal, and you can then proceed to print it out. By negating the call to *common_customer*, by placing a *not* in front of it, you then get a complete list of the duplicates.

If you would like to try your hand at converting a negative specification into a positive one, we have suggest your solving the following problem.[2]

Ms. Moneybags is fed up with the problems she has had with her safe. For the fifth time now, she has forgotten the combination, and each time she has had to have the safe cut open — a process both dirty and costly!

Now she has invented a locking mechanism using nine switches, each of which can assume one of two possible positions. Only one particular combination of switch settings for all nine switches will allow the safe to be opened. Since she has a terrible memory for such things, she has written the proper combination of switch settings, in a somewhat cryptic form, onto a piece of paper which is taped to the door of the safe! We quote:

[2] This is a modified version of a problem found in the book *Logeleien fuer Kenner* by Zweistein, published by Hoffman and Campe, Hamburg, West Germany (1980).

'Switches 6, 7 and 9 may not all be set keke. Only when 8 or 2 are not keke is 3 set baba. Switches 4 and 1 may not be set baba at the same time. If 8 is baba, then 9 is keke. If neither 6 is keke nor 2 is baba then switch 5 must be set baba. And when 2 is baba, then 1 is baba and 7 keke. If at least one of the switches 4 or 9 is set keke, then 3 must be set to baba. Switches 2 and 5 cannot both be set to baba. The same is true of switches 3 and 5. Switches 3 and 8 may not have the same setting. If switches 1, 7 and 9 must all be set to the same position, then this implies that keke means down and baba means up. Otherwise they have the opposite meaning.'

Ms. Moneybags now has no more problems opening her safe. At the same time, she is certain that a thief would have great difficulty decoding her instructions.

How must she set all the switches in order to open the safe?

If it were not for the problem discussed above, with respect to the built-in *not*, then you could practically write a solution by translating the conditions into Prolog. And yet, even given the limitations of *not*, the solution is not so difficult, albeit somewhat more troublesome. If you should have trouble finding a solution, however, we have provided one in Appendix C.

11.6   Selector Predicates

Another important technique for solving certain problems in Prolog involves the use of so-called *selector predicates* to reduce the number of objects building a set of possible choices.

To illustrate the method, let us assume we have a list of employees

```
Employees = [Emp|OtherEmps]
```

from which those are to be selected which are candidates eligible for a transfer to some other city. One of the criteria might be that the partner of a married employee must not have employment, since this would either force the family members to be separated or, if the partner quits his/her job, there are likely to be additional problems related to finding suitable work for that person at the new location.

In this case, we define the predicate *ineligible* as follows:

```
ineligible(Emp) :-
        (         is_married(Emp,Partner)
        ;         is_married(Partner,Emp)
        ),
        employer(Partner,_).
```

Naturally, one could extend this definition of ineligibility by any arbitrary number of additional criteria, i.e. rules.

We then use our new predicate to reduce (we hope) the number of employees eligible for consideration, i.e. to shorten the list:

```
transferable([Emp|OtherEmps],EligEmp) :-
        ineligible(Emp), !,
        transferable(OtherEmps,EligEmp).
transferable([],[]).
```

11.7 Skolem Functions

Perhaps you still recall the convention observed in identifying special characters in the predicates for word-oriented read functions (end of Chapter 9). We had the problem that we had to specify their names in a somewhat roundabout way, since we could not merely use some arbitrary identifier, such as 'comma' or 'eof', because these might occur as a *word* in the text being read.

As we mentioned at the time, the technique of referencing an object not by its name but rather via a function is of both great theoretical and practical importance in Prolog. In our sample program we used a *logical function char(X)* to give the members of a specific class of objects — the special characters — unique names.

This method of naming things is referred to in logic as a *Skolem function*. In principle, it is something which we do, unwittingly, all the time. When we don't know Mary's name, or perhaps it is ambiguous to speak of Mary because we know so many of them, then we often refer to the respective person as Mrs. Smith or my daughter or the librarian, i.e. by naming a *function* which uniquely characterizes and thereby identifies the corresponding object.

In this sense, we could describe *char(white)*, as used in the example from Chapter 9, as being the 'word for the character, which produces blanks on the paper or screen'.

To see just how fundamental this method really is, you need only think back to the very first chapter. From the very start we presented logical functions, which could be used as arguments to predicates. At the time we could not go into detail as to the purpose and useful application of this, as we lacked certain basic knowledge. Let us now make up for that omission.

Generally speaking, a logical function usually represents a value, which itself is dependent on one or more other values. Thus, the value set of the function

```
husband_of(Wife)
```

covers the names of all married men, when its argument *Wife* assumes the respective names of all married women.

The advantage of such logical functions is that they reduce the number of variables in a predicate by exploiting semantic dependencies. For example, in the predicate

is_married(Woman,Man)

we can eliminate the variable *Man* by introducing the function *husband_of*:–

is_married(Woman,husband_of(Woman))

or, to do justice to women's rights, we could also eliminate the *Woman*:

is_married(wife_of(Man),Man)

The practical result is a lesser number of 'genuine' variables to be managed in the problem, i.e. program. In the case of word-oriented read predicates, we were able to use the Skolem function *char(C)* to reduce the set of all possible special characters to a single variable C, whose value set covered the ASCII equivalent of all the special characters plus the atoms *white* and *end*. Programs using this feature are generally more readable and maintainable.

From the point of view of logic, the use of functions replaces the *existential quantifier*. Perhaps you noticed that the clauses used in Prolog are (implicitly) always *universal statements*. All variables X in the predicates we defined are universally valid, i.e. the statement specified by the predicate is true for all the possible values of X. This means that statements like

for every wife *Woman* there exists a husband *Man*

for every character C, which is not permitted in a word, there is a *special character* named

are not readily formulated as clauses. This leads to the problem whereby

is_married(Woman,Man)

could be interpreted as meaning *every* woman is married to every man.

The logical functions *husband_of* and *wife_of* enable you to make *existential statements* in an indirect fashion: for every existential quantifier in the logical specification of our problem, we define a Skolem function, e.g. *husband_of(Woman)* or *char(C)*, which explicitly names the object postulated by the existential statement, via the universally quantifying variable — *Woman* and C in our example.

This method may seem somewhat unorthodox in its indirectness, but it is an invaluable trick. Indeed, there is no other way to formulate the *existence* of a specific object or circumstance in Prolog (or any other logic-oriented language based on a predicate calculus)!

Thus, the ability to use Skolem functions is fundamental to practical Prolog programming skills. It often makes the difference between a clear and simple problem specification and a complex, programmer's nightmare!

11.8 Equivalence and Demodulation

Skolem functions for naming objects are especially common in logic problems and in *artificial intelligence* applications; therefore one should understand their definition — for purposes of specifying the problem — and be practised in their use — to solve the specified problem! The latter consists primarily of learning how to *substitute* atoms or other Skolem functions for *Skolem functions* occurring in clauses.

In the previous section, we said Skolem functions are often used to uniquely reference an object via its role or function, when we cannot yet know its name, e.g. *wife_of*(X) to refer to the wife of whomever X may be.

Frequently, a partial solution to a problem lies in finding out just what the real name of the object referred to by the Skolem function is, e.g. that the *wife_of*(*John*) is actually called *anna*. Or, similarly, that two Skolem functions are equivalent, e.g. *father_of*(*mother_of*(X)) and *grandfather_ of*(X).[3] In such cases, we would presumably want to replace the Skolem function with the simpler representation, i.e. the equivalent atom(s) or less deeply nested structures.

We shall now examine a generalized predicate

   replace(*What,With,In,Simplified*)

which conveniently does this for us (see Fig. 11.8).

```
replace(What,With,In,Simplification,true) :-
        replace(What,With,In,Simplification),
        not In == Simplification, !.
replace(What,With,In,Simplification,fail).

replace(What,With,What,With) :- !.
replace(_,_,In,In) :-
        atomic(In), !.
replace(What,With,In,Simplification) :-
        In =.. [Functor|Args],
        replace_in_list(What,With,Args,NewArgs), !,
        Simplification =.. [Functor|NewArgs].

replace_in_list(_,_,[],[]).
replace_in_list(What,With,[X|RestX],[Y|RestY]) :-
        replace(What,With,X,Y),
        replace_in_list(What,With,RestX,RestY).
```

Fig. 11.8   *The generalized replacement predicate*

---

[3] Please excuse us for ignoring the fact here that a person normally has two grandfathers. We merely wanted to avoid ungainly functor names, like *maternal_grandfather_of*(X), or multi-arity functors, like *grandfather*(*maternal, X*), merely to save space. Naturally, in practice such constructs are both useful and necessary to simplify expressions and resolve possible ambiguity.

The four-variable arguments can be structures of arbitrary complexity. Their respective function in the context of the predicate is indicated by the variable names. An example follows illustrating its use:

```
?- replace(f(x),y,
          [f(x),f(f(x)),g(f(x),f(f(x)),y,f(x)),
          x,[f(x),f(f(x))]],
          Simpler).
```

Simpler = [y,f(y),g(y),f(y),y,y),x,[y,f(y)]]

Such a substitution predicate is usually to be found in knowledge-based systems, where it serves as the basis for the mechanism for evaluating expressions with the help of equivalence facts. The process is referred to as *demodulation*. In systems for automatic theorem proving or non-numeric mathematics a *demodulation* is often made automatically after each step in the solution process, to simplify the intermediate results, e.g. to substitute a term like $x+0$ with x.

Demodulation is guided by equivalence facts, stored in the database, which are labeled with a particular functor, perhaps *equal*. A sample set of such facts might be

```
equal(sister(mother(X)),aunt(X)).
equal(sister(father(X)),aunt(X)).
equal(brother(mother(X)),uncle(X)).
equal(brother(father(X)),uncle(X)).
equal(mother(mother(X)),grandmother(X)).
equal(mother(father(X)),grandmother(X)).
equal(father(mother(X)),grandfather(X)).
equal(father(father(X)),grandfather(X)).
equal(daughter(mother(X)),sister(X)).
equal(daughter(father(X)),sister(X)).
equal(son(mother(X)),brother(X)).
equal(son(father(X)),brother(X)).
```

Notice that in all these facts, the argument of the Skolem function is a variable. Thus, they are *universal statements* with respect to the Skolem functions which are valid for arbitrary values of X. Such an X might conceivably represent another complex structure, i.e. a further Skolem function. Thus, given the above equivalences, the following fact must be correct:

```
equal(son(mother(landlord(father(mother(george))))),
      brother(landlord(grandfather(george)))) ).
```

It also helps to illustrate the principle of demodulation and its usefulness in problem solving: whereas 'george's mother's father's landlord's mother's son' is perhaps a more precise specification of a given person, it is hardly as understandable as 'george's grandfather's landlord's brother'!

Figure 11.9 shows a demodulation procedure *demod(Expression, Simplified)*, which reduces a given *Expression* to a simpler one, using *all* applicable *equal* predicates in the database. We call your attention to the fact that, due to the interchangeability of the arguments as input and output parameters in Prolog, equivalence predicates are inherently symmetric, i.e. *equal(a,b)* implies *equal(b,a)*. If you examine our demodulator, you will notice that we suppress this symmetry, i.e. we always substitute the second argument with the first and never the other way around (although this could be easily done)! Our *equal* predicates diverge semantically from the concept of equivalence and embody implicitly our concept of *simplification of terms*: the second argument of each fact is the simplification of the more complex first argument, which it is to replace.

The demodulation predicate is probably a bit confusing at first, because it consists of two recursions nested in one another. This is because the list of substitution pairs produced by *findall* (see Fig. 7.6) must, under certain circumstances, be repeatedly reprocessed. This is the case when a substitution occurring later in the *SubstList* results in an intermediate expression containing some object which, according to a substitution instruction earlier in the list, should be further simplified. Thus, the 'workhorse' predicate *demod_list* must continually reprocess the *IntermediateResult* as the *Expression* to be simplified, until no further substitutions are possible, i.e. the *Expression* passed in and the *IntermediateResult* passed out are identical.

```
:- [replace].

demod(Expression,SimplerExpr) :-
        findall([What,With],equal(What,With),SubstList),
        demod(SubstList,Expression,SimplerExpr).

demod(SubstList,Expression,SimplerExpr) :-
        demod_list(SubstList,Expression,
                IntermediateResult),
        (       Expression == IntermediateResult, !,
                SimplerExpr = IntermediateResult
        ;       demod(SubstList,IntermediateResult,
                        SimplerExpr)
        ).

demod_list([],Expression,Expression).
demod_list([[What,With]|Rest],Expression,SimplerExpr) :-
        replace(What,With,Expression,NewExpression),
        demod_list(Rest,NewExpression,SimplerExpr).
```

Fig. 11.9 *A Procedure for demodulating an* **Expression** *using* **equal** *predicates in the database*

The check for this situation is made in the ternary predicate *demod*(*SubstList,Expression,SimplerExpr*) in Fig. 11.9. It is, incidentally, a fine example of the functional difference between the two equality operators '=' and '==', a common source of problems for novice Prolog programmers. We employ '==' to check for *exact equality*, i.e. suppressing the unification mechanism, which could generate equality by instantiating variables in either of the expressions compared to make them equal. This is precisely what the 'simple equality' operator '=' does. And when the *Expression* passed in and the *IntermediateResult* are identical (==), then we use the simple equality (=) to assign the *IntermediateResult* to *SimplerExpr*.

A typical example for the use of demodulation is in differentiating mathematical functions. You can find this in so many books about nonnumeric mathematics, artificial intelligence or textbooks on programming in Lisp or Prolog, that we feel it would be superfluous to repeat the exercise here. If differentiation is something you are confronted with in your regular programming diet, then you probably see the use for demodulation in this frame, and we prefer not to deny you the pleasure of writing the solution yourself. If, on the other hand, you have little to do with such problems, then such an example would not be particularly instructive, and you should look for something closer to home — perhaps your family tree is big enough to warrant closer scrutiny?

12   KNOWLEDGE-BASED SYSTEMS

We have presented Prolog to you as a multi-purpose programming language and not, as you may well have expected when you purchased this book, as a special language for *artificial intelligence* applications or for building *expert systems* (although our examples with the Whatsits and *demodulation* clearly fall into this category). This has been intentional on our part! Being so well suited for such applications, Prolog usually gets ignored for more general purpose use, and we wanted to demonstrate its usefulness in less esoteric areas, to reduce this prejudice. On the other hand, we do not wish to dash your hopes, so we are closing with a small example of an expert system in this final chapter. It does not deal with a vital problem, so we have been able to keep the example small. Real expert systems are typically much larger. Nonetheless, our system does introduce you to the essential components of any expert system and shows you how they can be implemented using Prolog.

12.1   Expert Systems

Perhaps the most important application involving *artificial intelligence*, or to use more conventional terminology, *knowledge-based software*, is *expert systems*. They are intended to make the knowledge and experience of experts accessible and useful to other experts and to laymen too.

This knowledge, e.g. medical knowledge, typically cannot be reduced merely to a set of algorithms, as in traditional data-processing problems, but rather consists mostly of a collection of *facts* and *rules*, according to which the expert draws logical conclusions. Since this is precisely the method applied by Prolog, it is no wonder that this language is especially suited to modeling experts, i.e. to simulate their method of working.

The major areas of application for expert systems are:

- support for tasks requiring expert knowledge, e.g. making a medical diagnosis or engineering a structure,

- the provision of expert knowledge in the context of managerial decision making or for creating 'interactive handbooks' to guide in the repair of complex technical devices,

- for instruction and training, e.g. for learning how to classify plants or how to operate a given machine, etc.

In any case, expert systems are almost always dialog-oriented systems, interacting with the user via a friendly *front end*, e.g. a menu-driven or a limited natural-language interface.

Indeed the analysis of natural language was one of the first areas of application of Prolog. The syntax notation presented in Chapter 6 makes Prolog more suitable for such efforts than most conventional programming languages. Processing natural languages is nonetheless one of the most difficult programming tasks altogether and a topic for a book in its own right, so we shall not attempt even a superficial treatment. Instead we shall use a menu-driven approach, building on our experience from Chapter 8.

This front end should not be limited to prompting the user for problem-specific *case data* and then like an oracle, presenting her, with some results. It should be able to explain to the user *why* it is requesting a given piece of information, and upon presenting its result(s), *how* it came to the conclusion(s). Thus, our little system in Chapter 6, which provided information regarding the Widgets and the Whatsits, could not even be considered a model of an expert system, because it has no *explanatory component*.

The system we shall now present eliminates this shortcoming. When presented with a menu, the user can enter a '?', instead of one of the alternatives presented for selection, to learn *why* the system wants to know what is being asked. In addition, and this is a mark of a good *explanatory component*, entering another question mark in response to the explanation triggered by the first one yields a *further* supplementary explanation and not just a repetition of the original one.

Likewise, the system provides an explanation for the result(s), i.e. conclusion(s) reached. In this case, however, we shall see a radically simplified version of what a genuine, high-performance explanatory component would provide. The user is merely shown the sequential 'path' of user inputs which led to the given result(s). A more realistic, i.e. useful, approach would involve an annotation of the rules which were applied in reaching the conclusion. This is especially necessary if the system is to be employed for instructional purposes or if decisions of potentially grave consequence are dependent on the conclusion(s), as in medical diagnoses.

Thus, we have chosen an application area for our sample system where the consequences of the advice given are likely to be less weighty. Having helped the restauranteur in Chapter 10, we feel it is only proper that we now give the guest a bit of assistance. Therefore, our expert system is designed to give advice in the art of tipping.

12.2 Expert-system Shells

Now perhaps neither you nor your clients are especially interested in this (or some other, arbitrary) problem area, and are unwilling to make the not inconsiderable investment typically required to produce an expert system. Since this reluctance is not uncommon, the idea of having a *shell*, which is 'filled' with some knowledge base, to acquire an expert system for some specific field, has become popular. The shell provides the necessary data structures and mechanisms in as general a form as possible, e.g. an interactive user front end including an explanatory component, an *inference engine* to determine the strategy employed in interrogating the user and evaluating the information acquired, and other such software components yielding to generalization, definition and implementation.

Since, as you know, the Prolog interpreter itself implements an inference engine, you are probably wondering why we should go and implement another one using Prolog, to run as a shell under Prolog? A partial answer lies in the fact that one often employs strategies for evaluating information in expert systems, which are more complex than that of the very general, but very simple *resolution mechanism* in Prolog.

Expert systems often apply the principle of *goal stacks*, which we saw in Chapter 7. For one thing, the many different possible arrangements of new goals in the stack (LIFO, FIFO, etc.) makes it especially adaptable. For example, it makes it possible to control the dialog such that it seems most natural to the user, i.e. by dealing completely with some aspect (subproblem) of the main problem before going on to another.

The main advantage of the goal stack, however, is that it provides a simple, natural way of acquiring a history of the entire question-answer process – one need only record the goals already dealt with. And this, on the other hand, is easily done using a second stack! Or, in larger expert systems, where the demands on main memory are greater to begin with, one can store this information, along with intermediate results, incrementally in a file.

Such a protocol of goals evaluated is very useful for the explanatory components. This is obvious with regard to the *how* question: the system need only process the history from the oldest to the most recent entry, fashioning it into a form meaningful to the user and displaying it for her perusal.

It can also be used to answer the 'why' questions, especially to avoid repetition of a given explanation whenever the user repeats the '?' to get more details. Presumably the user wants to know what sense the requested information makes in the context of the previous request(s). Deriving an explanation, therefore, usually involves a stepwise retracing of the goals leading up to the current state or context.

Now you already saw how easily such goal stacks are implemented in Prolog in our matchmaking example of Chapter 7. Under the circumstances, then, you may wonder why such a 'trivial' feature should be implemented as a special, separate software tool, i.e. an expert-system shell. Wouldn't a few predicate modules, e.g. menu driver, some I/O routines and some procedures to administer the goal stack do?

You are not alone in your skepticism. Not all implementors of expert systems in Prolog build a shell. Many write them directly in Prolog, using libraries of procedures developed independently of the task at hand. Most expert-system shells described in journals and books or found on the market are either programmed in Lisp or even in conventional languages like Pascal or Basic. Because these languages do not offer the necessary mechanisms built-in, as does Prolog, shells certainly make more sense in those environments, assuming that you do not wish to spend the months or years needed to implement this functionality yourself.

Be that as it may, we have embedded our tipping knowledge base in such a shell. This can serve as a sample for other expert systems you might build, even if you do not find the problem of optimal tipping particularly important.

12.3 The Task of Acquiring Knowledge

The knowledge with which the expert system shell is to be provided must be appropriately prepared. This must either be done by the *expert* herself or by a *knowledge engineer*. The latter is a professional trained in *knowledge acquisition*, i.e. the skill of extracting the necessary facts and rules from the expert in the respective field and expressing them such that they can be manipulated by the shell.

Knowledge engineers are thus themselves experts in the field of knowledge preparation. It should then be no surprise that, for building large, complex expert systems the attempt is made to automate *their* task via 'meta-expert systems': *knowledge acquisition components* are intended to permit the expert herself, e.g. an experienced medical doctor, store her knowledge directly into the knowledge base of the system, e.g. a medical diagnosis system, via a dialog interface oriented towards a 'natural (professional) language'.

We shall not be going quite so far here. Instead, we assume that the knowledge base has been described in terms of Horn clauses. This is structured such that our shell can interpret the description with no further preparation.

It is advisable to select a notation for the knowledge base which closely reflects the flow of the dialog and the evaluation of information in the planned expert system. The structure should be general enough to accommodate arbitrary problem areas, e.g. all those where the consulting activity involves first collecting case data interactively and then letting the system draw its conclusions based on the rules in the knowledge base.

Let us illustrate this with a sample dialog from our proposed tipping adviser:

?– expert.

I am the *** minishell ***.
I can give you advice on

strategies for tipping

If you do not understand my questions,
enter a "?" instead of one of the choices presented.

Do you have enough money ?

    y – yes, plenty
    n – no

Your choice : **n**

Do you have a credit card ?

    y – yes
    n – no, I cannot pay anyway

Your choice : **y**
Do you ever want to dine in this restaurant again ?

    y – yes
    n – no

Your choice : **?**

If you never want to dine here again,
you can skimp on the tip.

Your choice : **?**

If you are not sure, then answer with yes.
Otherwise, you run the risk that should you
return, you will get poor service.

Your choice : **y**

Was the service satisfactory ?

      y – yes, in general
      n – no, absolutely not

Your choice : **n**

Do you have some loose change in your pocket ?

      y – yes
      n – no

Your choice : **?**

This is an excellent opportunity to dispose of it!

Your choice : **n**

How was the quality of the food and
the atmosphere in the restaurant ?

      e – excellent
      m – rather mediocre
      t – terrible

Your choice : **m**

Why do you think you might come back sometime ?

      w – cute waiter/waitress
      r – owner is a relative/customer/friend
      o – this is the only place for miles
      d – don't really know just why

Your choice : **o**

Can you write this off as a business expense ?

      y – yes
      n – no

Your choice : **n**

Having examined the information provided
I would advise :

      Give a tip of a bit less than 10 percent.

Because you answered the question
      Do you ever want to dine in this restaurant again ?

```
with
     yes
and
     Can you write this off as a business expense ?

with
     no
and
     How was the quality of the food and
     the atmosphere in the restaurant ?

with
     rather mediocre

Would you like another consultation (y/n) ? n

yes
?-
```

The dialog should be fairly self-explanatory. The loading of Prolog and the expert system were intentionally omitted. We start with the call to *expert*. The tipping adviser responds by introducing itself and posing the first question in the form of a small menu.

In two different places we show you the use of the '?' to find out *why* some information is being requested; in one case with a repeat for more details. You see that the system provides additional information as to why it asks for the information.

Most of the questions are yes/no decisions, but some menus illustrate that, naturally, there can just as easily be an arbitrarily large number of choices.

Whenever the system has acquired enough data to give some advice, it does so, indicating which responses led it to the conclusion it reached. If you find the system's explanation somewhat unconvincing, please remember that this is just a minishell with a small knowledge base for a rather unpretentious field of expertise.

12.4 Knowledge Representation

The flow of our sample dialog is largely the result of how the knowledge in our system is represented. In Fig. 12.1, you can see an excerpt of the *knowledge base* for the art of tipping. You might note the standardization of the representation. A complete version can be found in Appendix B. Let us walk through the knowledge base to familiarize ourselves with its structure.

To begin with, we find a fact *knowledgebase*(...). On the one hand, this serves as a label for the file, and on the other, its argument is used by the shell to generate an introductory text explaining the nature of the expert system to the user.

The next step entails consulting the *minishell*, i.e. our expert system shell, which we shall discuss shortly. Naturally, we could have done the reverse, i.e. consulted the knowledge base from within the shell, but that would mean the user would have to take two steps to activate the system: first call the shell and then inform it as to which expert she wishes to consult with. Such an approach might be more sensible in broad problem areas, where many expert systems each cover a sub-field of the overall one. In the case of our small system, however, the more direct method seems more appropriate. And the user typically has little interest in whether or not a shell is being used or whether all the predicates are packed into a single unit.

If you examined our sample dialog closely, you probably noticed that our system consists basically of two activities:

- the *collection of case data*, via situation-oriented interrogation, and

- the *evaluation of case data*, wherein the system applies certain rules to determine the significance of the user's responses.

```
knowledgebase('strategies for tipping').

:– [ minishell ].

question(start, 'Do you have enough money ?').
explain(start,
        ['If you cannot pay your bill as is,',' ...']).
explain(start, 'You should not...').
option(start,y, 'yes, plenty', [return]).
option(start,n, 'no', [creditcard]).

question(return,
         'Do you ever want to dine ... restaurant again ?').
explain(return,
        ['If you never want to dine here again,',' ...']).
explain(return, ['If you are not sure, ...',' ...']).
option(return,y, 'yes', [service,quality]).
option(return,n, 'no', [service]).

%          . . . . .

question(why_return,
         'Why do you think you might come back sometime ?').
explain(why_return,
                ['...',' ...']).
```

```
explain(why_return, '...').
option(why_return,w,
        'cute waiter/waitress', []).
option(why_return,r,
        'owner is a relative/customer/friend', []).
option(why_return,o,
        'this is the only place for miles', []).

%          . . . . .

assessment('Do not leave a tip, but ...') :-
        if(creditcard, n).

%          . . . . .

assessment('Give a tip of a bit less than 10 percent.') :-
        if(service, y),
        (
                if(return, n),
                if(deductible, y),
        ;       if(return, y),
                if(quality, y),
        ).

%          . . . . .
```

Fig. 12.1   Excerpt from a knowledge base

This division of labor is evident in the organization of the knowledge base.

The description of the data-capture activity is oriented toward flow of control between the menus used. It is an extension of the menu-generation principle already encountered in Chapter 8. Each menu has an identifying name; the first menu to be shown being labeled as *start*. Each menu embodies a *question* with a set of possible responses, i.e. choices. In contrast to the earlier menu generator, however, flow of control between menus is not a function of a boolean constant *true* or *fail*, i.e. success or failure, but rather of the fourth argument in *option* — a list of further questions of interest in the given context.

This list can have an arbitrary number of elements, reflecting the new questions arising from the given response. The elements themselves are actually the 'names' of the yet to be answered questions 'under the circumstances'. These are, in our simple, non-cyclic example, always questions which have really never before been asked. In more complex systems, this unlikely, artificial restriction could be eliminated by having the system record which questions have already been asked, together with the responses given, and treating this as already known, thus avoiding unnatural and irritating repetition.

Just how this shortcoming of our minishell affects the system's behavior can be seen, if you take the knowledge base as given in appendix B, and merely answer the first few questions with 'yes'. The question about the 'deductibility' of the expense will be repeated! Try walking through the part dealing with data collection to see if you discover where the problem lies.

The modifications necessary to eliminate this unprofessional behavior on the part of the minishell are almost trivial. Perhaps you should try and make this improvement? It should be a good incentive to study the program more closely and give you a solid footing for the remaining discussion.

You may already have guessed just what our minishell will be doing with the elements of the list of follow-up questions: it places them onto the *goal stack*, which is used to control the flow of dialog in the first phase.

In contrast to our earlier menus, each question (menu) is associated here with at least one, if not more, predicate(s) of arity 2, with the functor *explain*. The first argument is always the name connecting the explanation with a given question (menu). The second argument is the explanatory text itself. Since the latter may be quite lengthy, or may even contain variables serving as placeholders for information which is acquired during the interrogation (a possibility not exploited in our example), the text may appear either as an atom or a list of the constituent elements of the explanation. Such list elements are merely displayed in the sequence in which they occur, i.e. as lines.

If the user repeatedly asks why the system is requesting given information, by entering '?' as her selection, then the minishell merely presents the explanations, one after the other, as they occur in the knowledge base. If the user exhausts the pool, then the system starts repeating its explanations, beginning at the original one for the question at hand. If you wish to deepen your understanding of the problem, you might try making some corrective modifications here as well!

The second functional part of the dialog, the evaluation of the data collected, is conducted by a series of unary predicates with the functor *assessment*. You will recognize these immediately as Prolog rules; the respective expert in the problem area being dealt with probably will not, and in an optimal arrangement for knowledge acquisition, should not, have to do so.

The argument of the predicate *assessment* is the *Recommendation* made by the system. Its body consists of binary *if* predicates, each of which consists of the name of the question involved as the first argument, and the user's response as the second. As you see, these preconditions are connected as needed by the usual *and* and *or* (i.e. comma and semicolon) logical operators. Parentheses are used here, to insure the correct order of interpretation, when defining complex circumstances.

A given rule does not have to take all the user responses into consideration with its *if* predicates. It is the area expert's job to define which (sub-)set of the answers given are relevant to a given response by the system. In a forest of facts may stand a (few) tree(s) of knowledge!

Since our minishell activates these evaluating *assessment* rules directly as goals, it applies the first one encountered which is satisfied by the existing conditions. If none can be unified with the current set of circumstances, then the expert system is forced to admit that, having examined the facts, it too is helpless!

12.5　The Minishell

Having seen a sample dialog session and the underlying knowledge base, let us now turn our attention to the expert-system shell itself. Figure 12.2 contains the core elements of the minishell. As you can see, three additional modules get consulted:

menu　　　to manage flow of control between menus, including the explanatory components,

io　　　　containing specially tailored input/output predicates, and

evaluation　which evaluates the information provided by the user.

We shall examine the individual modules in the following discussion.

As you recall, the user invokes the expert system by entering:

　　?– **expert.**

The introductory text is displayed by the output predicate *banner*, whereafter the system enters an iterative loop via the predicate *repeat*. This loop consists of the *consultation* session itself, and the inquiry as to whether or not further consultation is desired. Please note that

● 　the *repeat* is necessary only because the *consultation* ends with a cut ('!'), and

● 　the predicate *repetition* is defined such that it *fails* whenever the user requests another consultation by entering 'y' (i.e. 'yes') as her choice.

The *consultation* is itself defined as an iterative loop. First, the *initialization* purges the database of any entries which may have been left over from a previous consultation. The next step is to provide the goal stack with its first goal. This is the name of the first question to be asked in the session about

```
:- [ -menu, -io, -evaluation ].

expert :-
        banner,
        repeat,
        consultation,
        repetition.

consultation :-
        initialization,
        repeat,
        not still_goals_left,
        evaluation, ! .

repetition :-   % fail (!) if another consultation desired
        write('Would you like another consultation (y/n) ? '),
        read_char(Char),
        Char \ = y.

initialization :-
        abolish(goal, 1),
        abolish(result, 2),
        abolish(reason, 2),
        asserta(goal(start)).

still_goals_left :-
        retract(goal(RuleName)),
        rule(RuleName).

rule(X) :-
        question(X, Question),
        menu(X, Question),
        response(X, ResponseCode, FollowUpRules),
        asserta( result(X, ResponseCode) ),
        register_goal( FollowUpRules ), ! .

register_goal([]).
register_goal([RuleName|RestOfRules]) :-
        register_goal( RestOfRules ),
        asserta( goal( RuleName ) ).
```

Fig. 12.2   The expert system shell minishell

to begin: *start* by convention. Now the goal stack can begin to be processed. This is carried out in the loop consisting of the following two predicates:

```
repeat,
not still_goals_left.
```

The goal just before the cut, *evaluation*, is not effectively part of this goal-stack processing loop, because it is only activated when the goal stack contains no further goals, causing *still_goals_left* to *fail* and *not* to be *true*.

As long as *still_goals_left* finds a goal in the goal stack it passes it, i.e. the *RuleName* or name of the next question to be posed the user, to the unary predicate *rule*. The predicate *rule*, in turn, uses two predicates, *menu* and *response*, from the menu and explanatory components (to be discussed in the next section), to fetch the *ResponseCode* entered by the user. In addition, *response* returns the list of *FollowUpRules* associated with the given choice *option* in the given knowledge base, via its third argument.

The *ResponseCode*, together with the name identifying the question asked, X, are then registered in the database, for later evaluation, as the binary predicate

result(X, ResponseCode).

The list of *FollowUpRules* is added to the goal stack by *register_goal*. During the next iteration of the loop in *consultation*, they will be fetched by *still_goals_left*, one after the other, thereby continuing the dialog with the user.

Consequently, the flow of the dialog depends entirely on where the new goals are stored in the goal stack, and in what order, should there be more than one new goal in the *FollowUpRules* list. Thus, the innocent-looking predicate *register_goal* embodies a significant design decision. This decision is especially critical in large knowledge bases and complex user dialogs, as it greatly influences the degree of user acceptance of the system:

> Which *strategy for conducting the dialog* is most natural for the user? If the flow of interrogation is too disconnected and erratic, i.e. jumping unexpectedly from topic to topic, then is the user not likely to find her own train of thought unnecessarily disrupted, associations getting lost, possibly leading to more uncertainty and mistrust in the system?

Since *still_goals_left* always fetches the first goal it finds on the goal stack, the dialog strategy is left entirely up to the predicate making the entries, *register_goal*. In this minishell implementation we assumed that the *FollowUpRules* associated with the question just answered by the user have immediate priority over any goals which might still be in the stack. Furthermore, the order in which these new, supplemental goals (rules) are to be satisfied is determined by the author of the knowledge base, i.e. it is the order in which the goals occur in the *FollowUpRules* list for the respective *option* associated with the question.

Take another look at the predicate *register_goal* to be sure you see just how it implements the above strategy. Can you think of any alternative strategies? Try modifying *register_goal* to implement them, and see how the dialog is affected.

12.6   Controlling Dialog Flow and the Explanatory Components

We shall now tackle the problem of I/O control, and with it the task of conducting a dialog via the menu driver. Let us look at Fig. 12.3. We surely need not discuss the predicates *menu* and *selection*, as they correspond so closely to the menu-generator predicates we saw in Chapter 8.

The explanatory component, i.e. the predicate *why*, is activated by the

```
menu(X, Question) :-
        screen_init,
        writelines(0, Question), nl,
        selection(X).

selection(X) :-
        option(X, ResponseCode, Response, ),
        tab(8),
        write(ResponseCode),
        write(' - '),
        write(Response), nl,
        fail.

selection(_) :- nl.

choice(X, RespCode, FollowUpRules) :-
        repeat,
        ask_for_choice,
        read_char(Char),
        (    option(X, Char, _, FollowUpRules),
             RespCode = Char, !
        ;    why(X, Char, RespCode, FollowUpRules), !
        ;    % no choice with response code entered
             write('\nDid not understand your answer, '
             write('please repeat\n\n'),
             fail
        ).

why(X, ?, RespCode, FollowUpRules) :-
        explain(X, ExplanatoryText),
        nl, writelines(0, ExplanatoryText), nl,
        ask_for_choice, read_char(RespCode),
        (    RespCode \= ?, !,
             option(X, RespCode, _, FollowUpRules)
        ;    fail
        ).
```

Fig. 12.3   The menu and explanatory components

ternary predicate *choice* as required. *choice* is an iterative loop, as the use of *repeat* indicates, which is executed until the user has entered a character which corresponds to one of *options* in the knowledge base associated with the currently active menu X.

The predicates *ask_for_choice* and *read_char* do precisely what their names suggest. They are part of the I/O module, which is shown in Fig. 12.4, and should be self-explanatory. If no *option* can be found corresponding to the character entered by the user, then the *why* predicate checks to see if it is a question mark, i.e. if the user is requesting an explanation for the question asked. If that is not the case, then the input was not meaningful in the current context, and *choice* displays an error message and then back-tracks to activate *ask_for_choice* again.

The predicate *why* fetches the first explanation, i.e. *explain*, for the given question X and displays it. It then precedes to *ask_for_choice* and reads the character entered by the user in response. If it is *not a question*

```
banner :-
      knowledgebase(KB),
      writelines(0,
          ['\nI am the *** minishell ***.',
          'I can give you advice on\n',
          KB,
          '\nIf you do not understand my questions,',
          'enter a "?" instead of one of the choices presented.'],
      nl ).

screen_init :-
      nl, nl.

ask_for_choice :-
      write('Your choice : ').

writelines(Indent, [Line|RestOfLines]) :-
      tab(Indent), write(Line), nl,
      writelines(Indent, RestOfLines), !.
writelines(_, []) :- !.
writelines(Indent, [Line]) :-
      writelines(Indent, [Line]).

read_char(Char) :-
      get0(C),
      name(Char, [C]),
      skip(10),
      ! .
```

Fig. 12.4   Input/Output predicates of the minishell

mark, then it proceeds to look for a matching *option*. If it finds none, then the *cut preceding* the activation of *option* causes *why* to suppress any alternative unifications and it merely returns to *choice* with a *fail*. Then *choice* prints the error message and reinitiates a prompt to the user for another choice. If, however, the user entered *another question mark* at this juncture, then the first goal in the parentheses is skipped (and with it the cut too!), and the alternative goal *fail* causes control to flow back to the beginning of the *why* predicate, and the *next* explanatory text for question X is then fetched from the knowledge base.

Thus, the backtracking mechanism built into Prolog enables us to program an explanatory component in a compact and, once the principle is understood, straightforward fashion.

Finally, a short explanation of the binary *writelines* predicate (Fig. 12.4) is perhaps warranted. The first argument is merely the number of columns (blanks) to be indented from the left margin for each line of text to be output; 0 suppresses any indentation. The second argument is a list of atoms, each such atom constituting a physical line of output. If at call time the second argument is not a list, it is converted into one. On the other hand, if the list contains a variable, then the instantiated value at call time will appear in that line. The predicate *banner* does just that, printing the respective 'title' of the expert system consulted, which is by convention stored in the fact *knowledgebase* and passed into the list via the variable *KB*.

12.7 Evaluating the Case Data

The final module of the minishell, shown in Fig. 12.5, serves to evaluate the case data, i.e. 'give the user advice', and ultimately to explain to her *how* it reached this conclusion. The predicate *evaluation* first checks the knowledge base, using *clause*, for the existence of at least one *assessment* rule. If none is found, then the expert system must inform the user that it has no advice (which it also does when it has advice, but none appropriate under the circumstances).

Assuming one or more were found, then they are activated, via the backtracking mechanism, one after the other, in the order in which they occur in the knowledge base, until the first one satisfying all the circumstances has been found. The cut following *assessment(Recommendation)* ensures that the first satisfactory *Recommendation* also remains the only one made! The *Recommendation* is then displayed at the user's terminal by *output* followed by our simplified explanation as to *how* that conclusion was reached, prepared by the predicate *reasoning*.

Let us look closely at just how the latter explanation is produced.

Notice that although the assessment predicates are drawn from the

```
evaluation :-
        clause( assessment(Recommendation), _),
        abolish( reason, 2),      % Remove old "reasons"
        assessment( Recommendation), !,
        output( Recommendation ).
evaluation :-
        output('I have no advice for you.').

if( RuleName, ResponseCode) :-
        % if condition true, i.e. there exists
        result( RuleName, ResponseCode),
        % then record the reason
        assertz( reason(RuleName, ResponseCode) ).

output( Recommendation ) :-
        screen_init,
        writelines(0,
            ['Having examined the information provided',
             'I would advise :']),
        nl, writelines(8, Recommendation), nl,
        write('Because you answered the question'), nl,
        reasoning.

reasoning :-
        retract( reason(RuleName, ResponseCode) ),
        question(RuleName, Question),
        writelines(8, Question),
        write('with'), nl,
        option(RuleName, ResponseCode, Legend, _),
        writeline(8, Legend),
        (       clause( reason(_,_), true),
                write('and'), nl, reasoning
        ;       !, nl
        ).
```

Fig. 12.5 *Main module of* minishell: *evaluation of results*

respective task-specific knowledge base (see Fig. 12.1) 'driving' the minishell, the *if* predicate activated in the *assessment* is defined in the *evaluation* module, shown in Fig. 12.5. The *if* predicate checks the protocol of user responses, recorded by the *minishell* predicate *rule* in the form of facts with the functor *result* (see Fig. 12.2), to determine if a *result* exists where the question identified by *RuleName* was responded to with the answer *ResponseCode*.

When *if* finds such a matching fact, then it keeps a protocol of its success by storing a fact *reason(RuleName, ResponseCode)* in the database. Then, if the assessment being made is altogether successful, the protocol contains an entry for all the *reasons* leading to the *Recommendation* made. The predicate *reasoning* need only gather them all together using *retract*. For each *reason found, the RuleName* and *ResponseCode* is then used to extract the user's literal answer from the associated *option*. These texts are then displayed in the order processed.

Naturally, if an *assessment* proves to be unsuccessful, i.e. not supported by the evidence in the *result* protocol, the *reasons* possibly gathered up until it *failed* must be eliminated, so as not to appear in the *how* explanation for a *Recommendation* which was assessed valid. This is taken care of by *evaluation*, which always calls *abolish* to purge any *reasons* which might still be in the database, before attempting the *assessment* of another *Recommendation*.

FURTHER READING

We hope we have sufficiently aroused your interest in Prolog and its many uses that you might now want to explore further applications or perhaps acquire more information regarding the theoretical basis and issues behind the language. With this in mind, we include the following brief summary of a number of articles and books, which *we* found instructive.

A textbook instrumental in spreading the word about Prolog and serving as a *de facto* standard definition of the language is

> W. F. Clocksin and C. S. Mellish, *Programming in Prolog*, Springer-Verlag, Berlin–Heidelberg–New York (1981).

There are newer editions in the meantime. It is a valuable reference book and provides a good supplement to the material we have presented, particularly if you are more interested in the theory of logic programming or for AI applications relating to the analysis of text and natural languages.

The inspiration for a number of examples we used in our text was found in an excellent collection of sample Prolog programs. Unfortunately, the book is not easy to get hold of, although we can recommend the effort:

> H. Coelho, J. C. Cotta and L. M. Pereira, *How To Solve It with Prolog*, Laboratorio Nacional de Engenharia Civil, Lisbon, Portugal (1982).

The programs are based on the Clocksin–Mellish standard, so if our programs ran on your system without any difficulty then these should too.

A good introduction to the idea of *programming in logic*, and thus to an aspect of Prolog which we intentionally treated only in passing, can be found in:

> R. Kowalski, *Logic for Problem Solving*, Elsevier–North-Holland, New York (1979).

We suggest this book for those readers who want to delve more into the fundamentals of Prolog and are looking, at the same time, for a practical introduction to the theory and application of *Horn clauses*.

If you prefer a briefer introduction, then take a look at an article by the same author:

R. Kowalski, *Logic Programming, BYTE* **10** (8) 161 (August 1985).

In that same issue you will find another good article:

C. Y. Cuadrado and J. L. Cuadrado, *Prolog Goes to Work, BYTE* **10** (8) 151 (August 1985).

In addition to some nice examples, e.g. finding the path through a labyrinth, this also contains some interesting discussions about further development of the language and *dedicated Prolog machines*, as well as short reports on contemporary projects: e.g. two simulations of dataflow mechanisms for signal processing with similar functionality. One was written in Prolog, the other in Ada. The Prolog version was not only completed significantly sooner, it also ran *faster* — and that despite the fact that the Prolog version was interpreted and the Ada version compiled!

The implementation of a Prolog programming environment (written *in* Prolog, of course) is the subject of

H. J. Komorowski and Sh. Omori, 'A Model and an Implementation of a Logic Programming Environment', *Proc. ACM SIGPLAN 85 Symposium on Language Issues in Programming Environments, SIGPLAN Notices* **20**(7) (July 1985).

The use of Prolog as a specification and prototyping language for the development of programs beginning with the necessary data structures — a technique known, in the commercial data processing world, as the Jackson Method — is explained in

L. Logrippo and D. R. Skuce, 'File Structures, Program Structures, and Attributed Grammars', *IEEE Trans. on Software Eng.* **SE-9** (May 1983).

As the title indicates, the authors present the processing of a file as a syntactic check and 'translation' into the desired output. To this end, they use an *attributed grammar*, which describes the organizational structure of the file and the processing of individual syntactic elements in it. This is expressed in Prolog, so that the data structure thus specified and the associated processing can be directly executed as a program.

An informal report on Prolog applied in a commercial problem area is afforded by

J. Malpas, *Prolog as a Unix System Tool*, Unix/World, Tech Valley Publishing, Mountain View, CA, (July 1985), p. 48.

The author comes to the conclusion that the non-algorithmic approach to problem description supported by Prolog corresponds closely to the philosophy behind the Unix tools *yacc* or *awk, sed*, etc. Furthermore, Prolog programs, like any others in the Unix environment, are easily integrated into the Unix system, as *filters*. And his enthusiasm for the potential of Prolog in a Unix environment is all the more convincing when one realizes that, from the description of his experience, he was apparently working with a Prolog system which lacked the tools we mentioned: e.g., the means to communicate directly with *shell* procedures via *pipes*, or the convenient interface for integrating C procedures into a Prolog program.

A Prolog dialect which diverges considerably from the Clocksin–Mellish standard is Micro-Prolog. If you need an introduction to this implementation, we can recommend:

K. L. Clark, J. R. Ennals and F. G. McCabe, *A Micro-Prolog Primer*, Logic Programming Associates, London.

The book is also interesting insofar as it presents *Simple Prolog*, an interface, written in Prolog, for the entry of rules in an (almost) natural language. And this could just as easily be implemented with Clocksin–Mellish Prolog.

Departing slightly from our stated theme, it might be worth mentioning two books which should certainly be of use to you, should you be running Prolog under Unix. Please note that neither of these books deals explicitly with Prolog:

B. W. Kernighan and D. M. Ritchie, *The C Programming Language*, Prentice-Hall, Englewood Cliffs, N.J. (1978).

an old standard, still hard to beat, and for those who are looking for a more in depth, practical introduction to the Unix system environment and how to program in it, we highly recommend:

B. W. Kernighan and Rob Pike, *The Unix Programming Environment*, Prentice-Hall, Englewood Cliffs, N.J. (1984).

It is one of the best books we know of about program development under Unix. It distinguishes itself, in particular, by its discussions of support utilities for software engineers, e.g. *make* and the like.

For those of you who wish to tackle the task of implementing your own Prolog system, or would like to apply some of the techniques used in Prolog to your own tasks, we should mention the collection of articles:

J. A. Campbell (ed.), *Implementations of Prolog*, Ellis Horwood, Chichester (1984).

For those of you who can read German, we can recommend the following texts.

The first illustrates the applicability of Prolog as a basis for *graphical applications*. It discusses the predicates needed to make this possible:

W. Huebner and Z. I. Markov, *Eine Graphik Erweiterung fuer Prolog auf der Basis von GKS*, Springer-Verlag, Berlin Goettingen Heidelberg (1985).

Their contribution discusses how the *GKS standard* can be supported in Prolog at two levels. At the lower level, the GKS primitives are implemented directly as procedures. Since these must be integrated into the control-flow structures of Prolog, it is an advantage, if you have an interface to a language like C, of the type we discussed in Chapter 10. The second level, existing above the latter, describes the pictures as objects, *declared* in the typical Prolog fashion. This higher level of abstraction is not nearly as elegantly and maintainably implemented in conventional languages.

A collection of reports dealing with experiences in applying Prolog to build expert systems is available in the form of the proceedings of a congress held by Nixdorf, a computer manufacturer which has done a great deal of practical research and development work using Prolog:

Stuart E. Savory (ed.), *Kuenstliche Intelligenz und Experten Systeme*, Oldenbourg, Munich (1985).

Especially interesting is a description of an expert system shell, called TWAICE, which has already found its way into commercial efforts at Nixdorf.

And finally we allow ourselves to mention a book dealing with a more general introduction to the purpose, construction and issues of expert systems, from the humble pens of:

Peter Schnupp and Ute Leibrandt, *Expertensysteme*, Springer-Verlag, Berlin Goettingen Heidelberg (1985).

This book is intended for non-software engineers, although it has been written such that professionals should find it interesting and, it is hoped, enlightening.

Appendix A   SIMULATION OF A DATABANK

The following C program can be used to simulate a databank for testing the predicates presented in Chapter 10 for interfacing to a databank.

```
#include <stdio.h>

typedef FILE        DB ;

#define MAXLINE 80
#define TRUE        1
#define FALSE       0
#define objp        ap[0]
#define attrp       ap[1]
#define valuep      ap[2]

char    *ap[3],
        objbuf[MAXLINE+1],
        dbname[ ] = "databank" ;

#define db_open(dbname,mode)      fopen(dbname,mode)

#define db_close(db)              fclose(db)

getattr(db,object,attribute,value)
   DB  *db ;
   char *object, *attribute, *value ;
{
   char *cp , *p ;
   int   i ;

   objp = objbuf ;
   while ( fgets(objbuf,MAXLINE,db) ) {
      p = objbuf, i = 0 ;
      while ( *(cp = p++) ) {
         if ( *cp == '\t' ) {
```

```
                *cp = '\0' ; ap[++i] = p ;
            } else if ( *cp == '\n' ) *cp = '\0' ;
    }
    if ( ( ( ! object || ! strcmp(object,objp) ) &&
        ( ! attribute || ! strcmp(attribute,attrp) ) &&
        ( ! value || ! strcmp(value,valuep) ) )
      return TRUE ;
    }
    return FALSE ;
}
```

The following sequential file was used in Chapter 10, together with the above simulation program, to test the C predicates for accessing a database. The individual fields of a given line are separated from one another by a single tabulator character.

Take out	sandwich	tuna salad
Take out	sandwich	roast beef on rye
Take out	sandwich	turkey on white
Take out	dessert	pastries
Take out	soup	french onion
Take out	side order	french fries
Take out	side order	onion rings
Take out	side order	coleslaw
Italian soup	minestrone	
Italian soup	tortelini	
Italian	appetizer	proscuitto crudo w/ cantelope
Italian	appetizer	carpaccio
Italian	main course	chicken cacciatore
Italian	side order	spinach
Italian	dessert	tiramisu
Greek	appetizer	satziki
Greek	appetizer	gigantos
Greek	main course	calamares
Greek	dessert	baklava
Thanksgiving	main course	turkey
Thanksgiving	side order	yams
Thanksgiving	side order	corn on the cob
Thanksgiving	dessert	pumpkin pie
Thanksgiving	dessert	apple pie
Thanksgiving	appetizer	chestnuts
Chinese	soup	wan tan
Chinese	soup	hot and sour
Chinese	appetizer	egg roll
Chinese	appetizer	fried noodles
Chinese	main course	lobster cantonese
Chinese	dessert	fortune cookie

Chinese	dessert	fruit compote
Chinese	side order	fried rice
Chinese	side order	mixed vegetables fukien
American	appetizer	shrimp cocktail
American	soup	clam chowder
American	soup	cream of mushroom
American	main course	southern fried chicken
American	main course	prime rib
American	dessert	apple pie
American	dessert	hot fudge sundae
American	side order	corn on the cob
American	side order	french fries
American	salad	waldorf
American	side order	spinach
American	salad	tomato

THE KNOWLEDGE BASE FOR TIPPING IN A RESTAURANT

```
/*
        The expert system 'Tips' gives advice with
        respect to tipping in a restaurant.
*/

:- [ -minishell ].

knowledgebase('strategies for tipping').

/*
        Rule-based knowledge
        ***************************

        Every rule has a name or identifier. The rule which
        is to be applied first must be called 'start'.

        A rule contains the following information:

        question( RuleName, ListOfLines ) :

        The question to be posed in connection with the
        application of the named rule.

        explain( RuleName, ListOfLines ) :

        One or more explanations (in the order of
        increasing detail) as to why the associated
        question is being posed.

        option( RuleName, Choice, Legend, FollowUpRules) :

        Choices to be presented as possible response to
        the associated question with legend and a (possibly
        empty) list of rules to be applied in follow up
        to this question.
```

The evaluation of the user responses for the
purpose of finally giving advice is left to
the assessment rules, which are formulated as
general Horn clauses, e.g:

```
assessment( Recommendation ) :–
          if( RuleName1, Choice1),
          if( RuleName2, Choice2),
                . . .,
          (      if( RuleName4, Choice4),
          ;      if( RuleName5, Choice5),
          ),
                . . .,
          If( RuleNameN, ChoiceN).
```

The evaluation goes through the assessment rules
sequentially, i.e. in the order in which they
appear in the knowledge base, and does not, for
example, try all the rules associated with a
specific RuleName first. The first Recommendation
encountered, whose assessment rule body can be
properly unified, is the one which gets presented.

```
*/

question(start, 'Do you have enough money ?').
explain(start,
        ['If you cannot pay your bill as is,',
         'then you certainly cannot leave a tip.']).
explain(start,
        ['You should not eat out if you cannot',
         'afford it.']).
option(start, y, 'yes, plenty', [return]).
option(start, n, 'no', [creditcard]).

question(creditcard, 'Do you have a credit card ?').
explain(creditcard,
        'I hope they accept it here.').
explain(creditcard,
        ['If you do not have a credit card either',
         'then you need a lawyer not an expert system!']).
option(creditcard, y, 'yes', [return]).
option(creditcard, n, 'no, I cannot pay anyway', []).

question(return,
        'Do you ever want to dine in this restaurant again ?').
explain(return,
        ['If you never want to dine here again,',
```

```
                    'you can skimp on the tip']).
explain(return,
                    ['If you are not sure, then answer with yes.',
                    'Otherwise, you run the risk that should you',
                    'return, you will get poor service.']).
option(return, y, 'yes', [service,quality]).
option(return, n, 'no', [service]).

question(service, 'Was the service satisfactory ?').
explain(service,
                    ['Unless the service was extremely poor,',
                    'you should leave at least a small tip.']).
explain(service,
                    ['Come on now, give them the benefit of the',
                    'doubt! After all they are only human.']).
option(service, y, 'yes, in general', [change, deductible]).
option(service, n, 'no, absolutely not', [change]).

question(quality,
                    ['How was the quality of the food and',
                    'the atmosphere in the restaurant ?']).
explain(quality,
                    ['I am trying to figure out why you think',
                    'you might ever come back here.']).
explain(quality,
                    'Unsure? Then things were probably mediocre.').
option(quality, e, 'excellent', [change,deductible]).
option(quality, m,
                    'rather mediocre', [why_return, deductible]).
option(quality, t, 'terrible', [why_return, deductible]).

question(change,
                    'Do you have some loose change in your pocket ?').
explain(change,
                    'This is an excellent opportunity to dispose of it!').
explain(change,
                    ['Think about the wear and tear on your trouser',
                    'pockets. The weight is greater than you think.',
                    'Take it from an expert!']).
option(change, y, 'yes', []).
option(change, n, 'no', []).

question(deductible,
                    'Can you write this off as a business expense ?').
explain(deductible,
                    ['If the IRS ends up paying the biggest share',
                    'then give the money to the waiter/waitress!',
                    'At least s/he did something to earn it!']).
```

```
explain(deductible,
        'I want to know if the IRS is paying for most of this').
option(deductible, y, 'yes', []).
option(deductible, n, 'no', []).

question(why_return,
         'Why do you think you might come back sometime ?').
explain(why_return,
        ['I want to know if your reason for returning',
         'justifies giving a bigger tip than normal.']).
explain(why_return,
        ['Then say you do not know why, since if you',
         'are not certain then the reason cannot be',
         'terribly significant.']).
option(why_return, w, 'cute waiter/waitress', []).
option(why_return, r,
       'owner is a relative customer friend', []).
option(why_return, o, 'this is the only place for miles', []).
option(why_return, d, 'do not really know just why', []).

assessment(['Do not leave a tip, but offer',
            'your services as a dishwasher']) :-
           if(creditcard, n).

assessment(
           'A tip of about 30 percent will increase your chances'):-
           if(why_return, w).

assessment(['15 percent if all is well between you',
            '25 percent if looking for improvement.']) :-
           if(why_return, r).

assessment('Give a tip of a bit less than 15 percent.') :-
           if(service, y),
(
                if(return, n),
                if(deductible, y),
        ;       if(return, y),
                if(quality, y),
           ).

assessment('A tip of about 10 percent is adequate.') :-
           if(return, n),
           if(service, y).

assessment(['Leave your small change,',
            ' but no more than 75 cents!']) :-
           if(return, n),
           if(service, n),
           if(change, y).
```

```
assessment(['Leave no tip at all, you could',
            'use the money better elsewhere']) :-
        if(return, n).

assessment('Go ahead and give a 20 percent tip!') :-
        if(return, y).
        if(deductible, y),
        if(service, y),
        if(quality, y).

assessment('O.K. Leave about 10 percent.') :-
        if(return, y).
        if(deductible, y).
```

SOLUTION TO THE SAFECRACKER PROBLEM

The following predicate *thief* figures out the correct positions of the switches for opening Ms. Moneybags' safe based on the contraints described in the puzzle in Section 11.5. The result is returned as *SwitchesList*. The code words *baba* and *keke* from Ms. Moneybags' instructions are already converted to their proper values of *up* or *down* in *SwitchesList* via a *maplist* procedure and the binary transformation predicates *keke_up* and *keke_down*.

The *not* at the end of the predicates causes no problems (why?).

```
/*

        **********************************************
        The Thief's Logic for Opening the Safe
        **********************************************

                S1 to S9 : switch positions,
                given as "baba" and "keke".
*/

thief(SwitchesList) :–
        /* switches 6, 7 and 9 cannot all be keke              */
        (       S6 = baba
        ;       S7 = baba
        ;       S9 = baba
        ),
        /* Only if 8 or 2 is not keke, then 3 is baba :         */
        (       ( S8 = baba ; S2 = baba ), S3 = baba
        ;       S8 = keke, S2 = keke, S3 = keke
        ),
        /* 4 and 1 cannot be baba at the same time:             */
        (       S4 = keke
        ;       S1 = keke
        ),
        /* If 8 is baba, then 9 is keke                         */
        (       S8 = baba, S9 = keke
```

```
;       S8 = keke
),
/* If 6 is not keke AND 2 is not baba,                          */
/* then 5 must be baba:                                         */
(       S6 = keke, S2 = baba
;       S5 = baba
),
/* If 2 is baba then 1 is baba and 7 is keke :                  */
(       S2 = baba, S1 = baba, S7 = keke
;       S2 = keke
),
/* If either 4 or 9 (or both) is keke,                          */
/* then 3 must be baba :                                        */
(       ( S4 = keke ; S9 = keke ), S3 = baba
;       S4 = baba, S9 = baba
),
/* 2 and 5 cannot both be baba :                                */
(       S2 = keke
;       S5 = keke
),
/* The same holds for switches 3 and 5 :                        */
(       S3 = keke
;       S5 = keke
),
/* 3 and 8 are not in the same position :                       */
(       S3 = keke, S8 = baba
;       S3 = baba, S8 = keke
),
/* If 1, 7 and 9 must be placed in the same                     */
/* position, then "keke" means down and "baba"                  */
/* means up. Otherwise they have exactly the                    */
/* opposite meaning.                                            */
(       S1 == S7, S7 == S9,
        maplist(keke_down,
                [S1,S2,S3,S4,S5,S6,S7,S8,S9],
                SwitchesList)
;       not ( S1 == S7, S7 == S9 ),
        maplist(keke_up,
                [S1,S2,S3,S4,S5,S6,S7,S8,S9],
                SwitchesList)
).

maplist(_,[],[]).
maplist(F,[X|RestX],[Y|RestY]) :-
        P =.. [F,X,Y], P,
        maplist(F,RestX,RestY).

keke_down(keke,down).
```

```
keke_down(baba,up).

keke_up(keke,up).
keke_up(baba,down).
```

Appendix D SURVEY OF THE STANDARD PREDICATES

The following is a survey of the major built-in predicates which can be found in a typical Prolog system. It consists of a brief summary of each of the predicates discussed.

The information is presented in a format adapted from the conventions observed in Unix manuals. A keyword appears in the top corners of each page, e.g.

abolish/2.

The name is that of the predicate, or operator, and the number following the slash indicates its arity.

Operators with non-alphanumeric names, e.g. '=..', ';' or '!' are referenced by name, i.e. *univ, or, cut* and so on.

Occasionally we have gathered a number of operators together into a group, such as 'term comparators' or 'value comparators'. In such cases, we have written the keyword beginning with an upper-case letter, to draw your attention to the category.

The functional description is based on the IF/Prolog implementation of the language. The survey covers a *subset* of all the predicates provided in the implementation.

This subset was selected such that the predicates described are likely to occur in the same form in other implementations, assuming that they too conform to the *quasi-standard* defined by Clocksin and Mellish.

Each description is broken down into the following sections:

SYNTAX shows how the predicate or operator is called.

DESCRIPTION gives an informal explanation of how the predicate or operator functions, i.e. what it does.

EXAMPLE illustrates the usage of the predicate or operator. This often consists of dialog excerpts or a predicate.

PECULIARITIES, as the label indicates, is a section which deals with any unusual, i.e. unexpected characteristics or behavior associated with the predicate or operator, of which the Prolog user or programmer should beware.

EXCEPTIONS describes the exception or error conditions which can arise when applying the predicate. This is generally more IF/Prolog dependent, i.e. you are likely to find deviations from the information provided here when using other Prolog systems.

In particular, you will find differences in the system messages issued. IF/Prolog uses Prolog atoms exclusively here, so that the trapping of exception conditions is easier for the user; many systems do not provide the same comfort, indeed some do not allow it at all. If the exception is not trapped, then IF/Prolog terminates automatically, as soon as it has finished notifying the user of the exception condition.

If the *EXCEPTIONS* section is missing, then that means that there are no such exception conditions associated with the respective predicate.

The *SEE ALSO* section contains references to other predicates or operators which in some way relate to the predicate being described. This might be a predicate with a similar function or merely one often used together with the current one or perhaps just one which is often confused with it.

NAME
abolish – delete all clauses with a given functor and arity

SYNTAX
abolish(functor(Arg1,...,ArgN))
abolish(Atom)

DESCRIPTION
abolish removes all clauses from the internal database with the given *functor*, i.e. *atom*. The value of the arguments is ignored; only their number, i.e. the arity established through them, is significant.

EXAMPLES
?– **abolish(result(Question, Result)).**
yes
?– **result(Question, Result).**
EXCEPTION : result : undefined_predicate
no
?–

PECULIARITIES
The argument must be instantiated with either a structure or an atom.
The storage freed in the database by deleting the clause is recycled as soon as any activations of the clause have ended.
When backtracking through *abolish*, the deletion of the clauses is *not* undone.

EXCEPTIONS
'*not_modifiable*', if it has been prohibited to modify the given predicate or atom, e.g. built-ins.
'*struct_expected*', if the given argument is neither a structure (i.e. function) nor an atom.

SEE ALSO
abolish/2, *retract*/1, *retract*/2

abolish/2   *abolish*/2

NAME
abolish – delete all clauses with a given functor and arity

SYNTAX
abolish(Functor, Arity)

DESCRIPTION
abolish removes all clauses from the internal database with the given *Functor* and *Arity*.

EXAMPLES
?– **abolish(appointment, 4).**
yes
?– **appointment(When, Who, Where, What).**
EXCEPTION : appointment : undefined_predicate
no
?–

PECULIARITIES
Both arguments must be instantiated, i.e. no variables at activation time (*abolish*/1 allows for variables in the functor argument list).
Storage occupied in the internal database by the deleted clauses is recycled, as soon as any respective active instantiations have completed their duty.
When backtracking through *abolish*, the deletion of the clauses is *not* undone.

EXCEPTIONS
'*not_modifiable*', if it has been prohibited to modify the given predicate or atom, e.g. built-ins.
'*atom_expected*', if the given argument, *Functor*, is not an atom.
'*integer_expected*', if the second argument, *Arity*, is not an integer value.
'*out_of_range*', if the second argument, *Arity*, is a negative value.

SEE ALSO
abolish/1, *retract*/1, *retract*/2

AND/2 (,)   *AND*/2 (,)

NAME
AND – logical *AND* operator (Conjunction)

SYNTAX
P , Q

DESCRIPTION
Logical *AND* is represented by a comma (,) in Prolog. The binary operator is successful if both its arguments, i.e. the predicates *P* and *Q*, end without failure.

EXAMPLES
```
complete_meal(A,S,M,D) :-
        appetizer(A),
        soup(s),
        main_dish(M),
        dessert(D).
```

PECULIARITIES
AND (,) binds more strongly, i.e. has a higher precedence than *OR* (;). Consequently, it is advisable to use parentheses to explicitly define and indicate the intended associativity in structures (typically clauses or *rules*) where semicolons are also used.

SEE ALSO
OR/2,

NAME

append – concatenation of two lists into a third

SYNTAX

append(List1, List2, ConcatenatedList)

DESCRIPTION

append tries to instantiate its arguments such that the *Concatenated-List* is a product of 'chaining' *List1* with *List2*.

Any two arguments must be instantiated at the time of activation, in which case the variable list is produced (if successful). If all three lists are instantiated at call time, then the predicate serves as a test, i.e. if *List1* and *List2*, when chained to one another, yield the *Concatenated-List*.

It is permissible to have some elements of the respective Lists be variable. The unification will instantiate these variable members, if possible, in order to satisfy the predicate.

EXAMPLES

```
?- append([a,b,c], L, [a.b.c]).
L = []
yes
?- append([X|Y], [d,e], [a.b.c,d,e]).
X = a
Y = [b,c]
yes
?-
```

NAME
arg – fetch the *n*th argument of a structure

SYNTAX
arg(N, S, A)

DESCRIPTION
arg returns the *Nth* argument of the structure *S* via the argument *A*. The first two arguments must already be instantiated to an integer value and a structure, respectively, at the time this predicate is activated. If the third argument is already instantiated too, then the predicate performs a test.

EXAMPLES
?– **arg(3, rent(apartment,'park ave',6000), Rental).**
Rental = 6000
yes
?– **arg(2, [x,y,z], L).**
L = [y,z]
yes
?–

PECULIARITIES
A list as the structure *S* (see second example) is treated according to its internal representation, i.e. a binary 'period' operator:
"[x,y,z]" becomes ".(x, .(y, .(z,[ ])))".

EXCEPTIONS
'*integer_expected*', if the first argument *N* is not an integer.
'*struct_expected*', if the second argument is not an integer.
'*out_of_range*', if the structure has fewer arguments than the position from which one is to be fetched.

SEE ALSO
functor/3, *Univ*/2

                                                                   Assert/1

NAME
Assert – enter a clause into the internal database

SYNTAX
asserta(Clause)
assertz(Clause)

DESCRIPTION
asserta enters the clause, with which *Clause* has been instantiated, at the *beginning* of the internal database.
assertz enters the clause at the *end* of the internal database.
If the clause contains uninstantiated variables, then these will be replaced by other, likewise uninstantiated, variables.

EXAMPLES
?– **assertz((is_subordinate_to(A,B) :– reports_to(A,B))).**
A = _G21
B = _G23
yes
?– **asserta(teststate(ok)).**
yes
?– **teststate(X).**
X = ok
yes

PECULIARITIES
Backtracking through *asserta* or *assertz* does *not* undo the assertion, i.e. the clause remains in the database!

EXCEPTIONS
'*insufficient*', if *Clause* is not adequately instantiated.
'*not_modifiable*', if asserting *Clause* would cause a non-modifiable clause, e.g. a built-in predicate, to be changed.

SEE ALSO
Assert/2, *retract*/1, *retract*/2

NAME
Assert – build a clause and enter it into the database

SYNTAX
asserta(Head, Body)
assertz(Head, Body)

DESCRIPTION
asserta takes the two arguments *Head* and *Body*, constructs the clause
Head:–Body and enters it at the *beginning* of the database.
assertz does the same except it places the new clause at the *end* of the
database.
Head must be either an atom or a structure, so that the functor of the
clause is unique.

EXAMPLES
?– **assertz((is_subordinate_to(A,B), reports_to(A,B))).**
A = _G21
B = _G23
yes
?– **asserta(teststate(ok), true).**
yes

PECULIARITIES
Backtracking through *asserta* or *assertz* does *not* undo the assertion,
i.e. the clause added remains in the database!

EXCEPTIONS
'*struct_expected*', if *Head* is not instantiated with either an atom or a
structure.
'*not_modifiable*', if *Head* has been instantiated to a non-modifiable
clause, e.g. a built-in predicate.

SEE ALSO
Assert/1, *retract*/1, *retract*/2

NAME
atom – tests if instantiation is a non-numeric atom

SYNTAX
atom(X)

DESCRIPTION
atom tests if its argument X is currently instantiated with a *non-numeric* atom.

EXAMPLES
?– **atom(otto).**
yes
?– **atom(15).**
no
?– **atom(Var).**
no

SEE ALSO
atomic/1, *integer*/1, *nonvar*/1, *struct*/1, *var*/1, *name*/2, *number*/2

NAME
> *atomic* – tests if instantiation is an atom or a number

SYNTAX
> **atomic(X)**

DESCRIPTION
> *atomic* tests if its argument X is currently instantiated with either an atom or a number.

EXAMPLES
> ?– **atomic(15).**
> yes
> ?– **atomic(Var).**
> no
> ?– **Var is 3+4, atomic(Var).**
> yes

SEE ALSO
> *atom*/1, *integer*/1, *nonvar*/1, *struct*/1, *var*/1, *name*/2, *number*/2

NAME
clause – search for a clause in the database

SYNTAX
clause(Head, Body)

DESCRIPTION
clause initiates a search of the internal database for a clause whose head is unifiable with *Head* and whose body is unifiable with *Body*. *Head* must be bound to a non-variable term, i.e. cannot be an uninstantiated variable at the time of activation, although a structure may contain variable arguments (see Example). If the clause searched for is a fact, then the second argument, *Body* unifies with *true*.

clause is successful if it can unify the clause described via the arguments with one in the database, otherwise it ends with *fail*.

EXAMPLES
```
?– asserta(david(killed,goliath)).
yes
?– clause(david(Deed,Whom),Z).
Deed = killed
Whom = goliath
Z = true
yes
?– clause(david(maimed,Whom),Z).
no
```

PECULIARITIES
When backtracking *clause* searchs for the next clause in the database unifiable with the given arguments. It ends with *fail* when it has found all such clauses.

EXCEPTIONS
'*insufficient*', if the first argument is not instantiated with an atom or a structure.

NAME
close – close the file named

SYNTAX
close(FileName)

DESCRIPTION
The input or output file named by *FileName* is closed. The current input or output file, as well as standard input and output (Unix), cannot be closed with this predicate.

EXAMPLES
```
switch(OldFile,NewFile) :-
        close(OldFile),
        telling(OldOut),
        tell(NewFile),
        told,
        tell(OldOut).
```

PECULIARITIES
This predicate is not commonly used, except when many files have been opened or created, and the operating system limit for same has been reached.

EXCEPTIONS
'*atom_expected*', if *FileName* is not an atom.
'*protected*', if the file is protected (e.g. Unix standard input and output).

SEE ALSO
See, Tell

compare/3   *compare*/3

NAME

compare – generalized term comparison

SYNTAX

compare(Op, Term1, Term2)

DESCRIPTION

compare(Op, Term1, Term2) instantiates the *Op* with $<, =$, or $>$ to indicate the relationship between the two terms *Term1* and *Term2*. This comparison is based on sort criteria for the respective term types:

variables	no order defined
integers	from *minint* to *maxint*
atoms	in ASCII code or alphabetical order
terms	first by arity,
	then by functor name (see atoms), then by arguments, whereby the above rules apply (including this one, recursively, in the event of a term as argument).

If *Op* is already instantiated at the time of activation, then *compare* functions as a test predicate.

EXAMPLES

```
?– compare(Op, abc, ab).
Op = >
yes
?– compare(Op, "abc", [97,98,99]).
Op = =
yes
?– compare(=, [a], T).
no
?– compare(Op, f1(abc), f1(abc, bcd)).
Op = <
yes
?– compare(Op, f1(abcd), f1(abcc)).
Op = >
yes
```

PECULIARITIES

compare(=, A, B) is equivalent to $A == B$.

SEE ALSO

Term comparison/2 (==), *Value comparison/2*

NAME
consult – reading Prolog texts/programs into the database

SYNTAX
consult('Filename')
reconsult('Filename')

DESCRIPTION
consult reads the file(s) named by the atomic argument (or a list of atomic names) and appends all the syntactically correct Prolog terms found therein to the internal database. Existing terms are left unchanged. *reconsult* does essentially the same as *consult* except that clauses in the internal database having the same functor (i.e. functor name and arity) head as the clauses to be read in will be removed before the latter are appended.

Instructions, i.e. terms beginning with the operator ':–', are executed immediately, whenever encountered in the file(s) consulted.

EXAMPLES
?– consult([program, '/usr/hps/prolog/vi']).
consult : file program loaded in 4 sec.
consult : file '/usr/hps/prolog/vi' loaded in 1 sec.
yes
?– [–program,module].
reconsult : file program loaded in 4 sec.
consult : file module loaded in 2 sec.
yes

PECULIARITIES
An abbreviated form of the consult commands consists of a list of files to be (re)consulted given as response to the '?–' prompt or as a goal in some rule body. Files to be *re*consulted are merely prefixed with a minus (–) sign (see second example above).

EXCEPTIONS
'*file_does_not_exist*', if a given file cannot be found.
'*atom_expected*', if a file name is not an atom. File names consisting exclusively of numerals will raise this error unless placed in single quotes.

Cut/0

NAME

Cut – remove all choice points in the current procedure

SYNTAX

!

DESCRIPTION

Cut (!) removes all choice points accumulated in the context of the procedure where it occurs. Procedure means *all* definitions of the effected clause, i.e. of the same functor with the same arity.

EXAMPLES

```
not_true(Goal) :- Goal, !, fail.
not_true(Goal).
```

(This procedure is essentially the definition of *not*.)

PECULIARITIES

Cut causes dynamic storage in the system to be freed, and thus may be of (admittedly limited) help in certain situations.

SEE ALSO

not/1

Debug   *Debug*

NAME
Debug – managing the debugging facilities

SYNTAX
debug
nodebug
debug_mode(FunctorName, Arity, Currently, Hereafter)

DESCRIPTION
debug turns on the interactive debugger.

nodebug turns it off again.

debug_mode is used to enable/disable the suppression of debugger output for a specific predicate, with the functor *FunctorName* having the *Arity* given. *Currently* is instantiated to *on* when the debugger is displaying output for the predicate, and otherwise to *off*. *Hereafter* is used to enable or disable the debugger output for the given predicate, by setting it to *on* or *off*, respectively.

EXAMPLES
?– **debug_mode(person,4,_,off).**
yes
?– **debug_mode(person,4,CurrentMode,CurrentMode).**
CurrentMode = off
yes

PECULIARITIES
debug_mode is *on* by default for any predicates loaded. Debugging facilities vary widely from system to system. Many provide merely a *trace* when *debug* is called.

EXCEPTIONS
For *debug_mode*:

'*atom_expected*', if *FunctorName* is not an atom.

'*integer_expected*', if *Arity* is not a number.

'*out_of_range*', if *Arity* is negative.

'*on/off_expected*', if *Hereafter* is neither *on* nor *off*.

SEE ALSO
spy/2, *Trace*

NAME

Display – output terms with operator transformation

SYNTAX

display(Term)
display_err(Term)
display_user(Term)
displayq(Term)
displayq_err(Term)
displayq_user(Term)

DESCRIPTION

display(Term) outputs its argument *Term* to the current output file, without the closing period, transforming operators into conventional functor syntax.

displayq(Term) does the same, except that atoms appear in the output in the single quotes, making them distinguishable as such for 'retrieval' with *read*.

display_user(Term) and *displayq_user(Term)* behave correspondingly, writing, however, always to the standard output (Unix: *stdout*).

display_err(Term) and *displayq_err(Term)* behave correspondingly, writing, however, always to the standard error output (Unix: *stderr*).

EXAMPLES

```
?- op(100,xfx,means).

?- display('Today',means,'Today').
means(Today,Today)
yes
?- displayq('Today',means,'Today').
means('Today','Today')
yes
```

PECULIARITIES

During backtracking the output predicates are skipped, i.e. the output will not be repeated.

SEE ALSO

read/1, *Write*/1

NAME
End Session – terminating a Prolog session

SYNTAX
bye
end
end_of_file
halt

DESCRIPTION
bye, end, end_of_file and *halt* terminate the current Prolog session and bring you back to the operating system.

EXAMPLES
?– **bye.**
IF/Prolog session ended

PECULIARITIES
Unix systems also accept the standard *EOF* signal to terminate a Prolog session. This is typically *<control>D*.

fail/0

NAME
fail – unsuccessful goal

SYNTAX
fail

DESCRIPTION
fail is always unsuccessful as a goal. It is used essentially in two situations:

1. to implement an iterative behavior, sending control flow back to an earlier predicate or to *repeat*, or
2. to specify the unconditional failure of a predicate, i.e. no backtracking to be attempted, when occurring in combination with a cut, i.e. '!, *fail*'.

EXAMPLES
```
interpreter :-
        Term = initialization, !,
        activate(Term),
        read(Term),
        fail.

not(P) :- P, !, fail.
not(P).
```

SEE ALSO
repeat/0, *true*/0

NAME
> *findall* – finds all terms satisfying a given predicate

SYNTAX
> **findall(T,GoalPred,TList)**

DESCRIPTION
> *findall* gathers all terms *T* in the database which satisfy the 'goal' predicate formulated in *GoalPred* into the variable *TList*.

EXAMPLES
> ?– **[user].**
> | **birthday(mary,['Jun',13]).**
> | **birthday(john,['Dec',7]).**
> | **birthday(anne,['Jun',2]).**
> | **end_of_file.**
> yes
> ?– **findall(N, birthday(N,['Jun',_]), Names).**
> Names = [mary,anne].
> yes
> ?–

NAME

functor – functor of a term (extractive/constructive)

SYNTAX

functor(Term,FunctorName,Arity)

DESCRIPTION

functor unifies *FunctorName* with the (outermost) functor of the structure in *Term*, and *Arity* with *Term*'s arity.

Either *Term* or *FunctorName* and *Arity* must be instantiated to some value. In the latter case (constructive), *Term* is instantiated as a 'generalization', i.e. a functor with the given *FunctorName* and *Arity*, and all its arguments uninstantiated. In the former case, the predicate functions 'extractively'.

EXAMPLES

?– **functor(date(5,5,1951),FuncName,Arity).**
FuncName = date
Arity = 3
yes
?– **functor(Construct,list,3).**
Construct = list(_G21,_G22,_G23)
yes
?- **functor([x,y,z],FN,Ar).**
FN = .
Ar = 2
yes

(Remember '$[x,y,z]$' is short for '$.(x,.(y,.(z,[])))$' !!)

PECULIARITIES

Term can actually be an atom as well, in which case the *FunctorName* is the value of the atom and the *Arity* is 0 (zero).

EXCEPTIONS

'*insufficient*', if the arguments are not sufficiently instantiated to either construct a *Term* or to extract the *FunctorName* and the *Arity*.

SEE ALSO

arg/3, *Univ*/2

NAME
Get – reading a character

SYNTAX
get0(C)
get(C)

DESCRIPTION
get instantiates a variable argument C to the ASCII equivalent of the next character in the current input stream. If the argument C is already instantiated with an integer value, then the system positions itself to the next character in the input stream corresponding to the ASCII equivalent designated by that value. *get* behaves identically, except that it automatically skips over non-printable characters in the process.

EXAMPLES
?– **write('Enter a carriage return:'), get0(AsciiEquiv).**
Enter a carriage return:
AsciiEquiv = 10
yes
?– **get(AsciiEquiv).** % entry preceded by blanks
   x
AsciiEquiv = 120
yes

PECULIARITIES
During backtracking *get0* and *get* are never choice points, i.e. they will always be skipped, and only on the way back down from a previous choice point will they be reactivated. In other words, no attempt is made to directly resatisfy, i.e. reinstantiate, C, and thus 'automatically' read the next character. This must be implemented via a loop.

SEE ALSO
skip/1, *repeat*/0

NAME

integer – check is argument is an integer value

SYNTAX

integer(X)

DESCRIPTION

integer checks if its argument X is instantiated with an integer value.

EXAMPLES

```
?– integer(5).
yes
?– integer(Var).
no
?– get0(X), integer(X).
a
X = 97
yes
```

SEE ALSO

atom/1, *atomic*/1, *nonvar*/1, *struct*/1, *number*/2

NAME
is – evaluation of an arithmetic expression

SYNTAX
Result is Expression
where Expression uses:
X + Y
X − Y
X * Y
X / Y
X mod Y
+X
−X

DESCRIPTION
is evaluates an arithmetic structure *Expression* according to the usual
rules of arithmetic and assigns the result to *result* or if this is instantiated with a value, tests the truth of the statement.

The arithmetic structure *Expression* can contain the usual binary (+,
−, *, /, *modulo*) operators, as well as the unary plus and minus. The
usual operator precedence applies, which can be modified by the use
of parentheses.

Every term *X* and *Y* in *Expression* must be instantiated with a numerical value of an arithmetic expression.

EXAMPLES
?– **R is (32/2 + 2) mod 9.**
R = 0
yes
?– **T1 is time, consult(anyfile), T2 is time,**
   Elapsed is T2 − T1.
consult: file anyfile loaded in 3 sec.
T1 = 13700
T2 = 13703
Elapsed = 3
yes

PECULIARITIES
Division is integer division (truncation).

There exist certain atoms which, as functors of arity 0, return numerical values. The following are such:

time returns the time of day in seconds.

dbsize returns the amount of memory set aside for the internal database.

dbused returns the current size of the active database.

maxint returns the largest integer representable in the implementation.

minint returns the largest negative integer representable in the implementation.

EXCEPTIONS

'*illegal_expression*', if one of the operands is not correctly instantiated.

'*divide_by_zero*', if divisor is zero.

'*out_of_range*' if the final result does not lie in the range *minint* to *maxint* (under-/overflow).

NAME
   is_predicate – declaration of a predicate

SYNTAX
   is_predicate(Functor,Arity)

DESCRIPTION
   is_predicate declares *Functor* as a predicate with the given *Arity*.
   The purpose of the declaration is to suppress the error message caused
   by calling a predicate as a goal for which no corresponding clause exists
   in the database. This is particularly important for predicates which
   serve as state indicators, based on their presence in or absence from
   the database.

EXAMPLES
   ?– **test state**
   EXCEPTION: test_state: undefined_predicate
   no
   ?– **asserta(is_predicate(test_state,0)).**
   yes
   ?– **test_state.**
   no
   ?– **asserta(test_state).**
   yes
   ?– **test_state.**
   yes

PECULIARITIES
   Care must be taken not to delete *is_predicate*, either using *abolish* or,
   inadvertently, by reconsulting a file containing a self-defined *is_predi-
   cate* clause, since the Prolog system itself uses this predicate internally,
   and thereafter will be unable to 'recognize' its own predicates.

NAME
Listing – list the contents of the internal database

SYNTAX
listing
listing(FunctorName)

DESCRIPTION
In the absence of an argument, *listing* outputs all the user-defined clauses in the internal database on the current output stream.

If a *FunctorName* has been given, then only those user-defined clauses with the named functor, independent of their arity, are listed.

listing can be used to search for erroneously defined clauses, etc., as well as for saving the current state of the database in an external file.

EXAMPLES
```
save(SaveFile) :-
                /* save the current state of the database */
                telling(CurrOutfile),
                tell(SaveFile),
                listing,
                told, tell(CurrOutfile).
```

PECULIARITIES
Built-in predicates are not included in the output.

EXCEPTIONS
'*atom_expected*', if *FunctorName* is not an atom.

NAME
member – check for element in a list

SYNTAX
member(X,List)

DESCRIPTION
member checks if the element X is in the *List* given or, alternatively, if variables are involved, if and how they would be instantiated for the membership to apply.

member presents a choice point; thus during backtracking alternative instantiations for variables are generated.

EXAMPLES
?– **member(b,[a,b,c]).**
yes
?– **member(b,[a,X,c]).**
X = b
yes
?– **member(X,[a,b,c]).**
X = a;
X = b;
X = c;
no
?– **member(a(X,Y), [a(1,2),b(3,4)]).**
X = 1
Y = 2
yes
?– **X = [a,_], member(b,X).**
X = [a,b,_]
yes

SEE ALSO
Unification/2

NAME
name – convert name of atom into a list (string)

SYNTAX
name(Atom,List)

DESCRIPTION
name converts the name representing *Atom* into a *List* of the ASCII
equivalents of the individual characters constituting the atoms name.
The transformation may also be from a list to an atom name.
At least one of the arguments must be instantiated to some appropriate
value.
If both arguments are instantiated then *name* tests the two for strict
equivalence.

EXAMPLES
?– **name('Prolog',L).**
L = [80,114,111,108,111,103]
yes
?– **name(A, [80,114,111,108,111,103]).**
A = Prolog
yes
?– **name(A, "Prolog")**
A = Prolog
yes
?– **name(X, "[80]"), name(X, L).**
X = [80]
L = [91,56,48,93]
yes

EXCEPTIONS
'*insufficient*', if neither argument is instantiated.
'*illegal_string*', if *List* does not represent a legal string.

SEE ALSO
atom/1, *atomic*/1, *number*/2

NAME
    nl – issue a new line to output

SYNTAX
    nl

DESCRIPTION
    nl places a new line control character (i.e. the Unix special character '\n') into the current output stream.

EXAMPLES
    ?– **write(new), nl, write(line).**
    new
    line
    yes

PECULIARITIES
    Some Prolog systems, like IF/Prolog, allow you to write the special character '\n' right into the atom. This would make the above example simpler:

    ?– **write('new\nline').**
    new
    line
    yes

NAME

nonvar – test if argument is instantiated to a nonvariable

SYNTAX

nonvar(X)

DESCRIPTION

nonvar checks if its argument X is currrently instantiated to a non-variable term.

EXAMPLES

```
?- nonvar(X).
no
?- X = value, nonvar(X).
X = value
yes
?- nonvar(a(X,Y)).
X = _G12
Y = _G13
yes
```

SEE ALSO

atom/1, *atomic*/1, *integer*/1, *struct*/1, *Unification*/2, *var*/1

NAME
   not – negation of success of goal

SYNTAX
   not Goal

DESCRIPTION
   not is a unary operator. If *goal* is successful, then *not* itself *fails*, and
   vice versa.
   not thus implements a *partial* logical negation.

EXAMPLES
   ?– **not member(a, [a,b,c]).**
   no
   ?– **not member(d, [a,b,c]).**
   yes

PECULARITIES
   Since *not* always implies a *fail* (either of itself or of the *Goal*), all instantiations made by *Goal* will always be *undone*, i.e. uninstantiated, when
   not has completed executing. Thus, *not* is suitable for testing only if a
   goal was successful, and not for determining which variable values
   were responsible for causing a *fail* to occur.

SEE ALSO
   fail/0

NAME
number – convert a number to a list (string)

SYNTAX
number(Atom,DigitList)

DESCRIPTION
number converts a numeric *Atom* into *DigitList* containing the ASCII equivalents of the constituent digits of the atom. The conversion may also be made in the other direction.

At least one of the arguments must be instantiated.

If both are, then *number* functions as a test of strict equivalence between the two arguments.

EXAMPLES
?– **number(123,[49,50,51]).**
yes
?– **number(N,[50,48,48,49]).**
N = 2001
yes

EXCEPTIONS
'*insufficient*', if neither argument is instantiated.
'*illegal_string*', if *List* does not represent a legal string.

SEE ALSO
integer/1, *name/2*

NAME
OR – logical *OR* operator (disjunction)

SYNTAX
P ; Q

DESCRIPTION
OR (;) implements a logical *OR*. If *P* is successful, then *Q* will not be
executed. If *P fails* then *Q* will be executed as the alternative to *P*.
Backtracking, however it may have been initiated, causes the alternative (*Q*) to be executed. A *cut* (!) encountered during execution of *P*
suppresses the execution of the alternative *Q*.

EXAMPLES
```
interpreter :-
        repeat, read(Command),
        (       Command = quit, !
        ;       execute(Command), fail
        ).
```

PECULIARITIES
OR (;) binds more weakly, i.e. has a lower precedence than *AND* (,).
Therefore, it is always wise to indicate the scope of the *OR* operator by
parenthesizing the affected goals.
On the other hand, one should avoid extremely complex, nested usage
of the *OR* operator when defining a rule. These are usually better
broken up into a set of simpler ones.

SEE ALSO
And/2. *Cut*/0

NAME

   op – declaration of an operator

SYNTAX

   op(Precedence,Associativity,FunctorName)

DESCRIPTION

   op declares *FunctorName* as an operator with the given numerical
   Precedence and the given *Associativity*. The latter is coded as follows:

fx, fy	– prefix operator,
xfx, xfy, yfx	– infix operator,
xf, yf	– postfix operator

   The *f* stands for the functor (operator) itself, *x* for a *term* containing
   operators of *lower* precedence, *y* for a *term* containing operators of
   equal or *lower* precedence.

EXAMPLES

   ?– **op(100,xfy,directs).**
   yes
   ?– **[user].**
   | **mary directs john.**
   | **bob directs jane directs fred directs alice.**
   | **end_of_file.**
   yes
   ?– **X directs Y.**
   X = mary
   Y = john;
   X = bob
   Y = jane directs fred directs alice;
   no
   ?– **op(100,yfx,directs).**
   yes
   ?– **X directs Y.**
   X = mary
   Y = john;
   X = bob
   Y = jane directs (fred directs alice);
   no

EXCEPTIONS

   '*integer_expected*', if *Precedence* is not an integer.

'*out_of_range*', if *Precedence* does not lie in the permitted range (implementation dependent).

'*operator_type_expected*', if *Associativity* not one of the abovementioned codes (atom).

'*atom_expected*', if *FunctorName* is not an atom (use single quotes if necessary).

put/1   *put*/1

NAME
put – output a character

SYNTAX
put(N)

DESCRIPTION
put(N) places the ASCII equivalent of the integer *N* into the current output stream. The value of *N* can, of course, be the integer result of an arithmetic expression.

EXAMPLES
?– **put(97).**
a
yes
?– **number(0,[Null]), put(Null+1).**
1
Null = 48
yes

PECULIARITIES
put is never a choice point, i.e. in case of backtracking it is skipped. The character output will *not* be output again, nor will the character be withdrawn from the output stream.

EXCEPTIONS
'*integer_expected*', if *N* is not an integer.
'*out_of_range*', if *N* does not have an ASCII character equivalent.

SEE ALSO
nl/0, *tab*/1

NAME
   read – input a term from current input stream

SYNTAX
   read(Term)

DESCRIPTION
   read fetches the next complete *Term* from the current input stream.
   Term must be syntactically correct and be terminated by a period ('.').
   The period, however, is *not* treated as part of the *Term* read.
   Syntax errors are reported to the reader on the display, as the attempt
   is made to read the *Term* in.

EXAMPLES
   ?– **read(Term), write(Term).**
   'The output has no period here –>'.
   The output has no period here –>
   Term = The output has no period here –>
   yes

PECULIARITIES
   read is skipped during backtracking, i.e. no attempt is made to instantiate *Term* with an alternative (the next) term in the input stream.

SEE ALSO
   Display/1, *Write*/1

NAME
repeat – loop entry point for backtracking

SYNTAX
repeat

DESCRIPTION
repeat is a goal which never fails. It is used to introduce an iteration, which begins with the *repeat* predicate and reaches as far as the next *unsuccessful* goal (possibly an explicit *fail*).
Its behavior can be described as

```
repeat.
repeat :- repeat.
```

repeat is only necessary if the initial predicate in an iterative loop is subject to possible *failure*. This is particularly the case where I/O is to be repeatedly made, since these are typically ignored during backtracking.

EXAMPLES
```
password(PW) :-
        repeat,
        % loop till correct
        write('Your password: '),
        % PW is instantiated with the input
        read(PW).
```

SEE ALSO
fail/0

NAME
retract – delete a single clause from the database

SYNTAX
retract(Clause)

DESCRIPTION
retract removes the first *Clause* it encounters in the database which unifies with the argument given. *Clause* must be instantiated enough to insure that the functor and the arity of the clause are unambiguous.

If no clause can be found in the database, which is unifiable with *Clause*, then *retract fails*.

After a successful *retract* the deleted instance of *Clause*, with any variables instantiated by the unification, is available in *Clause* for further processing.

EXAMPLES
```
?- retract(appointment([8,23,85], What)),
    write(What), nl, fail.
prologseminar
no
?- retract(appointment([8,23,85], What)).
no
```

PECULIARITIES
Clauses deleted by a *retract* are *not returned to the database* in the event of backtracking over the responsible *retract* goal. On the contrary, backtracking causes *Clause* to be instantiated with the *next fitting* clause, which then gets removed. In this way all corresponding clauses can be removed *recursively* from the database.

EXCEPTIONS
'*insufficient*', if *Clause* is not instantiated enough to uniquely identify a clause.

'*not_modifiable*', if *Clause* may not be deleted, e.g. built-in clauses.

SEE ALSO
abolish/1, *abolish*/2, *retract*/2

retract/2   *retract*/2

NAME
retract – delete a single clause from the database

SYNTAX
retract(Head,Body)

DESCRIPTION
retract removes the first clause it encounters in the database, whose *Head* and *Body* can be unified with the values given.

The predicate *fails* if a corresponding clause cannot be found.

After a successful *retract Head* and *Body* are instantiated with the corresponding parts of the clause deleted, together with any variables instantiated by the unification, and are available for further processing.

The *Body* of a fact is *true*.

EXAMPLES
?– **retract(appointment([8,23,85], What), Body).**
What = prologseminar
Body = true ;
What = buy_flowers
Body = not too_expensive(flowers);
What = dentist
Body = true ;
no

PECULIARITIES
Clauses deleted by a *retract* are *not returned to the database* in the event of backtracking over the responsible *retract* goal. On the contrary, backtracking causes *Clause* to be instantiated with the *next fitting* clause, which then gets removed. In this way all corresponding clauses can be removed *recursively* from the database.

EXCEPTIONS
'*insufficient*', if *Head* and *Body* are not instantiated enough to uniquely identify a clause.

'*not_modifiable*', if the clause identified may not be deleted, e.g. built-in clauses.

SEE ALSO
abolish/1, *abolish*/2, *retract*/1

NAME
See – switch input stream

SYNTAX
see(File)
seeing(CurrFile)
seen

DESCRIPTION
see makes the name *File* the current input stream, opening it if it has not yet been opened.
seeing unifies its argument *CurrFile* with the name of the current input file.
seen closes the current input file, except if it is *user*, i.e. the terminal keyboard.

EXAMPLES
```
open(File,read) :-
        /* open a file, without reading it immediately */
        seeing(Input), see(File), see(Input).
```

PECULIARITIES
The terminal keyboard is the (standard input) file *user*. It cannot be closed with *seen*.

EXCEPTIONS
'*atom_expected*', if *File* is not a legal atom (try enclosing in single quotes).

SEE ALSO
close/1, *Get*/1, *read*/1, *Tell*

NAME
skip – move ahead to a particular character in input stream

SYNTAX
skip(N)

DESCRIPTION
skip skips ahead in the input stream, positioning on the next occurrence of the ASCII equivalent of the integer N. The next predicate to read the stream will receive input starting at the character that follows this position.

If N is an uninstantiated variable, *skip* will instantiate it to the next character in the stream.

EXAMPLES
?– get(X), skip(10), get(Y).
1 is ASCII 49, newline is 10.
2 is ASCII 50.
X = 49
Y = 50
yes

PECULIARITIES
There is no real difference between the predicates $get0(N)$ and $skip(N)$.

SEE ALSO
Get/1

NAME
spy – set observation or breakpoints for debugging

SYNTAX
spy(Goal,Port) :– Condition.

DESCRIPTION
spy sets an observation or breakpoint for the given *Goal* and the
specified *Port*(*call, redo, exit, fail*) therein. If the state of the goal is
only of interest in certain situations, this can be specified as a *Condition*, appearing in the body of the *spy* clause.

When the debugger is run and the spy mode is enabled (debugger
command *S*), then Prolog stops and displays the state of the goal in
accordance with the specification of the *spy* predicate.

EXAMPLES
```
?– [user].
| spy( see(File), call) :–
|               File = secret; File = classified.
| end_of_file.
yes
```

PECULIARITIES
spy also functions when the debugger is running in (non-stop) mode
(debugger command *N*). In this way, one can suppress all debug displays except for those selected with *spy* for observation.

Some systems have a more primitive *spy* predicate, which only allows
the specification of the *Goal* and not the *Conditions* under which one
wishes to observe them.

SEE ALSO
Debug

NAME

struct – check for a structure

SYNTAX

struct(X)

DESCRIPTION

struct tests if its argument X is instantiated with a structure. This is purely a check for the syntactic object *structure* versus *atom*, etc. and says nothing about the semantics of the structure involved, should X prove to be one.

A structure is characterized as a functor followed by a left parenthesis, a non-empty argument list and a closing right parenthesis (or the equivalent of this, e.g. consider the operators).

EXAMPLES

```
?– struct(a(X,_)).
X = _G12
yes
?– struct(a).
no
?– struct([a,b,c]).
yes
?– struct(N is 1).
N = _G12
yes
?– struct( is(N,1)).
N = _G12
yes
?– struct(father(karl) :– true).
yes
?– struct( blurry(X) :– (write(x), nl, write(X)) ).
X = _G12
yes
?– struct( :– (blurry(X), write(X), nl, write(X)) ).
X = _G12
yes
```

SEE ALSO

atom/1. *atomic*/1, *integer*/1, *nonvar*/1, *var*/1

NAME
tab – output blanks

SYNTAX
tab(N)

DESCRIPTION
tab places N blanks into the current output stream.

EXAMPLES
?– **write('('), tab(5), write(') contains 5 blanks').**
(   ) contains 5 blanks
yes

PECULIARITIES
Despite its name, *tab* has nothing to do with the tabulator or the tabulation character (*ht*, ASCII code = 9).

SEE ALSO
nl/0, *put*/1

Tell   *Tell*

NAME
Tell – switch the output stream

SYNTAX
tell(File)
telling(File)
told

DESCRIPTION
tell makes the given *File* the current output stream.
If *File* is not open, i.e. does not exist, it is opened, i.e. created.
telling instantiates its argument to the name of the current output file.
If *File* is already instantiated then *telling* tests if the current output stream is associated with the named file.
told closes the current output file.

EXAMPLES
?– **tell(calendar), listing(appointments), told.**
yes

PECULIARITIES
The user's terminal display is the file called *user*. It cannot be closed with *told*.
Under Unix, ouput gets buffered in the system and under certain circumstances will not get physically written into the file until *told* has been activated.

EXCEPTIONS
'*atom_expected*', if File is not a legal atom.

SEE ALSO
close/1, *Display*/1, *put*/1, *See*, *Write*/1

NAME
Term Comparison – test for (non-)identical instantiation

SYNTAX
    X == Y
    X \== Y

DESCRIPTION
== *tests* if the terms *X* and *Y* are instantiated with identical terms. This is a strict comparison, i.e., in contract to the operator '=', no further unification is made in order to bring two terms containing variables into an identical form.

If uninstantiated variables occur in the same position in the respective terms, then the comparison is successful only if they are instantiated with the *identical* (internal global) variables.

\== tests if the two terms are currently *not* identically instantiated.

EXAMPLES
    ?– [a,b] == [a,b].
    yes
    ?– [a,X] = [a,b].
    X = b
    yes
    ?– [a,X] == [a,b].
    no
    ?– write(X), nl, write(Y), X == Y.
    _G28
    _G33
    no
    ?– X = Y, X == Y.
    X = _G28
    Y = _G28
    yes
    ?– X = a, Y = f(X), X \== Y.
    yes

SEE ALSO
compare/3, *Value Comparison*/2, *Unification*/2

Trace   *Trace*

NAME
Trace – execution trace

SYNTAX
trace
trace(ProtocolFile)
notrace
trace_mode(Functor,Arity,Current,Hereafter)

DESCRIPTION
trace produces a record or protocol of execution, i.e. the predicates activated, the variables instantiated, the flow of control during processing. If a *ProtocolFile* is named, then the output of the trace is written to that file, otherwise it is placed in the standard output stream (typically, the user's display).

notrace turns the trace mechanism off again.

trace_mode is used to enable or disable the tracing of a the given *Functor* of a given *Arity*. *Current* is *on* if the predicate is being traced and *off* otherwise. *Hereafter* is to be instantiated with *on* or *off*, to respectively enable or disable the inclusion of the predicate in the execution trace.

EXAMPLES
```
?- asserta( msg:- write(' Message') ).
yes
?- trace
?- trace_mode(msg,0,Curr,Curr).
Curr = on
yes
?- msg.
(18) CALL msg
(19) CALL write( Message) Message
(19) EXIT write( Message)
(18) EXIT msg
yes
?- trace_mode(msg,0,_,off).
?- msg.
(18) CALL msg Message
(18) EXIT msg
yes
?- notrace.
?- msg.
Message
yes
```

PECULIARITIES

When a predicate is loaded *trace_mode* is *on*, by default, for a predicate, when it is loaded.

EXCEPTIONS

For *trace(ProtocolFile)*:
'*atom_expected*', if *ProtocolFile* is not an atom.
For *trace_mode*:
'*atom_expected*', if *Functor* is not an atom.
'*integer_expected*', if *Arity* is not a number.
'*out_of_range*', if *Arity* is a negative number.
'*on/off expected*', if *Hereafter* is neither *on* nor *off*.

SEE ALSO

Debug

NAME
true – successful goal

SYNTAX
true

DESCRIPTION
true always succeeds.

true is the implicit body of a fact. Thus, it is used almost exclusively to specify the body of fact for clauses which access facts in the database, e.g. the predicate *clause*.

Occasionally, however, one uses it as an alternative goal in disjunctions, i.e. *OR* structures, which were used to determine a series of causes for the failure of a predicate. As a rule, however, the same can be achieved by other, more easily understood constructs together with the *OR* operator (';').

EXAMPLES
```
?– asserta(prologbook([2,21,86])).
yes
?– clause( prologbook(When), true).
When = [2,21,86]
yes
```

SEE ALSO
fail/0, *repeat*/0

Unification/2

NAME
Unification – unifiability of two arguments

SYNTAX
   X = Y
   X \= Y

DESCRIPTION
= is successful if the terms *X* and *Y* can be unified. If both arguments
are instantiated, then this is a test. Otherwise, it implies the instantiation of the variable arguments with the corresponding non-variable
arguments. The assignments can be made in both directions across the
operator!

\= is successful if both terms cannot be unified with one another. No
instantiation (assignment) takes place.

EXAMPLES
   ?– **X = 6 * 2.**
   X = 6 * 2
   yes
   ?– **6 * X = 6 * 2.**
   X = 2
   yes
   ?– **X is 6 * 2, Y = 6 * 2, X = Y.**
   X = 12
   Y = 6 * 2
   yes

PECULIARITIES
The second, i.e. right-hand argument of '=' is not allowed to contain
a variable from the first, i.e. left-hand, argument.

Most Prolog implementations do *not* check for the recursion that arises
from such an expression, because testing for circularity would make
the operation very inefficient. Instead, the interpreter goes into an
endless loop in such cases.

SEE ALSO
is/2, *Term Comparison*/2, *Value Comparison*/2

NAME
Univ – conversion structure to/from list representation

SYNTAX
F = .. L

DESCRIPTION
Univ (=..) is a binary operator whose left operand, i.e. argument, *F* is a structure and whose right one *L* is a list. The operation is successful if the two arguments, possibly via certain unifications, can be said to correspond to one another in the following sense:

The first element of the list *L* is the same as the functor of the structure *F*, and the remaining elements of *L* correspond to the arguments of the structure *F*.

This means that the number of elements of the list *L* must be one more than the arity of the structure *F*.

Univ is a generalized means to access and create arbitrary structures.

EXAMPLES
```
?- friday(2,18,86) =.. [friday,Month,18,86].
Month = 2
yes
?- F =.. [f,X,Y].
F = f(_G23,_G24)
X = _G23
Y = _G24
yes
```

EXCEPTIONS
'*insufficient*', if *F* or *L* is not sufficiently instantiated to permit a meaningful unification.

'*illegal_list*', if *L* is not a list.

SEE ALSO
arg/3, *functor*/3

NAME
Value Comparison – arithmetic comparison

SYNTAX
X < **Y**   **X** =< **Y**   **X** =:= **Y**   **X** =\= **Y**   **X** >= **Y**   **X** > **Y**

DESCRIPTION
The operators <, =<, =:=, =\=, >= and > compare numeric constants or variables instantiated with such values. The meaning of the operators are, respectively, *less than, less than or equal, equal, not equal, greater than or equal* and *greater than*.

The operators all return either *true* if the relationship holds between the given values, otherwise they *fail*.

EXAMPLES
```
?- X = 4, Y = 4, X <= Y.
yes
?- X = 4, Y = 5, X =:= Y.
no
?- X is 3 * 2, Y = 4, X > Y.
yes
?- X = Y, X =:= Y.
EXCEPTION: _G12 =:= _G28 : illegal expression
no
```

EXCEPTIONS
'*illegal_expression*', if (at least) one of the operands, i.e. arguments, is not instantiated with a numeric value.

SEE ALSO
compare/3, *is*/2, *Term Comparison*/2, *Unification*/2

NAME
  var – test if argument is instantiated

SYNTAX
  var(X)

DESCRIPTION
  var tests its argument X, to see if it is either uninstantiated or instantiated to (another) variable. In both cases it succeeds, otherwise it returns with *fail*.

EXAMPLES
  ?– **var(atom).**
  no
  ?– **var(X).**
  X = _G13
  yes
  ?– **X = a, var(X).**
  no
  ?– **X = Y, var(X).**
  X = _G13
  Y = _G13
  yes

SEE ALSO
  atom/1, *atomic*/1, *integer*/1, *nonvar*/1, *struct*/1

NAME
Write – Output term with operator

SYNTAX
write(Term)
write_err(Term)
write_user(Term)
writeq(Term)
writeq_err(Term)
writeq_user(Term)

DESCRIPTION
write places its argument *Term, without the closing period*, into the current output stream. Operator definitions are observed, i.e. *no* transformation to standard predicate format is made.

writeq does essentially the same, except that any atoms in single quotes which must have these quotes preserved, so that they can be correctly read in at some later date with *read*, retain the quotes in the output.

write_err and *writeq_err* behave like their counterparts above, except that the output always goes to the standard error stream (Unix: *stderr*).

write_user and *writeq_user* behave like their counterparts above, except that the output always goes to the standard output stream (Unix: *stdout*).

EXAMPLES
?– **op(100,xfy,loves).**
yes
?– **write('Ronnie' loves 'hamburgers').**
Ronnie loves hamburgers
yes
?– **writeq('Ronnie' loves 'hamburgers').**
'Ronnie' loves hamburgers
yes
?– **writeq(loves('Ronnie', hamburgers)).**
'Ronnie' loves hamburgers
yes

PECULIARITIES
The various *write* predicates are skipped over when backtracking, i.e. the output is not repeated.

As can be seen in the last example, user-defined operators are observed even if the term is expressed in standard format. Built-in operators cannot be passed as arguments expressed in standard format (syntax error).

SEE ALSO
Display/1, *read*/1

Appendix E   LIST OF OPERATORS

The following is a list of the built-in operators which are part of a typical implementation of Prolog. The precedence and associativity for each operator is shown in the middle and rightmost columns. The precedence values are typical in their relationship to one another but not necessarily with respect to their absolute values. Notice that some of the operators, like ':–' and '+', have both unary and binary definitions.

:–	1200	xfx
:–	1200	fx
?–	1200	fx
-->	1200	xfx
;	1100	xfy
->	1050	xfy
,	1000	xfy
not	900	fy
is	700	xfx
>=	700	xfx
=<	700	xfx
>	700	xfx
<	700	xfx
=\=	700	xfx
=:=	700	xfx
\==	700	xfx
==	700	xfx
=..	700	xfx
\=	700	xfx
=	700	xfx
–	500	fx
+	500	fx
–	500	yfx
+	500	yfx
*	400	yfx
/	400	yfx
mod	300	xfx

Appendix F — ASCII CHARACTER SET

The following table of ASCII characters and their decimal equivalents was produced using the procedure *ascii_table* illustrated in Fig. 9.6.

nul	0	sp	32	@	64	`	96
soh	1	!	33	A	65	a	97
stx	2	"	34	B	66	b	98
etx	3	#	35	C	67	c	99
eot	4	$	36	D	68	d	100
enq	5	%	37	E	69	e	101
ack	6	&	38	F	70	f	102
bel	7	'	39	G	71	g	103
bs	8	(	40	H	72	h	104
ht	9	(	41	I	73	i	105
nl	10	*	42	J	74	j	106
vt	11	+	43	K	75	k	107
np	12	,	44	L	76	l	108
cr	13	−	45	M	77	m	109
so	14	.	46	N	78	n	110
si	15	/	47	O	79	o	111
dle	16	0	48	P	80	p	112
dc1	17	1	49	Q	81	q	113
dc2	18	2	50	R	82	r	114
dc3	19	3	51	S	83	s	115
dc4	20	4	52	T	84	t	116
nak	21	5	53	U	85	u	117
syn	22	6	54	V	86	v	118
etb	23	7	55	W	87	w	119
can	24	8	56	X	88	x	120
em	25	9	57	Y	89	y	121
sub	26	:	58	Z	90	z	122
esc	27	;	59	[	91	{	123
fs	28	<	60	\	92	|	124
gs	29	=	61	]	93	}	125
rs	30	>	62	^	94	~	126
us	31	?	63	_	95	del	127

INDEX